VISUAL QUICKSTART GUIDE

FILEMAKER PRO 4

FOR WINDOWS AND MACINTOSH

D1466730

Nolan Hester

 Peachpit Press

Visual QuickStart Guide
FileMaker Pro 4 for Windows and Macintosh
Nolan Hester

Peachpit Press
1249 Eighth Street
Berkeley, CA 94710
(800) 283-9444
(510) 524-2178
(510) 524-2221 (fax)

Find us on the World Wide Web at: http://www.peachpit.com

Peachpit Press is a division of Addison Wesley Longman

Copyright © 1998 by Nolan Hester

Editor: Nancy Davis
Indexer: Emily Glossbrenner
Production: David Van Ness
Inhouse production: Amy Changar, Mimi Heft
Cover design: The Visual Group

Notice of rights
All rights reserved. No part of this book may be reproduced or transmitted in any form or by any means, electronic, mechanical, photocopying, recording, or otherwise, without prior written permission of the publisher. For more information on getting permission for reprints and excerpts, contact Gary-Paul Prince at Peachpit Press.

Notice of liability
The information in this book is distributed on an "As is" basis, without warranty. While every precaution has been taken in the preparation of this book, neither the author nor Peachpit Press shall have any liability to any person or entity with respect to any loss or damage caused or alleged to be caused directly or indirectly by the instructions contained in this book or by the computer software and hardware products described herein.

Trademarks
FileMaker, ScriptMaker, and Web Companion are registered trademarks of FileMaker Corporation. Windows is a registered trademark of Microsoft Corporation in the United States and/or other countries. Macintosh is a registered trademark of Apple Computer, Inc. in the United States and/or other countries.

Throughout this book trademarked names are used. Rather than put a trademark symbol in every occurrence of a trademarked name, we state we are using the names only in an editorial fashion and to the benefit of the trademark owner with no intention of infringement of the copyright.

ISBN: 0-201-69664-9

9 8 7 6 5 4 3 2

Printed and bound in the United States of America

♲ Printed on recycled paper

This book is dedicated to:
my father for hanging in there
through the chemo, my mother for
bearing the burden, and, as always,
to Mary for keeping me startled
and delighted ever since we first
collided in Albuquerque's high desert.

Acknowledgments:

Friends and colleagues too numerous to list here offered crucial support and understanding during my disappearance to write this book. Thanks to all of you.

Special thanks to:

Nancy Aldrich-Ruenzel for giving me the chance to write this book; Nancy Davis for being a great editor who blends red ink and kind words in just the right mix; David Van Ness for his usual calm competence and awesome talent; Amy Changar and Mimi Heft for making the production side of the book a pleasure; Peet's espresso grind Arabian mocha java for keeping me going; and Laika, my study buddy, for making me stop—no matter what—for evening walks.

TABLE OF CONTENTS

PART V: WEB PUBLISHING WITH FILEMAKER

Chapter 16: Preparing for Web Publishing 225

Chapter 17: Using Instant Web Publishing 237

Chapter 18: Using Custom Web Publishing 243

PART VI: APPENDICES

Appendix A: Installing FileMaker 255

Appendix B: Setting Preferences 265

TABLE OF CONTENTS

PART 1

GETTING STARTED

INTRODUCTION

Welcome to the Visual QuickStart Guide
for FileMaker Pro 4. If you've used earlier
versions of FileMaker, you know how easy,
flexible, and powerful the program is. If this
is your first time using FileMaker, you're in
for some pleasant surprises, including
discovering Web Companion, FileMaker's
most significant improvement in years.

Why FileMaker?

Anyone who's used FileMaker much will readily sing its praises. It's the most popular Macintosh database program, which explains why many folks assume it's a Mac-only program. In truth, it's now also the second most popular stand-alone database program for Windows users. Roughly three million copies of FileMaker have been sold, and Windows sales have tripled in the past two years.

Anyone who hasn't used FileMaker may wonder what the fuss is all about. Two words— clean, simple—explain FileMaker's appeal. It takes a few more words to explain what I mean:

- **The interface:** FileMaker's been around since the mid-1980s, a very long time in the world of software. Unlike some programs that age, however, FileMaker's interface—the menus, buttons, windows, and steps required to get work done—has grown simpler, not more complex. This simplicity, and the resulting consistency that appears across the program, make it easy for you to stay focused on your work instead of puzzling over the program itself.

- **Cross-platform consistency:** FileMaker works so consistently on Windows and Macintoshes that your databases can move with you as you, and those using your databases, switch between platforms.

- **Simple yet powerful:** Folks who carp that FileMaker isn't as powerful as, say, Oracle, miss the real point of FileMaker. Heavy-duty database programs are super: super powerful, super hard to learn. FileMaker isn't. An example: FileMaker lets you build Web databases without learning CGI (Common Gateway Interface) scripting. If you are lucky enough to know CGI, FileMaker can use your scripts. But it's nice you don't have to know it.

What's new in FileMaker 4?

If you're a brand-new FileMaker user, *all* of FileMaker 4 is new. For FileMaker veterans, version 4's features and tools are not that different from FileMaker 3. (By the way, while FileMaker's official name is FileMaker Pro 4, we'll just call it FileMaker throughout this book.) The biggest change is the addition of the Web Companion, which makes FileMaker much easier to use for publishing on the World Wide Web. Here's a quick rundown of FileMaker's new features:

Web publishing with Web Companion

Anyone who's struggled to maintain or update a Web site knows how databases make everything easier. But until now serving databases over the Web required a fair understanding of CGI. Now all you need is an Internet account and FileMaker with Web Companion, which offers two approaches:

- **Instant Web Publishing:** This approach takes your database and automatically creates one of two standard views—one for seeing one record at a time, another for seeing a series of records in table form. A no-muss, no-bother, nothing-fancy way to post data to the Web.

- **Custom Web Publishing:** This approach gives you more control over the appearance of your Web database, offers interactive features, and provides better security for your files.

Expanded Internet support

- **GIF and JPEG support:** Two key graphic formats used widely on the Web, GIF and JPEG, are supported in FileMaker layouts, container fields, and Web pages. When FileMaker sends a graphic to a Web browser, it can send a GIF or JPEG image. It can even convert an image stored in another format to JPEG so that the browser can display it. (GIFs are used for virtually all Web illustrations; JPEGs are the Web's most common format for photographs.)

■ **FileMaker to HTML exports:** Most FileMaker databases now can be converted automatically to HTML, the basic coding for displaying Web pages. You don't have to mess with HTML coding, unless you want to.

■ **URL support and scripting:** Any URL (Web address) appearing within a FileMaker database is "hot"—click it and FileMaker will launch your Web browser to view the linked page. FileMaker now also lets you write scripts to open URLs.

Other improvements

■ **New calculation functions:** Now you can determine a user's network protocol, the modifier key being pressed, the password belonging to a group, the current record number, and the number and kinds of objects in a layout.

■ **More Sort and Find options:** Exact field matches allow more precise Find requests. Related records can be sorted within a particular list view (or portal as FileMaker calls it)—or as part of a related list.

■ **Greater layout flexibility:** Fields and objects can be horizontal or vertical.

■ **Direct import of Excel spreadsheets:** Worksheets from version 4.0 through Excel 97 (Windows), and versions 4.0, 5.0, and Excel 98 (Mac) can be brought into FileMaker easily and cleanly. As they say, this is huge for anyone with lots of Excel data that also could be put to use in a database.

How to use this book

The key to this book, like all of Peachpit's Visual QuickStart Guides, is that word *visual*. As much as possible, I've used illustrations with succinct captions to explain FileMaker's major functions and options. Ideally, you should be able to quickly locate what you need by scanning the page tabs, illustrations, and captions. Once you find a relevant topic, the text provides details and tips to make everything go mo' better.

If you're new to FileMaker, you'll find it easy to work your way through the book chapter by chapter. By the final pages, you'll know FileMaker better than most of the folks who use it daily.

But if you've got an immediate FileMaker problem or question that you need answered right now, the book makes it easy for you to dive right in and get help quickly. For those of you who find even a QuickStart Guide too slow, consider jumping straight to pages 16–24 in Chapter 3, where FileMaker's menus and context-sensitive screens are explained with an extra serving of illustrations and screen shots.

HOW TO USE THIS BOOK

One program, one book for Windows and Macintosh

FileMaker was one of the first programs that performed similarly whether you were using a Windows or Macintosh computer. In fact, the two versions are so similar now that anyone comfortable with FileMaker in general will find it relatively easy to pick up and move to FileMaker on the other platform—a real boon for anyone working in today's typical office with a mix of PCs and Macs. Still, there are some differences between FileMaker's Windows and Mac versions.

- Minor differences—different looking menus, dialog boxes, window icons—are not highlighted in the text. I've alternated illustrations from both platforms when such differences aren't important to how FileMaker functions. But in many of the book's illustrations, you can't necessarily tell which platform is being used. As Lefty in the film *Donnie Brasco* would say, "Fuggedaboutit!"

- Small but *important* differences between the versions are handled like so: "Under the Help menu, select FileMaker Help (Windows) or Show Balloons (Mac)."

- Major distinctions are highlighted with two icons:

  Win This one marks special instructions or features for the Windows version of FileMaker.

  Mac This one marks special instructions or features for the Macintosh version of FileMaker.

Just remember: The computer's your friend, but do try to get some sleep now and then. Even FileMaker's no substitute for life.

Database Basics

2

If you're new to databases, this chapter covers some basic concepts that will help you start off on the right foot in tapping the power of databases. If you're already familiar with databases in general, you may want to skip ahead to Chapter 3, "FileMaker Basics," on page 15.

While you might not think of them as such, databases are everywhere: address books, cookbooks, television program listings, to-do lists scribbled on envelopes—examples abound. None of those examples involves a computer, but they illustrate a fundamental concept: databases *organize* information.

It slices! It dices!

An address book organizes information alphabetically. A cookbook organizes information by ingredient or by course. Television listings organize information by time and channel. To-do lists organize information by task and time. Each lets you find what you need precisely because of how the information is organized. A computer database is not so different except for one major advantage: it can quickly organize the *same* information in *multiple* ways.

In some ways, a database is like that late-night TV perennial, the Veg-o-Matic: It slices! It dices! It's ten kitchen tools in one! A database can slice the same basic information any number of ways: as address book entries, as mailing labels, as billing invoices—whatever's needed.

Content versus form

Understanding content vs. form is the key to tapping the real power of any database. Do not confuse what a database contains (the content) with how it looks (the form). As important as data may be, it's not what gives a database its power. Instead, the power is in the program's ability to organize—and instantly reorganize—the display of that data (**Figure 2.1**).

Many people use spreadsheet programs to organize and analyze data. At times a spreadsheet is the best tool for such work, but a database often offers far more flexibility. Spreadsheet information, for example, is confined to rows and columns. Database programs like FileMaker can break free of that grid to display data as tables, lists, address labels, or in almost any form you need.

Tapping the power behind any database boils down to understanding and effectively using just a few items: fields, records, and layouts. Let's take a look at the role of each in a database program like FileMaker.

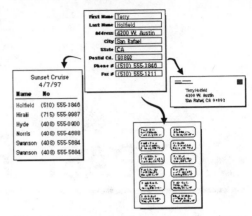

Figure 2.1 A database's real power comes from being able to display a single record's data in multiple ways.

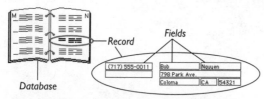

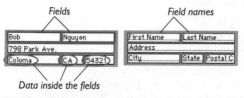

Figure 2.2 Every database organizes its information into individual records, which then contain fields for each bit of data.

Figure 2.3 Each field contains data but also carries a description, called a field name, which makes it possible to quickly manipulate even a large database.

Name	Home Phone
Dennis Smith	205-555-9876
Jennifer Norriz	702-555-4688
Jeremy Smith	503-555-4655
John Winford	414-555-9987
Julie Davidson	415-555-0900
Michael St. Lorant	415-555-0143
Pamela Day	712-555-5245
Sonia Long	508-555-6899

Figure 2.4 Smith before Norriz: Having only *one* name field highlights the problem of not breaking fields into the smallest pieces possible. Figure 2.5 shows a better approach.

First Name	Last Name	Home Phone
Julie	Davidson	415-555-0900
Pamela	Day	712-555-5245
Sonia	Long	508-555-6899
Jennifer	Norriz	702-555-4688
Dennis	Smith	205-555-9876
Jeremy	Smith	503-555-4655
Michael	St. Lorant	415-555-0143
John	Winford	414-555-9987

Figure 2.5 By breaking data into smaller pieces, such as adding *two* name fields, you gain more control over your information. This concept is crucial to building powerful, yet precise, databases.

Anatomy of a database

Databases often contain huge amounts of information, yet tiny pieces of that data can be fetched almost instantly. What's the secret? It's because everything within even the largest database is organized piece by piece into categories, or *fields* (**Figure 2.2**). Each field—the smallest unit within a database—contains information describing its contents. With that field information, the database can go to work. And by understanding the power of fields, so can you.

The field—the smallest unit

Fields let a database keep track of what information goes where. Each field contains data but also carries a description, called a *field name*. The field name helps the database sort, sift, and manipulate without necessarily needing to deal directly with the data itself. It can be a bit confusing, but remember: fields, field names, and the data inside the fields are three different things (**Figure 2.3**).

The more specific the fields you create within a database, the more powerful the database. Hang on to this idea as you learn more about FileMaker. For now here's an obvious example of why it's so important to make fields as specific as possible.

Though surely you wouldn't do this, imagine you've built an employee database with just one name field. With only a single name field, an alphabetical sort yields an immediate problem: Dennis Smith appears before Jennifer Norriz because D precedes J (**Figure 2.4**). Obviously that's not what you want. Creating two name fields lets you sort the last and first names alphabetically and independently (**Figure 2.5**). Obvious yes, but it's an idea that's easily forgotten in the heat of designing a new database. See Part III, starting on page 77, for more on defining and using fields with precision.

ANATOMY OF A DATABASE

The record— grouping related fields

Put a bunch of fields together and you have what FileMaker calls a *record*. A single record contains related information about a single topic, person, or activity. In an address book, for example, the equivalent of a record would be the entry for one person. That entry or record would contain several related items: the person's name, address, and telephone number. As you already know, those three items are equivalent to fields in a database.

The database— a group of related records

Combine a bunch of records on a single topic, for example customers, and you have a *database*. A database also can contain records on several related topics, such as customers, their addresses, invoices, and past orders. The ability to connect or relate *different* databases is what's meant by a *relational* database, like FileMaker.

One of the advantages of a relational database is that you can make such connections between databases without duplicating the information in each database. When you're dealing with thousands of records, that can save a lot of disk space—and lots of time.

The layout—
one record, many forms

A *layout*, sometimes called a *view*, is simply a way to control how the information in a database is displayed. When you first begin building FileMaker databases, you may find yourself occasionally confusing records with layouts. Again, the difference boils down to content versus form: One record (content) can have many different layouts (forms).

At its most basic, a record is *all* of the information for a single entry, while a layout shows a view of only the portion you need at the moment. Layouts also offer a way to hide everything you don't need at the moment. Let's go back to our paper address book example.

For each person in your book, you've probably listed their name, address, and phone number. If you're sending someone a birthday card, obviously you don't need to see their phone number. Similarly, if you want to call someone, you don't need their address. The paper address book shows you both. With databases, layouts enable you to show only what's relevant to the task at hand. So if you need mailing labels, you can take those address records and create layouts that only show the address. This notion of showing only what you need becomes especially important when you're working with a huge database containing dozens, or hundreds, of records and fields.

No matter whether you're using FileMaker or some other database program, these terms and concepts remain much the same. Now you're ready to delve into the particulars of FileMaker itself.

ANATOMY OF A DATABASE

FileMaker Basics

If you hate to read computer books, this chapter's for you. By taking a brief look at the menus assembled here and the explanations of how they and various commands work, you'll get a quick overview of FileMaker that will allow you to dive right in—if that's your style.

For readers who prefer a go-slow approach, this chapter's brief explanations also include page references to where in the book you'll find all the details you could want.

No matter which approach you prefer, this chapter provides a visual map for learning all of FileMaker's major functions.

FileMaker's screen and modes

No matter what you're doing in FileMaker, you will always be working in one of four modes: Browse, Find, Layout, or Preview. Because each mode is used for a different set of tasks, FileMaker's screen, menus, and their related options change from mode to mode.

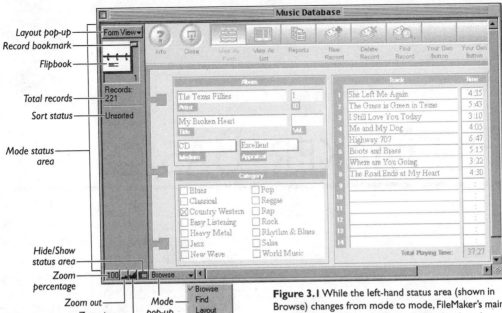

Layout pop-up
Record bookmark
Flipbook
Total records
Sort status
Mode status area
Hide/Show status area
Zoom percentage
Zoom out
Zoom in
Mode pop-up

Figure 3.1 While the left-hand status area (shown in Browse) changes from mode to mode, FileMaker's main screen always displays the flipbook icon, bookmark, zoom icons, and the mode status pop-up.

The FileMaker screen

Certain features of the FileMaker screen (**Figure 3.1**) remain constant: the flipbook icon at the upper left, the status area along the left side (unless you elect to hide it), the Zoom-in and Zoom-out icons, and the pop-up bar at the bottom of the screen, which lets you quickly choose your mode. As you switch from one mode to another, however, the left-hand status area displays a different set of tools and icons (**Figure 3.2**). The main record area also will change from mode to mode. For example, in Layout mode, the names of fields appear instead of the data itself.

Here's a quick rundown of the main elements of the FileMaker screen:

■ **Layout pop-up:** Clicking your cursor on the box reveals all the layouts for the current record. For more on using Layout mode, see Part III, "Creating and Designing Databases," on page 77.

■ **Record bookmark:** Using your cursor to click on and drag the bookmark allows you to quickly jump forward or backward through a database's records. For more on using the bookmark, see Chapter 4, "Viewing Records," on page 31.

■ **Flipbook:** This icon represents all the records in the current database. Clicking on the upper or lower pages of the flipbook moves you forward or backward one record at a time. For more on using the flipbook, see Chapter 4, "Viewing Records," on page 31.

■ **Current record, Total records:** The current record number tells you where you are among all the database's records, which is represented by the Total records number. By clicking on the Current record number, you can type in the number of a particular record you're seeking. For more information, see Chapter 4, "Viewing Records," on page 31.

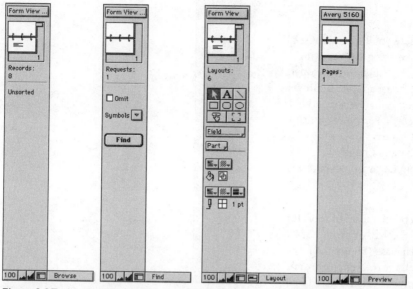

Figure 3.2 Tools and icons tailored to each mode appear in the left-hand status area as you switch from (left to right): Browse, Find, Layout, and Preview modes.

- **Sort status:** This simply tells you whether the records you're working with have been sorted or remain unsorted. For more on sorting records, see Chapter 5, "Finding and Sorting Records," on page 39.

- **Mode status area:** Running along the left-hand side of your screen, the status area displays the icons and tools for whichever mode you're in (**Figure 3.2**). For more on each mode's tools and icons, see pages 18–19.

- **Hide/Show status area:** Clicking on this icon allows you to hide or show the entire left-hand status area. This can be handy when you want to give the record itself as much screen space as possible.

- **Zoom percentage, Zoom in, Zoom out:** Clicking the Zoom-in and Zoom-out icons allows you to magnify or shrink your view of the current record. Clicking on the Zoom percentage box lets you toggle

between the current magnification view and the 100 percent view. This makes it easy, for example, to jump between an extreme close-up view (400 percent) and a regular view (100 percent) in a single click instead of the multiple clicks required by the Zoom-in and Zoom-out icons.

- **Mode pop-up:** This pop-up box at the bottom left of the screen displays FileMaker's current mode (**Figure 3.3**). By clicking on it, you can quickly move to another mode—just as you can by clicking on Mode in the menu bar. For more on modes, see the next section.

Figure 3.3 Click your cursor on the status mode pop-up and you can quickly switch to another mode.

Browse mode

Browse mode is where you'll spend most of your time if you're working with existing databases (**Figure 3.4**). Whenever you open a FileMaker database, it first appears in Browse mode. In Browse, you can view, sort, add, omit, and delete records. For more on using Browse mode, see Chapter 4, "Viewing Records," on page 31 and Chapter 5, "Finding and Sorting Records," on page 39.

Find mode

Find mode offers a powerful set of tools for locating individual records, or groups of records, within a database (**Figure 3.5**). In Find, you can search for records that match or don't match particular criteria based on text or mathematical values. For more on using Find mode, see Chapter 5, "Finding and Sorting Records," on page 39.

Figure 3.4 The status area for Browse mode appears to the left of the current record—though you can hide it if you want more screen space for the record.

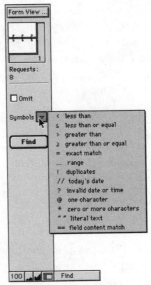

Figure 3.5 The Find mode status area offers tools for locating individual records, or groups of records, within a database.

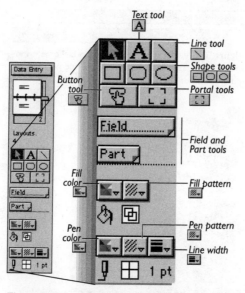

Text tool

Line tool

Shape tools

Button tool

Portal tools

Field and Part tools

Fill color

Fill pattern

Pen color

Pen pattern

Line width

Figure 3.6 The most elaborate of the four modes, the Layout mode's status area contains tools to control the appearance of the records and record views you design.

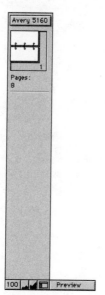

Figure 3.7 The Preview mode lets you control the appearance of printed FileMaker records.

Layout mode

Layout mode is where you design the appearance of the fields and records that display your data (**Figure 3.6**). In Layout, you can control every detail of fonts, field borders, button design—as well as the overall look of forms and entry screens. For more on using Layout mode, see Part III, "Creating and Designing Databases," on page 77.

Preview mode

Preview mode lets you control how your files look when printed (**Figure 3.7**). In Preview, you can set margins, get rid of unwanted gaps between fields, hide fields if you desire, and control how everything from reports to labels to envelopes print out. For more on using Preview mode, see Chapter 14, "Printing," on page 207.

FileMaker's menus

This section provides a quick run-through of FileMaker's eight to nine menus (**Figure 3.8**). The number of menus varies depending on which FileMaker mode you're in. Many of the menu commands and options are no different than those in any application: Open File, for example, is a fairly universal action. Commands specific to FileMaker are highlighted, below. Follow the page references for details on the various menu commands and options.

The File menu

As the name implies, all the commands within the File menu control actions related directly to file management (**Figure 3.9**). The File menu appears in all four FileMaker modes, with all its functions available.

- **New, Open, Close:** These first commands within the File menu operate much as they do in all programs.

- **Define, Access Privileges, Sharing:** All three commands control network-related functions. For more on determining which files can be seen on a network, who can see them, and which files can be shared, see Chapter 15, "Networking," on page 211.

- **Print Setup, Print:** These commands operate much as they do in all programs. For more information, see Chapter 14, "Printing," on page 207.

- **Import/Export, Save a Copy As, Recover:** These commands help you convert other database files to the current FileMaker format. For more on importing and exporting, see Chapter 7, "Converting Files," on page 67.

- **Exit/Quit:** Use this command to quit FileMaker.

Figure 3.8 FileMaker's menu bar offers eight menus in Browse, Find, and Preview modes (top) and nine menus in Layout mode (bottom).

Figure 3.9 The File menu's commands are available in all four modes.

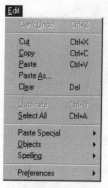

Figure 3.10 The Edit menu appears in all four modes, though not all functions are available in every mode.

The Edit menu

Most of this menu's commands operate just as they do in other programs—except for the fourth grouping explained below (**Figure 3.10**). The Edit menu appears in all four FileMaker modes, though not all its functions are available in every mode. (Dimmed items indicate functions not available within that mode.)

- **Paste Special, (Objects), Spelling:** Paste Special can be a tremendous time saver. Essentially, it lets you quickly reenter data from a previous record. It also allows you to instantly enter the current time, date, or user's name. For more on Paste Special, see Chapter 10, "Creating Layouts," on page 115.

  Win Choosing Objects takes advantage of a standard Windows feature, OLE (Object Linking and Embedding), which allows you to cut and paste data from other applications. The great advantage of OLE is that the data is updated automatically within the FileMaker record whenever it's changed in the original application. For more on Objects, see Chapter 10, "Creating Layouts," on page 115.

  Spelling offers the usual options. For more information, see Chapter 6, "Using Spell Check and Dictionaries," on page 61.

- **Preferences:** Setting FileMaker's preferences early on will save you time and frustration. The preference dialog boxes control a variety of items, including how FileMaker works with your modem, network, memory, and Web plug-ins. For more information, see Appendix B, "Setting Preferences," on page 265.

FILEMAKER'S MENUS

The Mode menu

FileMaker operates in one of four modes: Browse, Find, Layout, or Preview. Each mode is used for a different set of tasks and, so, the options offered under the Mode menu change depending on which mode you're in (**Figures 3.11–3.14**). In each of the four contextual mode menus, the top section remains the same, allowing you to quickly switch to another mode.

The rest of the menu changes based on which mode you're in, but the nice thing is that the arrangement and function remain consistent. Whether it's creating a new record in Browse mode, a new search request in Find mode, or a new layout in Layout mode, the command is the same. The commands for duplicate and delete work with the same cross-mode consistency.

The Select menu

The Select menu, available only in Browse and Find modes, contains commands used for finding and omitting records (**Figure 3.15**). Omitting records does not delete them but simply temporarily hides them so you can control which records you continue working with. For more information, see Chapter 5, "Finding and Sorting Records," on page 39.

The Show menu

The Show menu appears only in Layout mode and is used to help you control the appearance of records (**Figure 3.16**). The top half of the menu's selections (Size through T-Squares) gives you *document-wide tools* to help you create fields and objects within a record. The bottom half of the menu's selections (Buttons through Non-Printing Objects) lets you see the buttons and boundaries for *individual items* within the record. For more information, see Chapter 10, "Creating Layouts," on page 115.

Figures 3.11–3.14 In each of the four contextual Mode menus, the top section remains the same. While the other Mode commands change, the arrangement and function of the parts of the menu remain consistent.

Figure 3.15 Use the Select menu—available only in Browse and Find modes—for finding and omitting records.

Figure 3.16 Use the Show menu, which appears only in Layout mode, to control the appearance of records.

Figure 3.17 Use the Arrange menu, which appears only in Layout mode, to control the layering and grouping of objects as you design a layout.

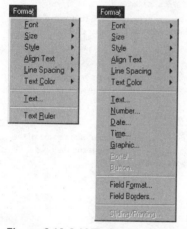

Figures 3.18–3.19 The Format menu appears in all modes except Preview, but offers the most functions in Layout mode (right).

The Arrange menu

The Arrange menu, which appears only in Layout mode (**Figure 3.17**), lets you control the layering and grouping of objects as you design a layout. For more information, see Chapter 10, "Creating Layouts," on page 115.

The Format menu

The Format menu appears in all modes except Preview, but offers the most functions in Layout mode (**Figures 3.18–3.19**). The availability of the functions also varies depending on what you've selected within the current record. In general, the functions within the Format menu start at the character level and move toward the field level. For more information, see Chapter 11, "Formatting and Graphics in Layouts," on page 157.

- **Font through Text Color:** The top six functions control attributes *at the character level* within a selected field.

- **Text through Button:** The second group of functions controls attributes at the field level, that is, what *type* of content the field contains: text, numbers, a date, a time, a graphic, portal (record view), or button.

- **Field Format, Field Borders, Sliding/Printing:** The third group of Format menu functions controls the style and behavior of the field *container*, that is, whether it's a standard field or one that offers a pop-up list or repeats itself.

The Script menu

Don't let this menu's unassuming appearance fool you (**Figure 3.20**). Choosing ScriptMaker will launch a powerful—and addictive—feature of FileMaker that enables you to automate many of the program's operations. For more information, see Chapter 12, "Using Templates and Scripts," on page 179.

The Window menu

This works much like the Window menu in most programs: The bottom half of the menu lists all currently open FileMaker databases, enabling you to arrange what's visible on your desktop (**Figure 3.21**).

The Help menu

If only FileMaker's Help menu were more, um, helpful (**Figure 3.22**). FileMaker has some of the best built-in help of any program, but it takes getting used to. For more information, see Appendix C, "Using FileMaker's Help and Tutorial," on page 273.

Figure 3.20 Use the Script menu to launch ScriptMaker, which enables you to automate many of FileMaker's operations.

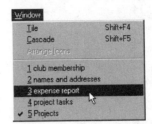

Figure 3.21 Use the Window menu to arrange multiple FileMaker databases on your desktop.

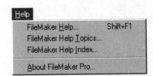

Figure 3.22 FileMaker's Help menu offers some of the best built-in help of any program, but the multiple options can seem confusing initially.

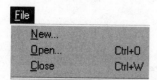

Figure 3.23 The commands for creating a new file, opening an existing file, and closing a file all reside under the File menu.

Opening and closing files

Opening and closing files in FileMaker works like most programs. Unlike many programs, however, FileMaker automatically saves data as you enter it. If by habit, you type Command-S, the Sort dialog box will appear. Just click Done and you'll be back to where you were with no harm done.

While FileMaker's save feature works automatically, you can control how often and under what circumstances saves take place. For more information, see Appendix B, "Setting Preferences," on page 265.

To open a file

1. If you haven't started the FileMaker program, do so now by either choosing Programs\FileMaker Pro 4.0\FileMaker from the Start menu (Windows 95) or double-clicking the FileMaker icon (Mac).

2. A dialog box will appear asking whether you want to create a *new* file using a template, create a new *empty* file, or open an *existing* file. Make your choice and click OK. For more information on templates see Chapter 12, "Using Templates and Scripts," on page 179.

3. If you've turned off the opening dialog box (see the Tip below), you still can open an existing file by clicking on the File menu bar, then selecting Open (**Figure 3.23**). Or use your keyboard: Ctrl O (Windows) or ⌘ O (Mac).

✔ Tip

- If you'd rather not see the dialog box that asks whether you want to open a template, a new file, or an existing file every time you launch FileMaker, check the "No longer show this dialog" box. In the future, when FileMaker starts up, you can then go directly to the File menu.

To create a new file

1. Click on the File menu, then select New (**Figure 3.23**).

To close a file

1. Because FileMaker automatically saves your data, closing a file is simple. You can close a file several different ways:

Click on the File menu, then select Close (**Figure 3.23**). The keyboard equivalents are: Ctrl W (Windows) or ⌘ W (Mac).

Win Click the close button in the record's upper-right corner (**Figure 3.24**) or double-click the FileMaker icon in the upper-left corner of the menu bar (**Figure 3.25**).

Mac Click the close box in the left corner of the record's title bar (**Figure 3.26**).

Figure 3.24 To close a Windows FileMaker file, click the close button in the upper right of the document.

Figure 3.25 You also can close a Windows FileMaker file by double-clicking the FileMaker icon at the far left of the menu bar.

Figure 3.26 To close a Macintosh FileMaker file, click the close icon in the upper left of the document.

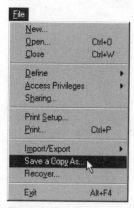

Figure 3.27 To make a backup copy of a record, select Save a Copy As under the File menu.

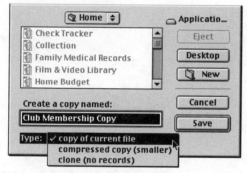

Figure 3.28 When making a backup copy, you can save it as a regular record, a compressed version, or a layout-only clone. Select one and click Save.

Though FileMaker saves your work as you go, you may want to make a copy of a database right before making a lot of changes to the original.

To save a copy of a database file

1. Click on the File menu, then select Save a Copy As (**Figure 3.27**).

2. When the dialog box appears, you can either accept the default name or type in a new name. Choose where you want to store the copy by navigating through the folder icons at the top of the dialog box. At the bottom of the dialog box (**Figure 3.28**), you also have the option to save the copy as a regular database file, a space-saving compressed file, or a clone. The clone option lets you save a database's layout, scripts, and field definition but without any data.

3. Once you've picked your file name, destination, and file type, click Save.

To quit FileMaker

1. From the File menu, select Exit (Windows) or Quit (Mac). The keyboard equivalents are: [Alt][F4] (Windows) or [⌘][Q] (Mac).

✔ Tip

■ If you don't quit FileMaker properly (for example, your machine crashes), the next time you open a FileMaker record the program will pause to run a consistency check. This takes only a moment, and then FileMaker is usually ready to go.

PART II:

WORKING WITH RECORDS AND FILES

VIEWING RECORDS

As eager as you might be to start creating your own database, the truth is you'll spend most of your time using FileMaker to view and modify *existing* records. Whether it's zipping through a big corporate health benefits database or working with your personal cookie recipes, knowing how to get around FileMaker records efficiently will save you lots of work over the long haul.

Opening a file

If you're working alone and this is your first time using FileMaker, you may not have any records to view. Never fear. To spare you the bother of having to create some records just for viewing, we'll be using some of the template records that came with your copy of FileMaker. If you already have a FileMaker database to work with, feel free to use it.

By the way, when you first open a FileMaker file it automatically appears in Browse mode, which enables you to look at a record without worrying about the layout or how it'll print. For more on each of FileMaker's four modes, see page 15.

To open a FileMaker database file

1. If you haven't started the FileMaker program, do so now by either choosing Programs\FileMaker Pro 4.0\FileMaker from the Start menu (Windows 95) or double-clicking the FileMaker icon (Mac).

2. A dialog box will appear asking whether you want to create a *new* file using a template, create a new *empty* file, or open an *existing* file. Select "Open an existing file..." and click OK (**Figure 4.1**). See Chapter 12, "Using Templates and Scripts," on page 179 to learn how templates can save you time in creating your own databases.

3. If you've turned off the opening dialog box (see page 25), you still can open an existing file by clicking File in the upper left of the menu bar, then selecting Open (**Figure 4.2**). Or use your keyboard: Ctrl O (Windows) or ⌘ O (Mac).

Figure 4.1 When FileMaker's opening dialog box appears, click "Open an existing file...".

Figure 4.2 You also can open an existing file via FileMaker's File Menu.

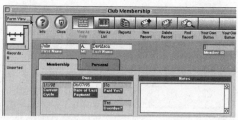

Figures 4.3 FileMaker's existing Club Membership file.

4. At this point, you can open a FileMaker file you may already have, in which case navigate your way through the dialog boxes to find it. If you don't have your own file, then continue with the following steps to open the existing example file featured in this chapter, Club Membership.

5. Navigate your way down to the file, Club Membership, nested inside these folders: FileMaker Pro 4.0 Folder\FileMaker Examples\Templates w-data\Business\. Open the file by clicking it directly, or clicking the Open button, or using the keyboard commands: Ctrl O (Windows) or ⌘ O (Mac). Now that you have the Club Membership file onscreen (**Figure 4.3**), we'll use it to explain how to view records, move from one record to another, and get around within individual records.

Viewing multiple or single records

FileMaker lets you view records two different ways: as single records using the Form View or as multiple records using the List View. Viewing one record at a time helps you see more detail within a particular record. Inspecting multiple records at the same time makes it easier to compare one to another.

To view multiple records

1. Our Club Membership example opens showing just one record (**Figure 4.3**). To view several records at once, click your cursor on the small Form View menu just above the flipbook icon in the upper left of the file. When the menu pops down, it will reveal your viewing choices.

2. Choose List View (**Figure 4.4**). The Club Membership file will shift to a list layout, enabling you to see as many individual records as your screen can accommodate (**Figure 4.5**).

To view a single record

1. To view one record at a time, click your cursor on the small List View menu just above the flipbook icon in the upper left.

When the menu pops down, hold down your cursor until it highlights Form View and release (**Figure 4.6**). The Club Membership file will shift back to the Form View layout with only one record showing (**Figure 4.7**).

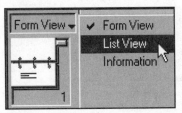

Figure 4.4 To see more than one record, click on the Form List menu above the flipbook and select List View in the pull-down menu.

Figure 4.5 The file will switch to the list layout, enabling you to compare one record to another.

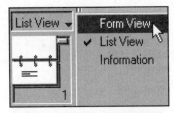

Figure 4.6 Toggling out of List View uses the same steps of clicking on the menu above the flipbook and selecting Form View in the pull-down menu.

Figure 4.7 After toggling, the file shifts back to the single-record view.

Figures 4.8–4.9 Buttons such as those built into the Club Membership layout offer another way to toggle from Form to List and back.

Another Form/List toggling option

■ Built-in buttons offer a convenient way to toggle from Form View to List View, and back. For more on creating such buttons, see page 188.

✔ Tips

■ The Club Membership file offers Form and List views because its designer created them (**Figures 4.8–4.9**). When you begin designing your own databases, remember how useful it can be to have different views of the same file.

■ There's no need to limit yourself to a single List View. Having a variety of views at your disposal can make it much easier to zero in on different aspects of your records. See page 115 in Chapter 10, "Creating Layouts," for more on creating various views of the same information.

Moving from record to record

FileMaker offers you three ways to quickly jump from record to record within a particular file. And, as with most things in FileMaker, you have several options within each view.

Navigating records in Form View

- Click on the flipbook's pages to move forward or backward—one record at a time. Click the lower page to move forward in the sequence (**Figures 4.10–4.11**); click the upper page to move back. A blank upper or lower page indicates there are no more records in that direction (**Figure 4.12**).

- To quickly skip ahead or back within the records, click and drag the flipbook's bookmark bar. Dragging it down will skip you ahead in the sequence; dragging it up moves you back (**Figures 4.13–4.14**).

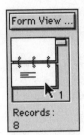

Figures 4.10–4.11 Click on the flipbook pages to move forward or backward one record at a time.

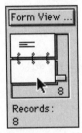

Figure 4.12 A blank page means you've reached the end of the record sequence.

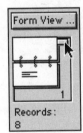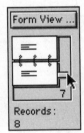

Figures 4.13-14 Jump ahead in the records by grabbing the bookmark bar and dragging it downward. Dragging it upward will let you move backward through the records.

Figure 4.15 Dragging the bookmark works in List View as well. Just grab, drag, and...

Figure 4.16 ... jump ahead in your records. Note how the black highlight in the thin bar left of the records now marks the Jennifer Norriz entry.

Figure 4.17 When in List View, you can click directly on any field and it will become highlighted. Once highlighted, you can change a portion or all of the data within the field.

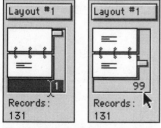

Figures 4.18–4.19 You can directly enter a record number by clicking the number just below the flipbook or by pressing the Esc key. Type in a new record number, press [Enter] (Windows) or [Return] (Mac), and you're there.

Navigating records in List View

- You can use the flipbook pages and book-mark bar in the List View as well (**Figures 4.15–4.16**).

- The List View also allows you to skip from record to record simply by clicking anywhere within the records visible on your screen (**Figure 4.17**). This is especially handy when you need to change data in one field within each record. Clicking directly on that field will highlight it, enabling you to begin entering your new data.

Navigating directly by record number

- If you know the number of a particular record, you can go right to it by clicking on the current record number (**Figure 4.18**), typing in the desired number, and pressing [Enter] (Windows) or [Return] (Mac) (**Figure 4.19**). Pressing [Esc] will automatically highlight the current record number, allowing you to work mouse-free. This method works in Form or List view.

✔ Tip

- When you're working in List View, a thin black bar just left of the records highlights the current record.

Moving within a record

Getting around within a single FileMaker record couldn't be easier, but as usual, there are several ways to do it.

Using your cursor to directly select a field works best when you need to change only a couple of items within a particular record. Using the Tab key generally works best when you're filling in new blank records or when you want to keep your hands on the keyboard. Both methods work in either Form or List View.

To move by direct selection

1. Click on any field you want to modify. Once the field becomes highlighted, type in your data (**Figure 4.20**). To reach another spot in the record, click your cursor on the desired field.

To move with the Tab key

1. After a record opens, press the Tab key to highlight the first field (**Figure 4.21**). Continue pressing the Tab key until you reach the desired field. To move backward among the fields, press Shift+Tab.

✔ Tips

- You can't tab to fields that contain calculations or summaries. But the contents of those fields are based on values set in other fields, so it's not really a problem. Just keep it in mind.

- FileMaker lets you set the tab order for all the fields in a record. Reordering the tabs is particularly handy if you need to reach only a few scattered fields within each record. For more on setting the tab order, see page 143.

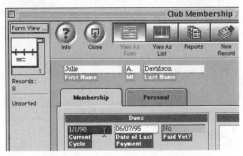

Figure 4.20 To enter data or modify a field, just click on it and type in your data once the field is highlighted.

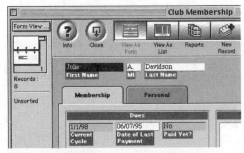

Figure 4.21 Press Tab once to reach the first field. Continue pressing Tab as many times as necessary to move forward to the desired field.

FINDING AND SORTING RECORDS

5

Finding and sorting records are like two halves of the same process. Together, they give you the power to spotlight particular records in a particular order. That ability allows you to complete such mundane work as correcting entry errors as well as big-picture tasks like analyzing trends.

With Find you can hunt down a record that needs changing without having to go through the records one by one. While records normally are displayed in the order they were created, the Sort command lets you arrange the view to what best suits your needs.

Virtually every Find or Sort you do can be set up as a script using FileMaker's ScriptMaker. Creating a script for a complicated Find allows you to save it for future use. For more information, see Chapter 12, "Using Templates and Scripts," on page 179.

Finding related field information in relational databases is covered in Chapter 13, "Creating Relational Databases," on page 191.

Finding records

Understanding a few key terms—the Find request and the found set, along with "and" versus "or" searches—will make it easier to use FileMaker's Find features.

The Find Request: What FileMaker calls a Find *request* simply represents all the criteria entered for a particular search. Whether they're plain or fancy, all the field criteria associated with a single search represent one Find request.

The Found Set: FileMaker calls the records returned in any search the *found set*, which represents only the records activated by the current Find request. The rest of the file's records still exist but are not displayed and make up what FileMaker calls the *omitted set*. For more information, see "Omitting records" on page 52 and "Deleting records" on page 54.

Working with a found set allows you to focus on tailoring it for sorting, printing, exporting, etc. You can return to working with the full set of records within a file at any time. To do so, choose the Find All command under the Select menu. Or use your keyboard: [Ctrl][J] (Windows) or [⌘][J] (Mac). In effect, this turns the entire file into the found set.

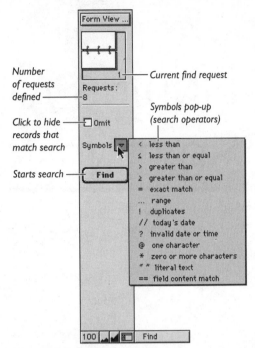

Figure 5.1 Switching to Find mode calls up search-related tools and buttons in FileMaker's left-hand status area.

And versus Or Searches: Find's features allow you to create wonderfully specific search requests but they all involve variations of two kinds of searches: the "and" search versus the "or" search.

Any time you create a Find request that looks for data in two or more *different* fields in a record, you're performing what's called a logical "and" search. FileMaker also calls this a *simple search*. If, for example, you create a Find request that asks for any records within a file where the city is San Francisco and the state is California, you're asking FileMaker to find records that contain San Francisco *and* California. Such "and" searches tend to narrow your search since you're not just looking for records containing California but a smaller group within that group that also contains San Francisco.

Any time you create a Find request that looks for *different* values within the *same* field, you're performing what's called a logical "or" search. FileMaker also calls this a *multiple search*. If, for example, you create a Find request for all records containing California or Arizona, that will require FileMaker to search the database's state field for two different values. Such "or" queries tend to widen your search.

Doing a simple search

The database used for examples in this section contains house sales information for my neighborhood collected from the county assessor: the address, the most recent sales price, when the house was last sold, the square footage, etc. It's intended to show how Find allows you to search the same information in a variety of ways.

To do a simple search for one item

1. You can't search for information in a particular field unless you have a layout with that field in it. Switch to the layout of your database that contains the field or fields you want to search.

2. Once the correct layout appears, click on the Mode menu and select Find (**Figure 5.2**). Or use your keyboard: Ctrl F (Windows) or ⌘ F (Mac). A blank version of the selected layout will appear.

3. In our example we want to find all the houses on Pomona Avenue, so type Pomona into the Street Name field (**Figure 5.3**). Click the Find button in the mode status area along the left-hand side of the screen (**Figure 5.1**), or simply press Enter (Windows) or Return (Mac). (You can also choose Perform Find from the Select menu but using the keyboard is much easier.)

4. Nine records appear that contain Pomona in the Street Name field (**Figure 5.4**). Notice that the left-hand mode status area shows the number of found records, along with the total record count.

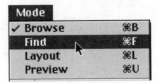

Figure 5.2 To start a search, select Find from the Mode menu.

Figure 5.3 Type into any field the data you're seeking.

Figure 5.4 Once you click Find, FileMaker switches to Browse and displays any records matching your search.

Figure 5.5 Entering data into multiple fields allows you to narrow your search, in this case to two-bedroom houses costing $200,000 or less.

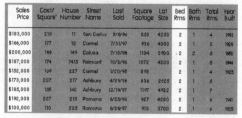

Figure 5.6 The search results show only records that match criteria in both fields.

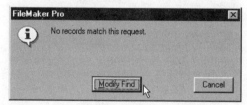

Figure 5.7 If no records match your request, click Modify Find.

To do a simple search for several items simultaneously

1. Select the database and layout you want to search. To start, click on the Mode menu and select Find, or use your keyboard: [Ctrl] [F] (Windows) or [⌘] [F] (Mac).

2. When a blank version of the layout appears, type your various criteria into the appropriate fields. In this example, we're searching for any two-bedroom houses costing $200,000 or less (**Figure 5.5**).

3. Click the Find button in the mode status area, or press [Enter] (Windows) or [Return] (Mac). The results show only records matching both request items (**Figure 5.6**).

✔ Tips

- If nothing in the database matches your search criteria, FileMaker will tell you and give you the chance to revise your search by clicking Modify Find (**Figure 5.7**).

- As long as each item you're requesting appears in a *different* field, you can make such requests as specific as you like: all two-bedroom, two-bath homes built since 1975 costing less than $200,000, for example. Many times this simple "and" search will be all you need. To search for different values within the *same* field, you'll need to make a multiple search request (see page 44).

- Once you've found a set of records, you can copy their data into another application, such as a spreadsheet, though FileMaker's field formatting will not be copied. Just use the copy command: [Ctrl] [C] (Windows) or [⌘] [C] (Mac).

DOING A SIMPLE SEARCH

Doing multiple criteria searches

What distinguishes a multiple criteria search from a simple search is that you're looking for several values within the *same* field. To go back to our real estate example, you may want to find homes on Pomona Avenue *and* San Carlos Avenue. Both items would appear in the Street Name field, so you'll need to make a multiple criteria search.

To do a multiple criteria search

1. Select Find from the Mode menu or use your keyboard: Ctrl F (Windows) or ⌘ F (Mac). Type what you're seeking into the relevant field. Do *not* hit Enter or Return just yet.
2. To add your second search item, choose New Request from the Mode menu. Or use your keyboard: Ctrl N (Windows) or ⌘ N (Mac). A duplicate set of blank fields will appear (**Figure 5.8**). Type what you're seeking into the duplicate of the field you used in the first request. Within the left-hand mode status area, the number of requests you've made within this set of records is displayed.

   If you want, you can continue to add multiple criteria by repeating this step.
3. When you're ready, click the Find button in the mode status area or press Enter (Windows) or Return (Mac) (**Figure 5.9**).

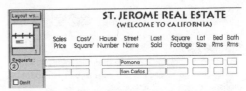

Figure 5.8 In a multiple criteria search, a second set of fields will appear—allowing you to look for several values within the *same* field.

Sales Price	Cost/ Square'	House Number	Street Name	Last Sold	Square Footage	Lot Size	Bed Rms	Bath Rms	Total Rms	Year Built
$240,000	189	115	San Carlos	11/12/97	1271	3900	2	1	7	1941
$163,000	216	11	San Carlos	8/6/96	853	4200	2	1	4	1948
$241,000	258	5	San Carlos	2/14/97	934	5000	2	2	4	1956
$250,000	139	200	San Carlos	9/30/96	1804	5000	2	2	9	1943
$201,000	204	216	San Carlos	1/20/97	983	4200	2	1	5	1940
$228,000	155	232	San Carlos	2/28/97	1474	4625	3	1	7	1948
$240,000	176	755	Pomona	5/29/97	1363	5400	3	2	7	1945
$218,000	195	145	Pomona	3/6/96	1119	4200				
$228,500	101	11	Pomona	8/15/97	2265	4280	4	2	9	
$192,000	207	215	Pomona	6/25/96	927	4280	2	1	6	1941
$230,000	147	200	Pomona	5/22/97	1567	4000	2	2	7	1938
$247,000	172	220	Pomona	7/12/96	1433	4000	3	1.5	8	1943
$291,000	203	116	Pomona	9/6/96	1432	4000	3	3	8	1950
$262,000	174	138	Pomona	6/6/97	1505	3600	3	1	8	1946
$211,000	196	146	Pomona	4/16/96	1067	4000	2	1	4	1944

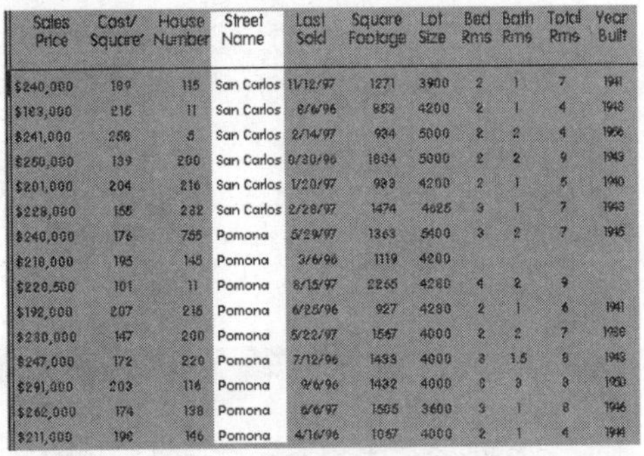

Figure 5.9 In this multiple criteria search example, the streets San Carlos *and* Pomona appear. Such searches can handle any number of requests for data in the same field.

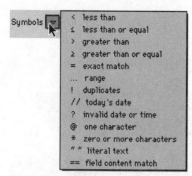

Figure 5.10 Click on the Symbols pop-up menu to access 13 choices for fine tuning your search. See Table 5.1 for details.

Refining searches

Within Find mode, the Symbols pop-up menu in the left-hand mode status area offers 13 choices for quickly fine tuning your search (**Figure 5.10**). Combined with the status mode area's Omit checkbox (for more information on Omit, see page 52), these tools can be a major help when trying to find a series of records amid hundreds (**Table 5.1**).

Table 5.1

Using Find's Symbols/Operators Pop-up Box

Use	To find	Type in field	Notes
<	Less than value to right of symbol	<200	
≤	Less than or equal to value to right	≤200	
>	Greater than value to right	>200	
≥	Greater than or equal to value to right	≥200	
=	Exactly value to right	=Pomona	Exact match *and* other values (e.g., will find Pomona <u>Ave</u>.)
==	Exact value in order & nothing else	==Pomona	Exact match with *no* other values (e.g., will not find Pomona <u>Ave</u>.)
...	A range of dates, times, numbers, text	... *or* .. (two periods)	Includes beginning and ending values; displays in A–Z, 1–10 order
!	Duplicate values	!	Finds *any* duplicate field entries—great for mailing lists
//	Today's date	//	
?	Invalid dates, times, or calculations	?	Finds *format* errors that can create calculation problems
@	*One* unknown or variable text character	@omona	A *one character* search that will find <u>P</u>omona and <u>R</u>omona
*	*Zero or more* unknown variable characters	P*a	No character limit: "P*a" finds Pomona but also Pia, Paula
" "	Text exactly as it appears	"Pomona"	Ignores letter case, so it will find "<u>P</u>omona" and "<u>p</u>omona"
==	Empty fields	==	Useful for finding missing data

To refine a search

1. Switch to the layout of your database that contains the field or fields you want to search. Click on the Mode menu and select Find, or use your keyboard: [Ctrl] [F] (Windows) or [⌘] [F] (Mac). A blank version of the selected layout will appear.

2. Click on the field you'll be searching. Now click on the Symbols pop-up menu in the left-hand mode status area and select the appropriate symbol or *operator*. (See **Table 5.1** for details on how each operator functions.) In this example, we want to find all the homes selling for less than $200,000. Select the first operator in the pop-up list, then type in 200,000 (**Figure 5.11**).

3. Click the Find button in the mode status area or press [Enter] (Windows) or [Return] (Mac). FileMaker will then display all the records meeting that criteria (**Figure 5.12**).

✔ Tips

■ You can use Find's Symbols pop-up box when making multiple criteria search requests as well as for simple searches.

■ If your search request criteria include finding the current date, time, or user name, use FileMaker's speedy Paste Special feature. Just click on the field you'll be searching, then choose Paste Special from the Edit menu and make a selection from the submenu. You can also use Paste Special while creating new records.

Sales
Price

<200000

Figure 5.11 Combining data you type in directly (200,000) with the pop-up menu's symbols (<) lets you quickly define a search for all entries of less than 200,000.

Sales Price	Cost/ Square'	House Number	Street Name
$183,000	215	11	San Carlos
$166,000	177	12	Carmel
$187,000	174	7415	Fairmont
$152,000	169	227	Carmel
$173,000	207	217	Ashbury
$185,000	155	140	Ashbury
$192,000	207	215	Pomona
$173,000	166	244	Ashbury
$191,000	165	309	Carmel
$100,000	110	225	Ramona

Figure 5.12 FileMaker switches to Browse mode and displays all records matching the <200,000 Find request.

REFINING SEARCHES

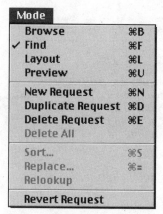

Figure 5.13 Commands for altering or modifying your most recent Find request reside under the Mode menu, but can be selected *only* if you're still in Find mode.

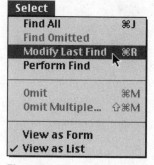

Figure 5.14 If you want to change a search but already are in Browse mode, choose Modify Last Find from the Select menu.

Modifying Find requests

FileMaker offers several commands for altering or modifying your most recent Find request. They all reside under the Find version of the Mode menu: New Request, Duplicate Request, Delete Request, and Revert Request (**Figure 5.13**). As long as you are still in Find mode, these commands can be used directly to revise your most recent search. However, if you've already performed the Find and are viewing the found records from within Browse mode, you'll need to take an additional step. (See "To modify your previous Find request" below.)

None of these commands can be applied to the previous search once you've done *another* search, which wipes out the previous search's criteria.

To modify your previous Find request

1. Make sure you've got the layout you want. If necessary, use the layout pop-up to select the right one.

2. Click on the Select menu and choose Modify Last Find (Ctrl R in Windows or ⌘ R on the Mac) (**Figure 5.14**).

3. When you've finished modifying your request, click Find or press Enter (Windows) or Return (Mac).

Making a new request

FileMaker calls this a *new* request but that's confusing. A more accurate name would be an *additional* request because you're adding search criteria to an existing Find request. This differs from simply modifying a Find because it's creating a logical "or" search and, so, requires searching *one* field for *two or more* criteria.

To add to a Find request

1. Switch to the layout you want.

2. If you're still in Find mode, select New Request from the Mode menu (**Figure 5.13**). Or use your keyboard: Ctrl N (Windows) or ⌘ N (Mac).

   If you've already performed the Find and now are in Browse mode, choose Modify Last Find from the Select menu (**Figure 5.14**). Or use your keyboard: Ctrl R (Windows) or ⌘ R (Mac). Now select New Request from the Mode menu or use your keyboard: Ctrl N (Windows) or ⌘ N (Mac).

3. A blank version of the selected layout fields will appear below the ones you previously filled in. Type your additional search criteria into the appropriate fields (**Figure 5.15**). Note: In this example only the street has been changed, but the price could be changed as well.

4. Continue adding requests just as you did in Step 2. When you've added all the requests, click Find, or press Enter (Windows) or Return (Mac).

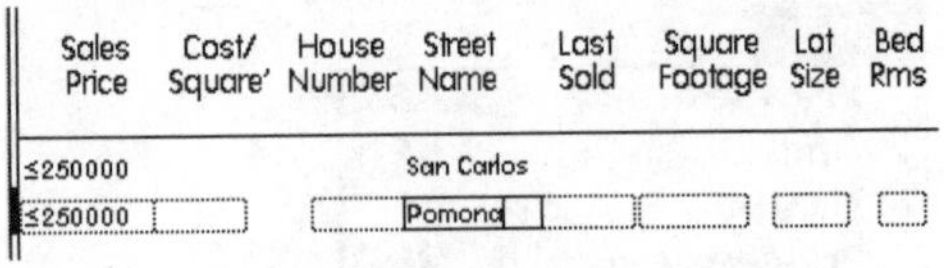

Figure 5.15 When you add a search request to an existing one (what FileMaker calls a New Request), a blank request form appears below the one you previously filled in.

✔ Tip

- This bears repeating because it can be so frustrating if you miss this step: Once you perform a Find (and so have wound up in Browse mode), you cannot modify that Find without first choosing Modify Last Find from the *Select* menu. Once you do that, you can then choose New, Duplicate, Delete, or Revert Request under the *Mode* menu without erasing the previous search criteria.

Sales Price	Cost/ Square'	House Number	Street Name	Last Sold	Square Footage	Lot Size	Bed Rms	Bath Rms	Total Rms	Year Built
≤200000			Pomona	≥1/1/91	≥1200		≥2	≥1.5		≥1960

Figure 5.16 While still in Find mode, use the flipbook icon to click to the previous Find request you want to duplicate.

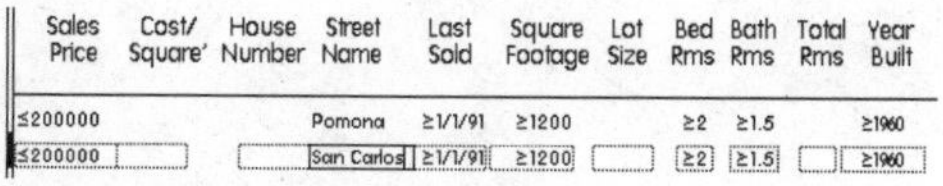

Sales Price	Cost/ Square'	House Number	Street Name	Last Sold	Square Footage	Lot Size	Bed Rms	Bath Rms	Total Rms	Year Built
≤200000			Pomona	≥1/1/91	≥1200		≥2	≥1.5		≥1960
≤200000			San Carlos	≥1/1/91	≥1200		≥2	≥1.5		≥1960

Figure 5.17 Using the Duplicate Request command saves time if you only need to change a few of the previous Find request's criteria.

To duplicate (and then change) a Find request

1. Switch to the layout you want.

2. If you're still in Find mode, use the flip-book icon to click to the previous Find request you now want to duplicate (**Figure 5.16**).

   If you've already performed the Find and now are in Browse mode, choose Modify Last Find from the Select menu (Ctrl R in Windows or ⌘ R on the Mac). Use the flipbook icon to click to the previous Find request you now want to duplicate.

3. Select Duplicate Request from the Mode menu (**Figure 5.13**). Or use your keyboard: Ctrl D (Windows) or ⌘ D (Mac).

4. A duplicate request will appear. You can then alter the appropriate fields—saving yourself a bit of time (**Figure 5.17**).

5. Repeat the steps until you've duplicated (and then changed) all the requests you need. Click Find, or press Enter (Windows) or Return (Mac).

DUPLICATING A FIND REQUEST

To delete a Find request

1. Switch to the layout you want.

2. While still in Find mode, use the flipbook icon to click to the Find request you want to delete.

If you've already performed the Find and now are in Browse mode, choose Modify Last Find from the Select menu (Ctrl R in Windows or ⌘ R on the Mac). Now use the flipbook icon to click to the Find request you want to delete.

3. Select Delete Request from the Mode menu (**Figure 5.13**). Or use your keyboard: Ctrl E (Windows) or ⌘ E (Mac).

✔ Tips

■ You can delete as many Find requests as you like—until there's just one left, which you cannot delete.

■ The Delete All command is not used for deleting Find requests. For more information about Delete All, see "To delete a group of records," on page 55.

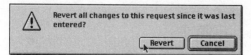

Figure 5.18 Choosing Revert Request from the Mode menu triggers an alert dialog box. Click Revert to correct a mistake or Cancel to leave things as they are.

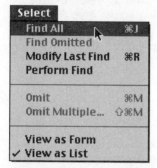

Figure 5.19 To display all the database's records, choose Find All from the Select menu.

Reverting requests

This command lets you correct entries while you're creating a Find request. It does not return you to where you were before you performed a Find. But it will let you start fresh on building the current Find request—no matter how many fields you've already filled in within that request.

To revert a request

1. You must be in Find mode, filling out a Find request. When you make a mistake, choose Revert Request from the Mode menu (**Figure 5.13**).

2. When the warning dialog box appears, click Revert (**Figure 5.18**). All the fields within that Find request will become blank, allowing you to start fresh.

To find all records

1. Choose the Find All command from the Select menu (**Figure 5.19**). Or use your keyboard: Ctrl J (Windows) or ⌘ J (Mac).

Omitting records

Omitting records does not delete them from your database but simply hides them from view. In that sense, omitted records are the reverse of the *found set* generated by a Find request. When you perform a Find, the records *not* shown are what FileMaker calls the *omitted set*. Used with the Find and Sort commands, the Omit command allows you to quickly make a selection and then *invert* it by finding all the records *not* in that selection.

To omit one record

1. In Browse mode, select the record you want to omit.

2. Choose Omit from the Select menu (**Figure 5.20**). Or use your keyboard: [Ctrl] [M] (Windows) or [⌘] [M] (Mac).

To omit more than one record

1. In Browse mode, select the first record of the group you want to omit.

2. Choose Omit Multiple from the Select menu (**Figure 5.21**). Or use your keyboard: [Shift] [Ctrl] [M] (Windows) or [Shift] [⌘] [M] (Mac).

3. A dialog box will appear asking how many records you want to omit. In our real estate example, we sorted the records to place together the six Ashbury records we want to delete (**Figure 5.22**). Since we'd selected the first Ashbury record in Step 1, we enter 6 and click the Omit button (**Figure 5.23**). The Ashbury records have been omitted—not deleted, just hidden. The "Records: 50" and "Found: 44" in the left-hand status area confirm that six records have been omitted (**Figure 5.24**).

Figure 5.20 To hide a record from view, select it, then choose Omit from the Select menu. Omitting records does not delete them but simply tucks them out of sight.

Figure 5.21 Choosing Omit Multiple from the Select menu hides a group of records—starting with the first one you select.

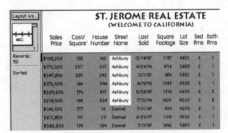

Figure 5.22 In the example, the far-left thin black bar indicates the first of the six Ashbury records that will be omitted.

Figure 5.23 When the Omit dialog box appears, type in the number of records you want to hide, then click Omit.

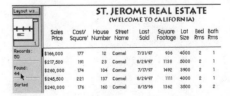

Figure 5.24 All six Ashbury records have been hidden. The "Records: 50" and "Found: 44" in the left-hand status area confirm that six records have been omitted.

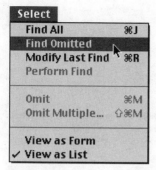

Select

Find All	⌘J
Find Omitted	
Modify Last Find	⌘R
Perform Find	
Omit	⌘M
Omit Multiple...	⇧⌘M
View as Form	
✓ View as List	

Figure 5.25 Because omitted records are only hidden, choosing Find Omitted from the Select menu restores them to view.

		Sales Price	Cost/ Square'	House Number	Street Name	Last Sold	Square Footage	Lot Size	Bed Rms	Bath Rms
		\$229,000	174	817	Ashbury	8/25/97	1314	4000	2	2
		\$219,000	156	838	Ashbury	7/12/96	1400	4200	2	2
		\$173,000	207	217	Ashbury	4/29/96	836	2625	2	1
		\$185,000	155	140	Ashbury	12/19/97	1197	4922	2	1
		\$247,500	259	242	Ashbury	11/7/97	956	3852	2	1
		\$173,000	166	244	Ashbury	4/19/96	1045	3852	3	1

ST. JEROME REAL ESTATE
(WELCOME TO CALIFORNIA)

Records: 50 — Found: 6 — Unsorted

Figure 5.26 The six previously hidden records return to view after choosing Find Omitted.

To bring back omitted records

1. Remember: Omitting a record does not delete it but simply removes it from the found set. To bring it back, choose Find Omitted from the Select menu (**Figure 5.25**).

2. The six records omitted in our previous example appear and are now the found set (**Figure 5.26**). The *previous* found set of 44 records are now omitted. It takes some getting used to, but the Find Omitted command's back-and-forth toggle nature becomes very handy when used with the Find and Sort commands.

✔ Tip

- Whenever you select the Find Omitted command it will display any records not already on the screen—even if you have every single record displayed. In that case, the Find Omitted command will display *no* records. Select Find Omitted again and up pop *all* the records. When you think about it, it makes sense.

Deleting records

Unlike the Omit command, which just hides records, the Delete command really does zap records and all the data inside them. Once you delete them, they're gone: no undo, no going back. To play it safe, consider making a backup copy of a file before you embark on a record-deleting session.

Think about this for a second. First create a copy of the file—just in case. If you're only looking to start with a fresh empty version of the layout, consider creating a clone of the existing database. Cloning gives you an empty database but does so by copying an existing database's layout without touching the original. See "To save a copy of a database file" on page 27 of Chapter 3.

To delete a single record

1. In Browse mode, select the record you want to delete. In our real estate example, we've selected an unwanted blank record (**Figure 5.27**).

2. Choose Delete from the Mode menu. Or use your keyboard: Ctrl E (Windows) or ⌘ E (Mac).

3. As a safeguard against accidentally deleting a record, FileMaker presents a warning dialog box (**Figure 5.28**). If you're sure, click the Delete button.

4. The selected record is then deleted (**Figure 5.29**).

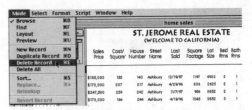

Figure 5.27 First select the record you want to delete (in this case a blank record on the right), then choose Delete from the Mode menu (left).

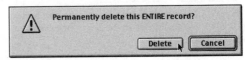

Figure 5.28 FileMaker presents a warning dialog box to make sure you really want to delete a record. If you're sure, click Delete.

ST. JEROME REAL ESTATE
(WELCOME TO CALIFORNIA)

Sales Price	Cost/ Square'	House Number	Street Name	Last Sold	Square Footage	Lot Size	Bed Rms
$185,000	155	140	Ashbury	12/19/97	1197	4922	2
$173,000	207	217	Ashbury	4/29/96	836	2625	2
$247,500	259	242	Ashbury	11/7/97	956	3852	2
$173,000	166	244	Ashbury	4/19/96	1045	3852	3
$229,000	174	817	Ashbury	8/25/97	1314	4000	2
$219,000	156	838	Ashbury	7/12/96	1400	4200	2

Figure 5.29 The blank record disappears after the Delete command is invoked.

Figure 5.30 To delete a group of records, select them, and then select Delete All from the Mode menu.

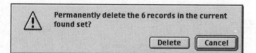

Figure 5.31 To keep you from accidentally deleting a group of records, FileMaker asks for confirmation of the number selected. If you're sure, click Delete.

To delete a group of records

1. Use the Find or Omit Multiple commands to select a group of records to delete.

2. Once you've selected the group of records, choose Delete All from the Mode menu (**Figure 5.30**). (To keep you from accidentally invoking the command, Delete All has no keyboard equivalent.) As a second safeguard, FileMaker presents a warning dialog box that notes how many records are about to be deleted (**Figure 5.31**). If you're sure, click the Delete button.

To delete all records in a database

1. If you truly want to delete all the records, choose Find All from the Select menu.

2. Choose Delete All from the Mode menu.

3. Again, FileMaker presents a warning dialog box asking if you really want to delete that many records. Remember: There's no undo for this command. If you're sure, click the Delete button.

Sorting records

FileMaker stores records in the order they were created but that's no reason for you work with them in that somewhat random order. Using the Sort command, you can rearrange the order for browsing, printing, or updating. FileMaker uses the found set concept discussed under "Finding records" to search through select fields and then arrange the records as you desire.

FileMaker offers three basic ways of arranging the records: ascending order, descending order, and a custom order based on a list you create. If, like me, you can hardly keep right and left straight, let alone what's ascending and descending, "How FileMaker Sorts What" (**Table 5.2**) should help.

To run a simple sort

1. Use any combination of the Find, Omit, and Delete commands to first narrow your selection of records for sorting. Of course, you can always sort the entire file.

2. Choose Sort from the Mode menu (**Figure 5.32**). Or use your keyboard: Ctrl S (Windows) or ⌘ S (Mac).

3. The Sort Records dialog box will appear (**Figure 5.33**). On the left side is a list of the fields in your file. Select the field you want to sort with by clicking on an item in the left list, then click the Move button in the middle to place it in the right-hand window.

   By default, the field will be sorted in ascending order. If you want to change the type of sort, first click the field in the right-hand list, then click on the appropriate radio button (Ascending, Descending, or Custom) in the lower-left area of the Sort Records dialog box (**Figure 5.34**). For more information, see "To set (or reset) a custom sort order," on page 60.

Table 5.2

How FileMaker Sorts What		
CONTENT	ASCENDING	DESCENDING
Text	A to Z	Z to A
Numbers	1–100	100–1
Time	6:00–11:00	11:00–6:00
Dates	1/1/98–12/1/98 Jan. 1–Dec. 1	12/1/98–1/1/98 Dec. 1–Jan. 1

Figure 5.32 The Sort command can be found under the Mode menu.

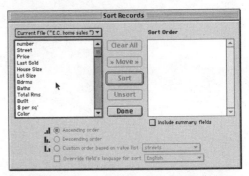

Figure 5.33 The Sort Records dialog box allows you to control which fields are sorted, the type of sorting used, and the order in which the sort occurs.

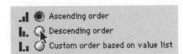

Figure 5.34 After you've selected a field, you can change the type of sort by clicking the appropriate radio button (Ascending, Descending, or Custom) in the lower-left area of the Sort Records dialog box.

Figure 5.35 The Sort Records dialog box's six buttons (Move and Clear never appear at the same time) control most Sort actions.

4. Click the Sort button in the middle of the dialog box or simply press [Enter] (Windows) or [Return] (Mac). If you want to adjust the results, choose Sort from the Mode menu again or use your keyboard: [Ctrl][S] (Windows) or [⌘][S] (Mac).

✔ Tip

■ The Sort order will remain in place until you perform a new sort.

To use the Sort dialog buttons

Whenever you run a sort, the Sort Records dialog box will appear. Most sort actions are controlled by six buttons (only five appear at any one time) running down the middle of the dialog box (**Figure 5.35**).

■ **Clear All:** Click this button to remove all sort fields in the dialog box's right-side Sort Order list.

■ **Move:** This button appears only after you click a field name in the dialog box's *left-side* list. Click Move to place a field name in the *right-side* Sort Order list.

■ **Clear:** This button appears only after you click a field name in the *right-side* Sort Order list. Click Clear to remove a field name from that list.

■ **Sort:** Click this button to start the sort itself.

■ **Unsort:** Click this button to return your file to its status before the sort was performed.

■ **Done:** Click this button to close the Sort Records dialog box without performing another sort.

Running multiple sorts

A multiple sort allows you to precisely arrange the order of your database records. When you sort more than one field at once, the precedence is based on the order in the Sort Records dialog box. Fields listed first in the box's right-side list will take precedence over fields listed later. Looking at our real estate example, if the Street field is listed before the Number field the records will be first sorted by the street name (A to Z) and then by the address number (1 to 100) (**Figure 5.36**).

To run a multiple sort

1. Use any combination of the Find, Omit, and Delete commands to first narrow your selection of records to sort. Of course, you can always sort the entire file.

2. Choose Sort from the Mode menu (**Figure 5.32**). Or use your keyboard: Ctrl S (Windows) or ⌘ S (Mac).

3. The Sort Records dialog box will appear (**Figure 5.33**). Select the left-side field name you want to first sort by. Click the Move button in the middle to place the field name in the right-hand Sort Order list.

	Sales Price	Cost/ Square'	House Number	Street Name	Last Sold
Records: 50	$185,000	155	140	Ashbury	12/19/97
	$173,000	207	217	Ashbury	4/29/96
Sorted	$247,500	259	242	Ashbury	11/7/97
	$173,000	166	244	Ashbury	4/19/96
	$229,000	174	817	Ashbury	8/25/97
	$219,000	156	838	Ashbury	7/12/96
	$166,000	177	12	Carmel	7/31/97
	$217,500	191	23	Carmel	8/29/97
	$260,000	174	104	Carmel	7/17/97
	$245,500	221	137	Carmel	8/29/97

Figure 5.36 By controlling the sort order within the Sort Records dialog box, all Ashbury homes appear first (with their house numbers in ascending order), followed by all the Carmel homes.

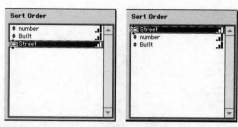

Figure 5.37 To change the sort order, use your cursor to drag the selected field name up or down in the order.

4. Continue selecting field names on the left side and placing them in the right side by using the Move button. Remember: Their relative precedence is set top to bottom. If you need to change the right-side order, click and hold your cursor over the double-arrow just left of the field name and then drag up or down. The field name will move, altering the sort order precedence (**Figure 5.37**).

5. Pick the *type* of sort (Ascending, Descending, or Custom) for each right-side field name by clicking on the name, then clicking on the appropriate radio button in the lower-left area of the Sort Records dialog box.

6. When you're ready, click the Sort button or simply press ⟨Enter⟩ (Windows) or ⟨Return⟩ (Mac). The records will then appear in the sorted order. If you need to adjust the sort order, choose Sort from the Mode menu again or use your keyboard: ⟨Ctrl⟩⟨S⟩ (Windows) or ⟨⌘⟩⟨S⟩ (Mac). Since you can unsort with the click of a button, feel free to experiment a bit to get a full sense of how different sorts work.

Setting sort orders

The Custom sort order is determined by a *value list*. Such lists—and their order—are typically created when fields are first being defined (see Chapter 9, "Defining Fields," on page 85). However you can change the order of a value list—and thereby the Custom sort order—any time.

To set (or reset) a custom sort order

1. Choose Sort from the Mode menu or use your keyboard: Ctrl S (Windows) or ⌘ S (Mac).

2. The Sort Records dialog box will appear. If the field name for which you want to create a custom sort order is already listed in the right-side list, click on it there and go to Step 4.

3. If the field name for which you want to create a custom sort order has not yet been selected and moved to the right side, click on its name in the left-side list. Now click the Move button, which will place the field's name in the right-side list.

4. By default, the field's sort type is Ascending. To change the type to a Custom order, click the radio button labeled "Custom order based on value list," wait for the pop-up menu to appear, and choose "Define Value Lists" (**Figure 5.38**).

5. Type an easy to recognize name into the Value List Name box and click Create (**Figure 5.39**).

6. In the large box in the lower right, type in the list of values exactly in the order you want the sort to occur (**Figure 5.40**). Click Save, then click Done.

7. Now sort the records using the Custom order for the Street field. The records will sort out in the order of the names in the Streets value list (**Figure 5.41**).

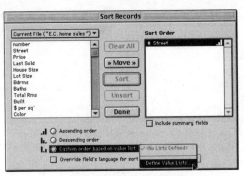

Figure 5.38 Click the radio button labeled "Custom order based on value list," wait for the pop-up menu to appear, and choose "Define Value Lists."

Figure 5.39 Give the value list an easy-to-recognize name, then click Create.

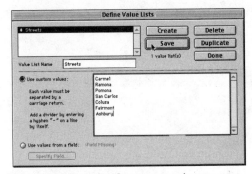

Figure 5.40 To set the Custom sort order, type your values into the large text box in the lower right in the exact order you want.

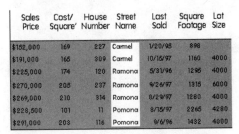

Sales Price	Cost/ Square'	House Number	Street Name	Last Sold	Square Footage	Lot Size
$152,000	169	227	Carmel	1/20/95	898	
$191,000	165	309	Carmel	10/15/97	1160	4000
$225,000	174	120	Ramona	5/31/96	1295	4000
$270,000	205	237	Ramona	9/26/97	1315	6000
$269,000	210	314	Ramona	8/29/97	1280	4000
$228,500	101	11	Pomona	8/15/97	2265	4280
$291,000	203	116	Pomona	9/6/96	1432	4000

Figure 5.41 Once you run the Custom sort, the record sequence mirrors the order of the value list.

USING SPELL CHECK AND DICTIONARIES

6

Each FileMaker record can be spell checked by FileMaker's built-in *main dictionary*, which contains an impressive 100,000 words, and by a special *user dictionary* of up to 32,000 words. If you frequently use special terms not commonly found in a dictionary—medical terms or irregular trademarks like FileMaker—you'll want to create one or more user dictionaries.

By default the main dictionary checks all FileMaker files, while you select which files are checked by a user dictionary. In fact, each FileMaker database can be linked to its own user dictionary. This allows you to link a medical database to a user medical dictionary or link a music-oriented database to a user dictionary of performing artists' names. Once that file-to-dictionary link is made, you need not specify it again.

In any case, you create the user dictionaries—either by importing an existing text file of your own special terms or by adding words one by one to an empty user dictionary created by FileMaker.

One more thing: FileMaker gives you the option to check your spelling as you type. For more information, see Appendix B, "Setting Preferences," on page 265.

To check spelling

1. When you have a record or layout to spell check, click on the Edit menu and select Spelling. The pop-up menu will then offer you the choice of checking the spelling of only what you've already highlighted (Check Selection), the record currently on your screen (Check Record), or the records browsed in the current session (Check All) (**Figure 6.1**). Choose one and release your cursor.

2. The Spelling dialog box will appear (**Figure 6.2**). If the dictionary says the selection is spelled correctly, click Done. If FileMaker suspects that the word is mis-spelled, it will display one or more possible replacement words. Click the one you prefer—or type in your own choice—then click the Replace and Done buttons.

   If, as in Figure 6.2, the word isn't in FileMaker's dictionary because it's a formal name or special term, you can click Skip or Learn, then click Done. Clicking Learn will add the word to the current user dictionary. If you have not created a special dictionary for this file, FileMaker will automatically create one within the Claris folder and name it USER.UPR (Windows) or User (Mac).

✔ Tip

■ If the field or file you're spell checking is password protected or access to it is otherwise restricted, you won't be able to change a misspelling.

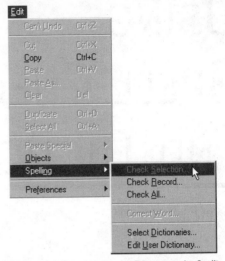

Figure 6.1 Found under the Edit menu, the Spelling pop-up menu offers you three spelling selection choices.

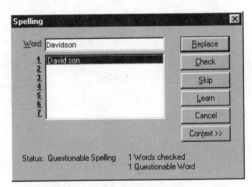

Figure 6.2 Within the Spelling dialog box, you can choose from six ways of dealing with a word's spelling, including seeing the word in context.

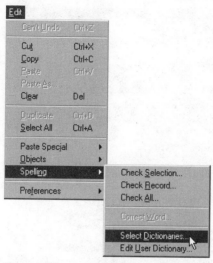

Figure 6.3 To create or select a dictionary, select Spelling under the Edit menu, then choose Select Dictionaries.

Figure 6.4 Within Windows' Select Dictionaries dialog box (Windows on left, Mac on right), you can choose FileMaker's *Main Dictionary* or a specially created *User Dictionary*.

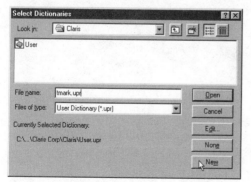

Figure 6.5 On Windows: Give your new user dictionary an easy to remember name, such as tmarks for a special trademark dictionary. Be sure to include the suffix .upr.

To create a user dictionary

1. Click on the Edit menu, select Spelling, and when the pop-up menu appears, choose Select Dictionaries (**Figure 6.3**).

2. Within the Select Dictionaries dialog box (**Figure 6.4**), click your cursor on the pop-up menu Files of type (Windows) or Select Dictionary Type (Mac) and select User Dictionary.

Win Within the File name text box, type what you want to call your new user dictionary. Make it something recognizable, such as "tmarks" for a special trademark dictionary. Be sure to include .upr at the end of the file name (**Figure 6.5**). When you're done, click New.

Mac Within the Select Dictionaries dialog box, click New. In the dialog box that appears (**Figure 6.6**), type a name for your new user dictionary. Make it something recognizable, such as "tmarks" for a special trademark dictionary. Click Save.

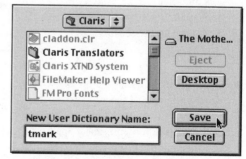

Figure 6.6 On the Mac: Type in a name for your new user dictionary, then click Save.

CREATING A USER DICTIONARY

To select or switch dictionaries

Once you've created more than one user dictionary, you'll need to select which one—if any—you want to apply to any new FileMaker databases. You can also use these steps to switch your main dictionary from US English to UK English.

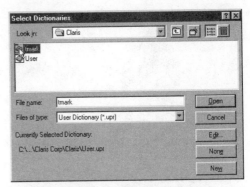

1. Click on the Edit menu, select Spelling, and when the pop-up menu appears, choose Select Dictionaries (**Figure 6.3**).

2. Within the Select Dictionaries dialog box, click your cursor on the pop-up menu Files of type (Windows) or Select Dictionary Type (Mac) (**Figure 6.4**). When the choices—Main Dictionary and User Dictionary—appear, release the cursor on User Dictionary. (When you want to change your main dictionary, choose Main Dictionary.)

3. Pick which user dictionary you want assigned to the current FileMaker database by double-clicking its name in the main window of the Select Dictionaries dialog box (**Figure 6.7**). If you've stored the dictionary in another folder, navigate your way there and double-click it.

   This also is where you can switch your main dictionary. If necessary, use the dialog box's main window to navigate to the dictionary you're seeking.

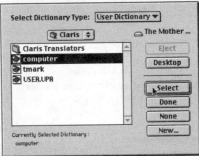

Figure 6.7 Pick a dictionary by double-clicking its name within the main window of the Select Dictionaries dialog box (Windows at top, Mac at bottom).

✔ Tip

■ Occasionally, you may want to check words only against the main dictionary and not use any user dictionaries. To do so, click on the Edit menu, select Spelling, and then choose Select Dictionaries. Within the Select Dictionaries dialog box, click the None button.

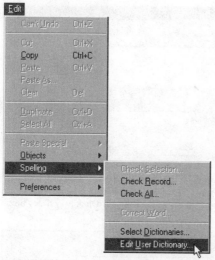

Figure 6.8 To edit a dictionary, click on the Edit menu, select Spelling, and then choose Edit User Dictionary.

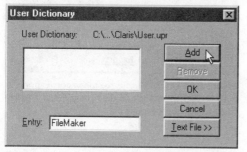

Figure 6.9 Within the User Dictionary dialog box, type in the word you want, then click Add or Remove.

To edit a user dictionary

Editing a dictionary allows you to add and remove words one by one or to import an existing text file of special terms you've created in another application.

1. First make sure you've selected the right dictionary to edit. (For more information, see "To select or switch dictionaries," on page 64.) Next, click on the Edit menu, select Spelling, and when the pop-up menu appears, choose Edit User Dictionary (**Figure 6.8**).

2. Within the Entry text box, type in the word you want to add to the dictionary. To remove words, navigate through the list within the top text box, click on the word you want removed, and click Remove (**Figure 6.9**). You can continue adding or removing words one by one until you're done. If you've already built a list of special terms in another application, you can use this dialog box to import them as a text file (see "To import or export a text file" on page 66.)

3. When you're done editing the dictionary, click OK to close the dialog box.

EDITING A USER DICTIONARY

To import or export a text file

1. You must first convert your original special-terms file to text so that FileMaker can recognize it. For example, if you created the list in Microsoft Word use that application's export feature to convert it to a text file.

2. Within FileMaker, click on the Edit menu, select Spelling, and when the pop-up menu appears, choose Edit User Dictionary (**Figure 6.8**).

    Win In the User Dictionary dialog box, click Text File and then click the Import or Export buttons when they appear (**Figure 6.10**). (You can use this same process to export a user dictionary you've built within FileMaker to use in another application.)

    Mac To see the Import/Export buttons, click on the triangle just right of Text File (**Figure 6.11**). Click the Import or Export buttons.

3. Use the dialog boxes to navigate your way to the file you want to import. Once you find it, click Open, then OK (Windows) or Save (Mac).

4. When you're done importing or exporting, click OK to close the User Dictionary dialog box.

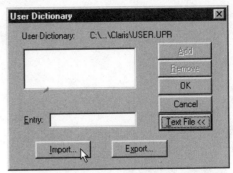

Figure 6.10 To import (or export) a file of special terms, click Text File, and then click the Import or Export buttons within the User Dictionary dialog box.

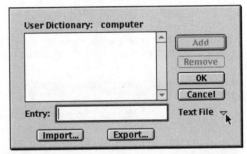

Figure 6.11 On the Mac: To see the Import/Export buttons, click the triangle to the right of Text File within the User Dictionary dialog box.

CONVERTING FILES

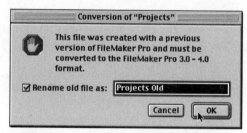

Figure 7.1 A warning dialog box asks you to rename older FileMaker databases you convert to version 4.

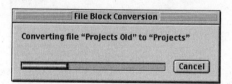

Figure 7.2 FileMaker displays a status dialog box while the conversion occurs.

No software program is an island. This chapter focuses on using FileMaker to build bridges by converting files from older FileMaker versions, bringing data from other application files into FileMaker (importing), and formatting FileMaker data so that other programs can use it (exporting). The chapter also discusses the unspeakable: how to recover data if a FileMaker file should ever become damaged.

To convert files from earlier FileMaker versions

1. While running FileMaker version 4, choose Open from the File menu ([Ctrl][O] in Windows/[⌘][O] on the Mac) and select the older FileMaker file. Click Open.

2. A dialog box will appear alerting you that the older file will be converted and asking you to name the new file (**Figure 7.1**). Click OK. A dialog box will appear showing the conversion process (**Figure 7.2**) and a new version of the data will appear in Browse mode.

Importing data into FileMaker

Moving data into FileMaker is easier than you might think. The trick is picking a file format for the source document that FileMaker can handle. Fortunately, you have many choices. (See **Table 7.1**, "Using FileMaker with Other File Formats," on page 71.) And thanks to FileMaker's ability to match source data to individual fields (**Figure 7.3**), the incoming data can be quickly put to use.

To import data into an existing FileMaker database

1. Make a backup copy of your original data and the FileMaker file you're importing it into.

2. Open the source file—that's the one you'll be importing data from. Save the file in one of the formats listed in **Table 7.1** on page 71. Close the source file.

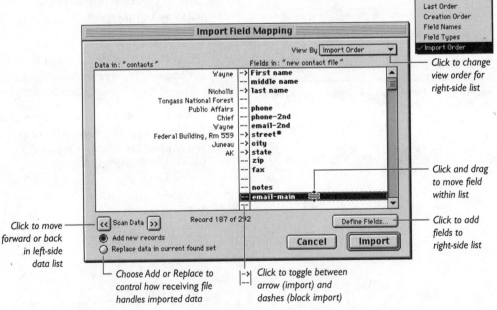

Figure 7.3 The Import Field Mapping dialog box gives you precise control over the data imported—and its order.

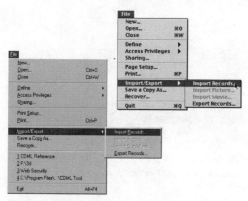

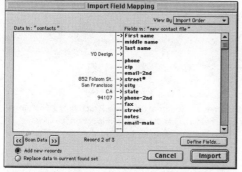

Figure 7.4 To import data into FileMaker, choose Import/Export from the File menu, then select Import Records.

Figure 7.5 Imported data often needs some tweaking: There's no field for the company name and the Zip field doesn't match with the data.

Figure 7.6 Once you've finished matching up the data fields, FileMaker displays the newly imported records in Browse mode.

3. Launch FileMaker, make sure you're in Browse mode ([Ctrl][B] in Windows/[⌘][B] on the Mac), and choose Import/Export from the File menu and select Import Records from the submenu (**Figure 7.4**).

4. When the Import Field Mapping dialog box appears, check to see if the data listed in the left-side window is properly matched with the field names on the right side. Many times, as in our example (**Figure 7.5**), a few things will need fixing: The ZIP code's set to import into the "phone-2nd" field and there's no field for the company name (YO Design). Click the name of a mismatched field (like Zip) and use the double-arrow to drag it down until it's across from the correct data (like 94107). To activate the import, click the center column to turn the double dash into an arrow. To add a field (like Company) to the FileMaker database, click the lower right Define Fields button.

5. Decide whether you want the source data to *add to* or *replace* the records already in the FileMaker database and click the appropriate radio button in the lower left of the dialog box.

6. Once you've tweaked the source-to-database mapping to your satisfaction, click Import. FileMaker will display the newly imported records in Browse mode (**Figure 7.6**).

IMPORTING DATA INTO FILEMAKER

Importing graphics or movies

You can import graphics or QuickTime movies into a FileMaker database only if you've already defined a container-type field to hold it. (See "To define a field" on page 88.)

To import graphics or movies

1. Make sure you're in Browse mode ([Ctrl] [B] in Windows/[⌘] [B] on the Mac), and select the container field by clicking on it.

2. To import a graphic, choose Import/Export from the File menu and select Import Picture from the submenu (**Figure 7.7**).

   To import a movie, choose Import/Export from the File menu and select Import QuickTime (Windows) or Import Movie (Mac) from the submenu (**Figure 7.8**).

3. When the dialog box appears, use the pop-up menu to select the appropriate file format, then find the file and click Open (**Figure 7.9**).

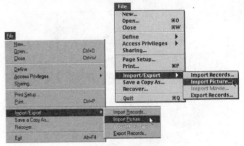

Figure 7.7 To import a graphic, which only a container-type field can handle, choose Import Picture from the File Menu.

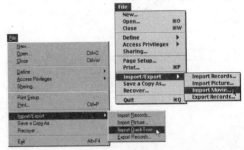

Figure 7.8 To import a movie, which only a container-type field can handle, choose Import QuickTime (Windows) or Import Movie (Mac) from the File Menu.

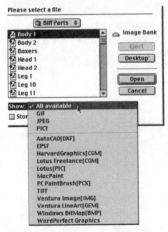

Figure 7.9 Use the pop-up menu to select the appropriate graphic file format.

Table 7.1

Using FileMaker with Other File Formats

FILE EXTENSION	FORMAT	WHAT FILEMAKER CAN DO WITH FORMAT
.FP3 or .FileMaker	FileMaker	Import data from FileMaker (v2, 2.1, 3, or 4) Export data to FileMaker (v3 or 4)
.TAB or .TXT	Tab-separated text	Exchange data with almost any application, including Claris Impact
.CSV or .TXT	Comma-separated values; Comma-separated text	Exchange data with BASIC programs
.SLK	SYLK	Exchange data with spreadsheet applications
.DIF	DIF	Exchange data with spreadsheet applications, such as VisiCalc
.WKI or .WKS	WKS	Exchange data with Lotus 1-2-3. FileMaker can import both formats but only exports .WKI
.BAS	BASIC	Exchange data with Microsoft BASIC programs
.MER	Merge	Combine Merge file data with main file text
.CWK or .CWS	ClarisWorks	Import data from ClarisWorks 4.0 database files
.HTM or .HTML	HyperText Markup Language table	Export FileMaker data as an HTML table for Web use
.DBF	DBF	Exchange data with dBASE III and dBASE IV
.XLS	Excel	Import data from Microsoft Excel (v4.0-97)

To import records from another FileMaker database

1. Before you import the FileMaker *source* records, use FileMaker's Find and Omit commands to expand or narrow the Found Set to just the records you'll want. Use Sort to put them in the order you want. They'll appear in that same order in the new FileMaker file.

2. Open the FileMaker *destination* database (the one you'll be importing records into). If you'll be replacing particular records, use FileMaker's Find, Omit, and Sort commands to expand or narrow the Found Set to only the records you'll be replacing.

3. Make sure you're in Browse mode (Ctrl B in Windows/⌘ B on the Mac) and choose Import/Export from the File menu and select Import (**Figure 7.4**).

4. When the Open File dialog box appears, use the pop-up menu to select the type of file you want to open. (See **Table 7.1**, "Using FileMaker with Other File Formats," on page 71.)

5. Click Open.

6. When the Import Field Mapping dialog box appears (**Figure 7.5**), check to see if the data listed in the left-side window is properly matched with the field names on the right side and tweak as necessary.

7. Click Import.

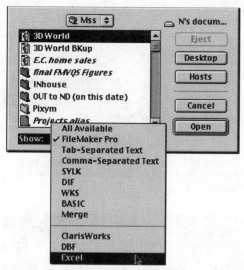

Figure 7.10 Use the Open File dialog box's pop-up menu to pick a format for the incoming data.

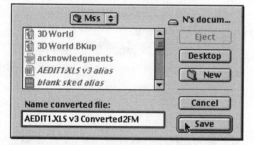

Figure 7.11 Give the converted data a clear name and click Save.

To import data into a new FileMaker database

1. Make a backup copy of your original data. Within FileMaker, choose Open from the File menu (Ctrl O in Windows/ ⌘O on the Mac).

2. When the Open File dialog box appears, use the pop-up menu to select the *format* of the file you want. (See **Table 7.1** "Using FileMaker with Other File Formats," on page 71.) In our example, we've selected Excel for the Microsoft spreadsheet (**Figure 7.10**). Click Open.

3. A dialog box will appear listing a new name for the file you're converting (**Figure 7.11**). Change it as you wish, then click Save.

4. Once the new file opens (the time required depends on the file's size), the old application's data will appear within the FileMaker database (**Figure 7.12**).

✔ Tip

■ If there's lots of data within the other application document that you won't need in the FileMaker database, it's often easier to weed it out using the original application *before* you import it into FileMaker.

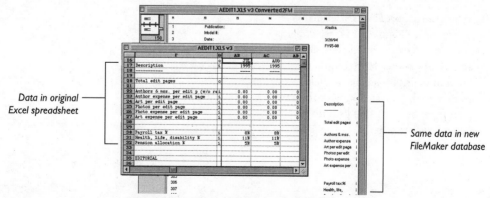

Data in original Excel spreadsheet

Same data in new FileMaker database

Figure 7.12 The data, and even some of the layout, of the Excel spreadsheet ported cleanly over to FileMaker.

Exporting FileMaker data

It's easy to export FileMaker records into another application—just as long as the receiving application can read one of the formats listed in **Table 7.1** on page 71. FileMaker's layouts can't be exported, but you can use FileMaker to arrange the record fields in the same order as a particular layout, as well as select exactly which records are exported.

To export FileMaker records

1. Before you export the FileMaker database, use FileMaker's Find and Omit commands to expand or narrow the Found Set to just the records you'll want. Use FileMaker's Sort command to then put the records in the order you want them to appear within the receiving document.

2. In Browse mode (Ctrl B in Windows/ ⌘ B on the Mac), choose Import/Export from the File menu and select Export Records from the submenu (**Figure 7.13**).

3. When the Export Records to File dialog box appears, name the file and select the folder where you want to store it. Use the pop-up menu to select a file format accepted by the application you're exporting to and click Save (**Figure 7.14**).

4. When the Export Field Order dialog box appears (**Figure 7.15**), select fields you want to export in the left-side list, and use the center Move button to place them in the right-side list of fields to be exported. Use the double-arrows to rearrange the right-side list into the desired export order.

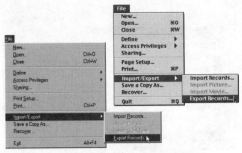

Figure 7.13 To export data out of FileMaker, choose Import/Export from the File menu and then select Export Records.

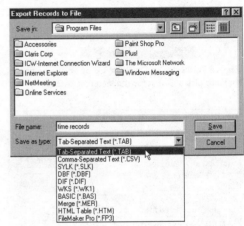

Figure 7.14 Use the pop-up menu within the Export Records to File dialog box to pick a format accepted by your target application.

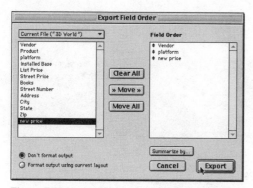

Figure 7.15 Use the Export Field Order dialog box to pick and order the FileMaker fields you're exporting.

5. Choose one of two format options listed in the dialog box's lower left. Use the "Format output using current layout" button to export, for example, commas and dollar signs along with the numbers in any fields you've formatted that way. Use "Don't format output" if you just want to export the raw, unformatted data.

6. Click Export. FileMaker will then place the data into a file based on the format you chose in Step 3, which you can now open in the other application.

✔ Tips

- If you're exporting records containing subsummary data, other applications may not be able to handle FileMaker's summary fields directly. You'll need to take the extra step of clicking on any summary fields among those fields you've moved into the Export Field Order dialog box's right-side list (**Figure 7.15**). Once you highlight the summary field, click the "Summarize by…" button and use the dialog box that appears to choose the field or fields used by the summary field. (See "Using calculation and summary fields" on page 109.)

- Not every export format can handle the multiple values contained in FileMaker's repeating fields. Work around this by cloning the original file that contains the repeating fields (see "To save a copy of a database file" on page 27). Then divide the repeating field data into separate records by selecting "Splitting them into separate records" within the Import Options dialog box. (See "Using repeating fields" on page 102.)

EXPORTING FILEMAKER DATA

Recovering damaged files

A file can become damaged from any number of causes: a sudden power loss, a disk drive crash, a corrupted bit of software. Most of the time, if you close and reopen the file, FileMaker will perform what it calls a consistency check and everything will be fine. If that doesn't work, you can try to rescue the file with FileMaker's Recover command.

To recover a damaged file

1. If you suspect that the file's been damaged, close it immediately (Ctrl W in Windows/⌘ W on the Mac).

2. Choose Recover from the File menu (**Figure 7.16**).

3. Use the Open Damaged File dialog box when it appears to navigate your way to the damaged file. Click Open.

4. By default, FileMaker will add the word "Recovered" to the end of the file's old name (**Figure 7.17**). If you like, type in another name. Click Save.

5. As it runs through a number of steps to recover the file, FileMaker will display a series of status dialog boxes (**Figure 7.18**). When FileMaker's done, a status report dialog box appears—hopefully with good news (**Figure 7.19**). Click OK.

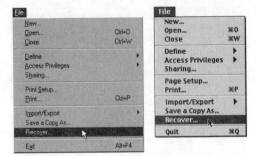

Figure 7.16 Make sure to first close a possibly damaged FileMaker file, then choose Recover from the File menu.

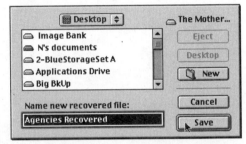

Figure 7.17 When it opens a damaged file, FileMaker automatically adds "Recovered" to its previous name.

Figure 7.18 While FileMaker's trying to recover a file, it will display a series of status dialog boxes.

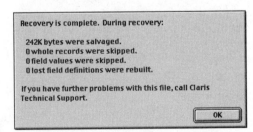

Figure 7.19 May the news always be this good: FileMaker provides a detailed report on how many records, fields, and values were recovered.

PART III

CREATING &
DESIGNING DATABASES

PLANNING DATABASES

If you're building a database from scratch, congratulations. You're free to do it right. Of course, you still have to start from scratch. It's a bit like building a new house versus restoring an old one. The new house gets a new foundation using the latest materials but it also starts as a clean—and very blank—sheet on the drafting table. With renovation, if the foundation's crumbling, you've got a big old house to somehow hold in place while you do the repairs.

No matter where you start, however, you'll not be entirely free of constraints. If you're building a database for your department, at some point, you'll probably need to share some data with another department. Even the home office worker will want, from time to time, to share information with others. In either case, you may have to export your FileMaker data to another format. By planning carefully, you can make even that task relatively easy.

How about a SlowStart®?

You know the saying: Hurry now, wait later.
The time you spend in this little chapter with
nothing more than a notepad and your
thoughts will save you hours of frustration
later at the keyboard. This is the secret to databases: they're not really about data, they're
about people and how they work together. As
odd as it might seem initially, the data itself
doesn't dictate the database design. Instead,
the processes and procedures among people
within an organization's various groups drive
the design. The very same data in a different
organization might need a completely different design.

Any time you build a database, you inevitably
face questions about the group it's intended
for: Where does this information come from?
Who knows this? Who needs this? Why do
we do it that way? Before you veer into an
existential thicket, here's the point: Take time
to understand the users' needs—along with
their organization's structure and information
flow—and you'll build a better database.

That, of course, means talking to people
about how they use information. Even organizations that don't already have a database
still have information flows, whether it's hidden in memos, spreadsheets, or the brains of
those folks you find in every office who
know where everything's kept and who did
what, when, and why. Talk to them. Not just
at the beginning of the design process, but at
every step. They know more about their needs
than you do. Unless, you are the user. In that
case, have a little heart-to-heart with your
own self. You'll probably learn something.

Follow the paper

Paper can be an important clue to how people use data in any organization. Look for which reports get printed out regularly and what overhead slides get used in meeting after meeting. Both are signs of what people find useful. Examine not just what they *contain* but what *form* they take. You'll find great ideas for what should be in the database and what layouts will be most useful. Don't just mimic the hard copy, of course, but those papers will help you more than pushing people to jump feet first into an electronic approach.

The same go-slow, pay-attention approach applies in looking at your organization's existing databases. Likely, you'll find them everywhere: inventories, billings, and mailing lists. Some will still be in use, others long dormant. Almost any database older than five years is going to be full of overlapping, redundant information, simply because stalwarts like dBASE II and III did not support relational databases. Don't slight them, however. Even if they're a bit creaky, they may contain useful data that you can import once you've built a new database.

In puzzling all this through, you may have some false starts. Don't worry. Unlike some database programs that force you to anticipate all your needs up front, FileMaker's very forgiving: You can always go back and add fields, layouts, scripts, or even new databases as you need them.

You must remember this...

■ Once you've done the planning, start listing the fields you'll need for all the information you'll want to track. If you're building a customer database, for example, you'll want the obvious fields for names, addresses, and phone numbers. You may also want a field or two or three for things like a customer's email address, pager number, and weekend message service. Don't forget that you're not limited to just fields for text and numbers. How about a picture field in the product catalog? And while you can't predict the future, the best databases anticipate growth and change. Need a crystal ball? Talk to those users again. To get started on using fields, see Chapter 9, "Defining Fields," on page 85.

■ Next, list the possible layouts you'll need. Assign a separate layout to each task: mailing labels gets its own layout, so do order invoices, summary reports, etc. You should also consider creating a different layout for each type of user. The sales folks, for example, probably need to see different data than the accountants.

All the action won't be on the screen, so you'll also need to think about layouts for printed reports, again using the layout-per-task rule of thumb. For more information, see Chapter 10, "Creating Layouts," on page 115. To make layouts easy on the eyes and easy to understand, see Chapter 11, "Formatting and Graphics in Layouts," on page 157. By the way, thanks to FileMaker's lookups and portals, layouts aren't confined to showing data from just one database. For help, see Chapter 13, "Creating Relational Databases," on page 191.

■ You don't have to start from scratch in building your layouts. Chapter 12, "Using Templates and Scripts," on page 179 shows you how to customize some of the 44 templates built into FileMaker. The chapter also shows you how to use scripts to automate multi-step actions, which makes it easier on the user. Creating scripts can also be a great way, for example, to find, sort, and highlight a group of records that show a pattern only FileMaker-savvy users could unearth without a script.

■ Finally, list the various databases you'll need, creating a separate database for each major category of information. For example, it's much better to create one database for products and another database for vendors rather than combine all that information in a single database. That's where FileMaker's relational abilities come in. Again, take your time. Building relational databases calls on everything else you'll learn in this section: defining fields, creating and formatting layouts, and using scripts. For more information, take a look at Chapter 13, "Creating Relational Databases," on page 191.

DEFINING FIELDS

Creating records in FileMaker is a multi-step process of defining fields, setting entry options for those fields, and setting relationships among the fields. This chapter covers each step in turn.

Controlling the *appearance* of your database and its records is covered separately in Chapter 10, "Creating Layouts," starting on page 115.

Choosing a field type

FileMaker's eight different types of fields are assigned via the Type radio buttons within the Define Fields dialog box (**Figure 9.1**). For step-by-step instructions on using this dialog box, see "To define a field" on page 88. But first, here's a quick rundown on the best uses for each field type:

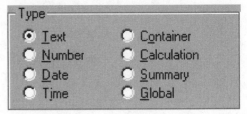

Figure 9.1 Choose your field type via the Type radio buttons in the Define Fields dialog box.

- **Text:** A text field can contain up to 64,000 characters (letters, symbols, and numbers as text). Text fields can be sorted (usually A–Z or Z–A) and used in formulas. Even items that might not at first blush seem to be text sometimes should be placed in text fields. For example, telephone numbers usually contain non-numeric hyphens or slashes, and, so, are best made into text fields.

- **Number:** A number field can contain up to 255 characters (numbers or other characters, which will not be treated as numbers). Number fields can be sorted (1–100 or 100–1) and used in formulas for calculations and summary fields.

- **Date:** Date fields must contain at least the day and month of a date. Date fields can be sorted (earliest-latest or latest-earliest) and used in formulas for calculations and summary fields.

- **Time:** Time fields can only contain the hours, minutes, and seconds of a time. Time fields can be sorted (earliest-latest or latest-earliest) and used in formulas for calculations and summary fields.

- **Container:** Container fields hold graphics, sounds, QuickTime movies, or Object Linking and Embedding (OLE) objects. Container fields cannot be sorted, but can be used in formulas for calculations and summary fields. While container fields cannot contain text or numbers, you can create related text or number fields to describe a container field's contents. The related text or number fields can be sorted—offering a work-around for the no-sort limitation on container fields. For more information, see "Understanding formulas," on page 104 and "Using calculation and summary fields," on page 109.

- **Calculation:** Calculation fields display the results of calculations made using other fields and, so, cannot have values typed directly into them. The result can be text, a number, date, time, or container. With the exception of summary functions, calculation fields operate on data *within single records*. For more information, see "Using calculation and summary fields," on page 109.

- **Summary:** Like calculation fields, summary fields cannot have values entered directly into them. Instead, they display summary values based on other fields in the database. In general, summary fields operate on data *from a group of records*. For more information, see "Using calculation and summary fields," on page 109.

- **Global:** Global fields display the same value in every record within a database. That value can be text, a number, date, time, or container. Typical uses include displaying boilerplate text or a company logo within each record. Container fields can be used in formulas for calculations and scripts. Since global fields appear in every record, they cannot be used to find records within a database.

CHOOSING A FIELD TYPE

Defining and changing fields

As you create fields for your database, you'll need to assign names and field types (for example, text or number), then choose how they will be displayed. The following steps cover most field types. For information on defining calculation and summary fields, see page 109.

To define a field

1. To create a field, click Define in the File menu and select Fields (**Figure 9.2**). Or use your keyboard: Ctrl Shift D (Windows) or Shift ⌘ D (Mac).

2. When the Define Fields dialog box appears (**Figure 9.3**), type the name of your first field in the Field Name text box.

3. Choose the type of field you want from the lower-left section of the dialog box (**Figure 9.4**). For more on deciding which field type best suits your needs, see "Choosing a field type," on page 86.

4. Once you click the Create button, the name of your new field will appear in the center window of the Define Fields dialog box (**Figure 9.5**).

5. At this point, you can repeat the steps to create another field. Or you can further define your field by highlighting its name in the center window of the Define Fields dialog box and then clicking the Options button. For more information, see "Setting field entry options," on page 90.

6. When you've finished creating fields (you can always add more later), click Done. FileMaker will then display the created fields in Browse mode. To dress up a field's appearance and layout, see Chapter 10, "Creating Layouts," on page 115.

Figure 9.2 To create a field, click Define in the File menu and select Fields.

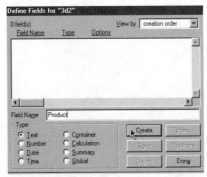

Figure 9.3 Assign a name to a new field within the Define Fields dialog box.

✔ Tips

- In naming your fields, FileMaker prevents you from using any of the symbols or words it needs to calculate functions: , (comma), +, -, *, /, ^, &, =, >, <, (,), ", ;, :, AND, OR, XOR, NOT. You also cannot use words that are also the names of FileMaker functions, such as "Status," "Count," or "Sum." One last thing: Don't start a file name with a period or a number.

- When defining a Global field, you'll need to take an extra step once you're back in Browse mode: Enter your desired information into the Global field in any record. Now select a new record—presto, the Global field is filled in.

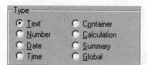

Figure 9.4 The lower-left section of the Define Fields dialog box offers eight field types to choose from.

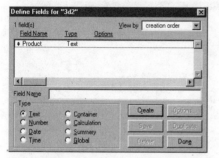

Figure 9.5 Once you create a field, its name appears in the list of fields within the Define Fields dialog box.

To delete or add a field

1. Open the Define Fields dialog box:
   Ctrl Shift D (Windows) or Shift ⌘ D
   (Mac).

2. To *delete* a field, click on its name in the center window, then click the Delete button. When the warning dialog box appears, again click Delete.

   To *add* a field, type the new field's name into the Field Name text box, check one of the radio buttons in the lower left Type area, and click the Create button.

3. When you're ready, click the Done button.

To change a field's name or type

1. Open the Define Fields dialog box:
   Ctrl Shift D (Windows) or Shift ⌘ D
   (Mac).

2. To change the *name* of a field, click on its name in the center text window and type in a new name.

   To change a field's *type*, highlight the field in the center text window, then find and check your new type choice among the eight radio buttons in the lower left Type area.

3. Click the Save button, then click the Done button.

DEFINING AND CHANGING FIELDS

Setting field entry options

FileMaker's Entry Options dialog box offers several powerful tools for speeding data entry and ensuring it meets certain standards. If more than one person will be entering data into the database, these options can reduce keyboard mistakes and problem-generating format variations. The options can be set while you're defining fields—or added later.

FileMaker lets you customize your field entries for four general areas: Auto Enter, Validation, Repeating fields, and Storage Options. For more information, see page 92 (Auto Enter), page 94 (Validation), page 102 (Repeating fields), and page 96 (Storage Options).

To set field entry options

1. Whether you want to set entry options for a new field or add them to an existing field, the steps are the same: Click Define in the File menu and select Fields. Or use your keyboard: Ctrl Shift D (Windows) or Shift ⌘ D (Mac).

2. In the center window of the Define Fields dialog box, select a field, then click the Options button (**Figure 9.6**). Or use the shortcut: double-click in the list on the field you want.

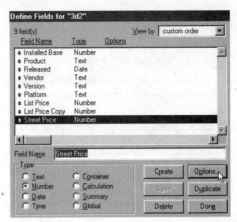

Figure 9.6 Double-click the field whose entry options you want to modify and click the Options button.

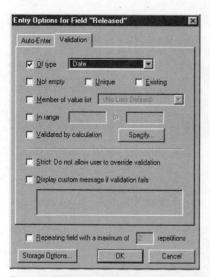

Figure 9.7 The Auto Enter and Validation settings share the upper half of the Entry Options dialog box with only one of the two appearing at a time.

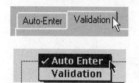

Figure 9.8 To switch between the Auto Enter and Validation settings, click the tab in Windows (top) or the pop-up box on the Mac (bottom).

3. When the Entry Options dialog box appears, make your selections. Of the two functions occupying the upper half of the dialog box (Auto Enter and Validation), only one appears at a time (**Figure 9.7**). Click the tab (Windows) or the pop-up box (Mac) to reach the other function (**Figure 9.8**). The Repeating field check-box and the Storage Options button are always visible at the bottom of the dialog box. Once you're done, click OK.

4. The Define Fields dialog box reappears. If you want to set entry options for another field, repeat steps 2 and 3. Once you're ready, click Done.

Though you've changed the entry options for a field, its *display* remains the same until you change the layout. For more information, see "To format a repeating field" on page 103, "To format a value list field" on page 100, and Chapter 10, "Creating Layouts," on page 115.

Auto Enter options

Follow the steps in "To set field entry options" on page 90 to reach the Auto Enter options (**Figure 9.9**). Here's how each functions:

- **Creation Date, Time, Name:** Use the first checkbox and its related pop-up box (**Figure 9.10**) to have the date or time when a record is created or modified entered automatically. It can also automatically enter the name of the person who originally created the record or the name of the person who most recently changed the record. Your choice here must conform with the type of field you've created: If you've already defined the field type as Date, the Creator Name and Modifier Name choices won't be available.

- **Serial number, next value, increment by:** Use these checkboxes to generate a unique number for every record in a database. It's particularly useful for invoices and other records that need one-of-a-kind identifiers. Once you've checked the "Serial number" box, you can then use the "next value" box to set the starting number for the next record. Starting numbers can include text at the front, such as A100 or Bin10. Use the "increment by" box to control whether the serial numbers increase in steps of 1, 2, 5, 10, or whatever.

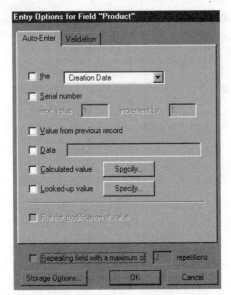

Figure 9.9 The Auto Enter panel's seven checkboxes control the automatic entry of values into selected fields.

Figure 9.10 The Auto Enter pop-up menu triggers the entry of times, dates, or names related to when a field is created or modified.

■ **Value from previous record:** This checkbox can save you a bit of keyboarding if you're creating a series of records where some of the fields need to contain the same value.

■ **Data:** Use this checkbox and the related text window to have a bit of text or a number automatically appear in a particular field.

■ **Calculated value:** Use this checkbox and the Specify button to automatically enter the results of any formula you choose. For more information, see "Using calculation and summary fields" on page 109.

■ **Looked-up value:** Use this checkbox and the Specify button to enter a value from another database. For more information, see Chapter 13, "Creating Relational Databases," on page 191.

■ **Prohibit modification of value:** This checkbox only becomes active if you've checked one of the previous boxes. Use it to ensure that a field's data isn't improperly changed. For more information, see the "Strict, Display custom message" choices under Validation options.

SETTING AUTO ENTER OPTIONS

Validation options

Follow the steps in "To set field entry options" on page 90 to reach the Validation options (**Figure 9.11**). These options ensure that data entered in the fields you select is correctly formatted.

- **Of type:** Use this checkbox and its related pop-up box (**Figure 9.12**) to automatically create a Number, Date, or Time type of field.

- **Not empty, Unique, Existing:** Use the first checkbox to make sure a field isn't skipped during data entry. The other two checkboxes work in opposing ways—Unique ensures that a record contains a one-of-a-kind value while Existing ensures that the value is the *same* as that of another field.

- **Member of value list:** Use this checkbox and its related pop-up box to present the user with a predefined list of entry choices. Value lists may be the single best tool in speeding data entry and preventing typos in records. For more information, see "Using value lists" on page 97.

- **In range:** Use this checkbox to ensure that the data entered falls within the range of the text, numbers, dates, or times you specify in the two entry boxes.

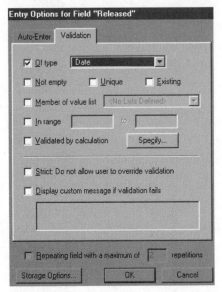

Figure 9.11 The Validation panel's nine checkboxes ensure that data entered into selected fields is correctly formatted.

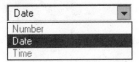

Figure 9.12 The "Of type" checkbox and its nearby pop-up box control the automatic entry of a number, date, or time.

SETTING VALIDATION OPTIONS

- **Validated by calculation:** Use this check-box and the Specify button to double-check a value against a chosen formula.

- **Strict, Display custom message:** These two checkboxes control what users see if the data they enter doesn't meet the criteria you've already set in the Validation dialog box. By checking Strict, you prevent users from simply clicking OK and ignoring Warning dialog boxes. This can be necessary if, for example, the field's value is used in a calculation and must be in one form only. If you check Strict, however, it's always good to also check the Display custom message box and write a message that will explain why the entry was not accepted—and what users might do to conform to the field's requirements. The message can contain up to 255 characters.

Storage options (indexing)

FileMaker's Entry Options include setting storage options (indexing) for any text, number, date, time, and calculation field. Indexing creates an alphabetical (or numeric) list of all the values in the selected field, greatly speeding finding records—once the index is created. But indexing also increases your database's size and can slow down running large files. For that reason, FileMaker gives you field-by-field control of which, if any, fields are indexed. Indexing can also be used to store results for calculation fields. (See "To store calculation results" on page 113.)

To set indexing

1. Select a field to index by following the steps in "To set field entry options" on page 90 to reach the Entry Options dialog box. Click the Storage Options button (**Figure 9.13**).

2. The Storage Options dialog box (**Figure 9.14**) gives you three index settings: On, which creates an index for the selected field; Off, which blocks FileMaker from indexing the field; and Automatically turn indexing on if needed. The third choice, which becomes available when you check the Off radio button, allows indexing only if you later use the field in a search or as part of a relational database. Make your choices, and if necessary, reselect which language the index will use by using the bottom pop-up menu.

3. Click OK. The Define Fields dialog box reappears. If you want to set indexing for another field, repeat steps 1 and 2. When you're finished, click Done.

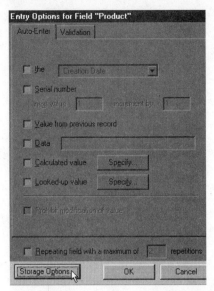

Figure 9.13 Click the Storage Options button at the bottom of the Entry Options dialog box to set indexing for a selected field.

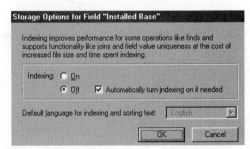

Figure 9.14 Within the Storage Options dialog box, click On or Off to control indexing for a selected field.

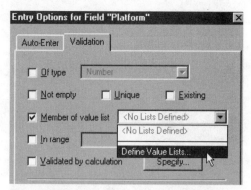

Figure 9.15 To create a value list while defining a field, press your cursor on the pop-up box next to the "Member of value list" checkbox, then select Define Value Lists.

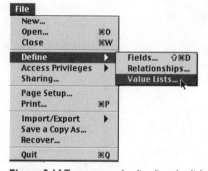

Figure 9.16 To create a value list directly, click Define in the File menu and select Value Lists.

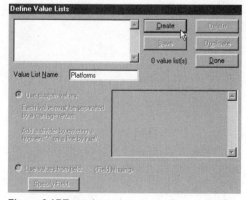

Figure 9.17 Type what you want to call your value list in the Value List Name text box and click Create.

Using value lists

By offering users a predefined list of field entry choices, value lists save lots of time and aggravation. The more people you have entering data into a database, the more important value lists become in maintaining record consistency and accuracy. Don't worry about locking yourself in: Like so many things in FileMaker, value lists can be altered any time. A quick-and-dirty explanation for formatting value lists is included in this section, but you'll want to read Chapter 10, "Creating Layouts," on page 115 to get a fuller sense of your formatting options for value lists.

To define a custom value list

1. While value lists often are created at the same time you create a field, they exist independently of any particular field and can be created directly.

   To create a value list while defining a field, follow steps 1-3 in "To set field entry options" on page 90. When you reach the Validation panel, select the third checkbox, "Member of value list." Hold your cursor down on the pop-up box immediately to the right and select Define Value Lists (**Figure 9.15**).

   To create a value list directly, click Define in the File menu and select Value Lists (**Figure 9.16**).

2. When the Define Value Lists dialog box appears, type what you want to call your value list into the Value List Name text box. Click the Create button (**Figure 9.17**).

   By default, the name of your new Value List will appear in the upper-left window, the "Use custom values" radio button will be selected, and your cursor will appear in the lower-right box—ready for you to enter the custom values you want. (You can also create a value list

   (continued)

using values from an existing field. See the following steps, "To define a value list using another field.")

Type in your first value, then press Enter (Windows) or Return (Mac) to begin a new value (**Figure 9.18**). When you're done adding values to the list, click Save. To create another value list, repeat steps 2 and 3. When you've finished creating lists, click Done.

Though you've made the field into a value list, its *display* will not change until you change the layout. See "To format a value list field" on page 100 for a quick rundown. For more information, see Chapter 10, "Creating Layouts," on page 115).

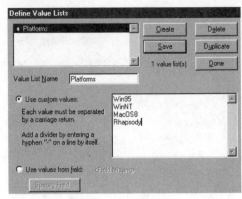

Figure 9.18 Build your value list (separating each value with a carriage return), click Save, and then click Done.

✔ Tip

■ If you have a long list for a Value List, make it easier to read by typing in some hyphens, *s, #s (or whatever) on a line of their own, then pressing Enter (Windows) or Return (Mac) to start a new line with a new value.

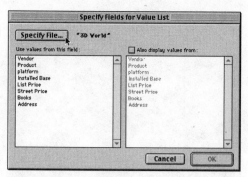

Figure 9.19 If you want to use values from the *current* database's fields, double-click the entry in the left list. To reach a field in *another* database, click the Specify File... button.

To define a value list using another field

1. Follow the preceding steps of "To define a custom value list." When the Define Value Lists dialog box appears, by default it is set to "Use custom values." Instead, select the radio button in the lower left, "Use values from field," and click Specify Field.

2. A dialog box appears listing all the fields within your current database (**Figure 9.19**). If one of these suits your purposes, select it, and click OK. More likely, you'll want to use values from a field in another FileMaker record, so click the Specify File button in the upper left.

3. Navigate your way to the FileMaker database file you want and open it. A new dialog box will appear listing all of that database's fields. Select the one you want to use and click OK. Those values will now be used in your pop-up list.

4. Again, you'll need to switch to Layout mode to format how you want the value list to appear. See the following steps, "To format a value list field," for a quick rundown. For more information, see Chapter 10, "Creating Layouts," on page 115.

To format a value list field

1. If you haven't already defined your value list, see "To define a custom value list" on page 97. When you're ready to format a field, switch to Layout mode (Ctrl L for Windows, ⌘ L on the Mac). Select the field you want to format by clicking on it.

2. From the Format menu, choose Field Format (**Figure 9.20**). The Field Format dialog box will appear (**Figure 9.21**).

3. Click on the second radio button, which will activate the adjacent "Pop-up list" menu, as well as the "using value list" pop-up menu to the right (**Figure 9.22**).

4. Select which style you want for your value list: Pop-up list, Pop-up menu, Check boxes, or Radio buttons (**Figure 9.23**). Also select from the second pop-up menu the value list you created for the field when you defined it earlier.

5. The Style section of the Field Format dialog box includes three other checkboxes to make your value list formatting more flexible for the user (**Figure 9.21**). The first two checkboxes can work as double-edged swords so consider whether you want to give users that flexibility or whether you'd prefer to limit entries to what's in the value list.

   Select the "Include 'Other…' item" if you want to let users enter a value that's not in your value list. This formatting option can be added to every value list format except the Pop-up list. If the user picks the "Other…" choice, a dialog box will open, allowing the user to add another value (**Figure 9.24**).

   Select the "Include 'Edit…' item" if you want to let users change the choices in your value list. This choice can only be used for the Pop-up list and Pop-up menu formats. If the user picks the "Edit…"

Figure 9.20 To format a field, select Field Format from the Format menu.

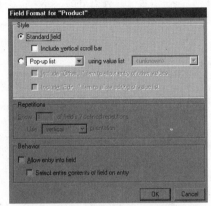

Figure 9.21 The Style section (highlighted in light grey) controls the *appearance* of the value list.

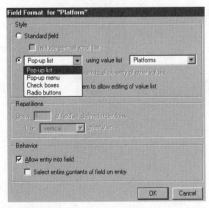

Figure 9.22 Clicking on the Style section's second radio button allows you to choose a format for your value list.

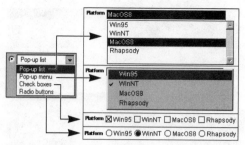

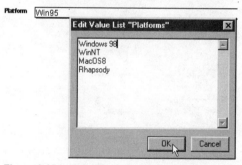

Figure 9.23 From top to bottom: The same field's value list formatted as a pop-up list, a pop-up menu, a series of checkboxes, and a series of radio buttons.

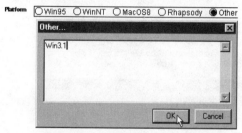

Figure 9.24 Including the "Other..." choice allows users to *add another* item to a value list.

Figure 9.25 Including the "Edit..." choice allows users to *change* an existing value list any way they like.

choice, a dialog box will open allowing the user to change an existing value or add more values to the list (**Figure 9.25**).

6. When you're done making your selections, click OK. The dialog box will close. Switch to Browse mode ((Ctrl) B for Windows, ⌘ B on the Mac) and your field will appear with its new formatting.

✔ Tip

■ Which value list style best suits your needs? The Pop-up list and Pop-up menu options simply show a blank field—with no clue that it holds multiple choices—unless the user clicks on it. That's handy if you don't have much screen space or want a clean, simple look. The checkbox and radio button options let the user immediately see all the choices for the field. Checkboxes allow multiple selections, while radio buttons only allow one selection at a time.

Using repeating fields

Repeating fields let you create a single field that accommodates more than one value—saving you the trouble of creating multiple fields that might not always be needed. A quick-and-dirty explanation for formatting repeating fields is included in this section. But to get a fuller sense of your formatting options see Chapter 10, "Creating Layouts," on page 115.

To define a repeating field

1. Within the Define Fields dialog box, double-click the name of the field you want to define as repeating (**Figure 9.26**).

2. When the Entry Options dialog box appears, click the checkbox near the bottom labeled "Repeating field with a maximum of __ repetitions." Fill in the blank with the number of repetitions you want. Click OK (**Figure 9.27**).

3. The Define Fields dialog box will reappear; click Done. Though you've now defined the field as repeating, its display will not change until you change the layout. See "To format a repeating field" on the next page for a quick rundown. For more information, see Chapter 10, "Creating Layouts," on page 115.

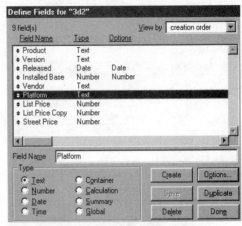

Figure 9.26 To *define* a repeating field, double-click the field's name within the Define Fields dialog box.

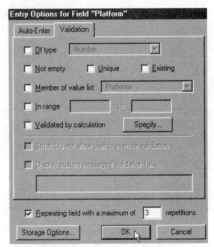

Figure 9.27 Within the Entry Options dialog box, fill in how many times you want the field to repeat and click OK.

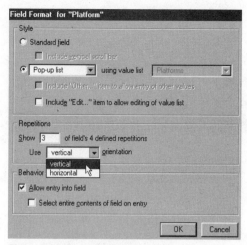

Figure 9.28 The Field Format dialog box lets you choose how many times you want the field to appear and its orientation.

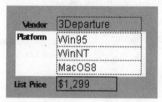

Figure 9.29 The repeating field's new vertical format appears when you switch from Layout to Browse mode.

To format a repeating field

1. Switch to Layout mode (Ctrl L for Windows, ⌘ L on the Mac). Select the field you want to format by clicking on it.

2. From the Format menu, choose Field Format and the Field Format dialog box will appear. Within the box's Repetitions section, enter how many times you want the field to appear and choose its orientation (**Figure 9.28**). Vertical will stack the fields; horizontal will place them side by side. Click OK.

3. FileMaker will return you to the Layout view of the field and the rest of the record. Switch to Browse mode (Ctrl B for Windows, ⌘ B on the Mac) to see the new format (**Figure 9.29**).

✔ Tip

■ In the above example, the repeating fields appear as Pop-up lists, but you can use the Style section's pop-up menu to have them appear in any of the other three formats. The two pop-up formats work best for repeating fields, however, since the checkbox and radio button options will produce a blizzard of boxes and circles.

Understanding formulas

Formulas are used in two kinds of FileMaker fields: calculation fields and summary fields. For the most part, formulas used in calculation fields operate on data in the *current* record. Formulas used in summary fields operate on data from *more than one* record.

Beneath a sometimes confusing raft of terms and definitions, formulas are simple. Using a set of specific instructions, formulas take data from one or more fields, calculate or compare or summarize it, and then display the results. That's it. The twist comes in that word *specific*: Formulas must be constructed in a set order, or syntax. Mess up the syntax and the formula won't work properly, if at all.

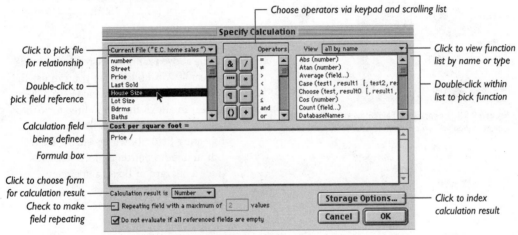

Figure 9.30 Within the Specify Calculation dialog box, formulas are built in the center formula box using pieces taken from (upper left to right) the field reference list, the keypad and scrolling list of operators, and the functions list.

Syntax and the parts of a formula

You'll build most of your formulas within the Specify Calculation dialog box (**Figure 9.30**), which will go a long way in helping keep your syntax straight. The dialog box works like a construction kit with tools to let you assemble the necessary field references, constants, operators, and functions. Once the formula is run, it spits out results, whose form you also control. Before you start, however, take a moment to understand some of the key terms used in formulas.

Field References: A field reference directs a formula to use the value in the field it's named after. The left-hand list within the Specify Calculation dialog box displays all the field references in the selected database.

Constants: As the name implies, a constant is a fixed value used in a formula. It remains the same from record to record. A string of text, a number, a date, or a time can all be constants. Each of these types of constants must be typed in a particular format for the formula to recognize which type of constant it represents. For more on the required formats, see **Table 9.1**, "Constants," below.

Table 9.1

Constants		
FOR THIS TYPE DATA	**REMEMBER TO**	**EXAMPLES**
Text	Enclose text in quotes (")	"Welcome to FileMaker" "94530-3014"
Number	Do not include currency symbols or thousand separators (, or ;)	80.23 450000
Date	Use the value as parameter of the Date function or the TextToDate function. See Appendix E, "Date functions," on page 289.	Date(3,13,1998) TextToDate("03/13/1998")
Time	Use the value as parameter of the Time function or the TextToTime function. See Appendix E, "Time functions," on page 289.	Time(10,45,23) TextToTime ("10:45:23")

UNDERSTANDING FORMULAS

Expressions: An expression is simply a value or any computation that produces a value. Expressions can contain field references, constants, and functions, and can be combined to produce other expressions. For more information, see **Table 9.2**, "Expression examples."

Operators: Operators enable a formula to compare the contents of two (or more) fields. Insert operators into your formulas using your keyboard or the keypad and scrolling list within the Specify Calculation dialog box (**Figure 9.31**). Operators combine expressions and resolve what operation should be performed on the expressions. For example, the addition sign, +, is simply an operator that combines the value appearing before it with the value appearing after it: Subtotal + Tax.

Mathematical and text operators are used with, surprise, numbers and text. Comparison operators compare two expressions and return a result of True or False, in what is known as a Boolean expression. Logical operators compare two or more conditions, such as whether the Cost field is more than $200,000 (the first condition) *and* the Square footage field is less than 1,000 (the second condition). For more information, see **Tables 9.3–9.6**.

Table 9.2

Expression examples	
TYPE OF EXPRESSION	EXAMPLE
Text constant	"FileMaker"
Number constant	80.23
Field reference	Cost per square foot
Function	TextToDate
Combination of expressions	(Price/House Size)*0.10

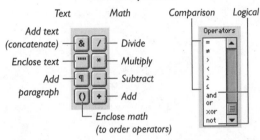

Figure 9.31 Build formulas using the keypad and scrolling list, which contain text, math, comparison, and logical operators.

Table 9.3

Mathematical operators (see Figure 9.31)			
SYMBOL	NAME	DEFINITION	EXAMPLES
+	Addition	Adds two values	2+2, Subtotal+Sales Tax
-	Subtraction	Subtracts second value from first	2-1, Total-Discount
*	Multiplication	Multiplies value	Subtotal*Sales Tax
/	Division	Divides first value by second	Total/Units
^	Exponentiation	Raises first value to power of second	$(A^2 + B^2)$ returns A^2B^2

Note: Exponentiation (^) Symbol not part of operators keypad, use regular keyboard ([Shift] [6])

Table 9.4

	Text operators (see Figure 9.31)		
SYMBOL	NAME	DEFINITION	EXAMPLES
&	Concatenation	Appends the text string on right to end of text string on left	"AAA" & "BBB" returns "AAABBB"
" "	Text constant	Marks beginning and end of text constant. Quotes with no text between them indicate a blank space. Text in formula without quotes is interpreted as a field name or function name. To mark a quote mark within a text constant, precede it with another quote mark.	"Welcome to FileMaker" returns as Welcome to FileMaker " " returns an empty (null) value "Welcome to our "favorite" place" returns as Welcome to our "favorite" place
¶	Return marker	Inserts a paragraph return in a text constant	"Welcome to¶Filemaker" returns Welcome to FileMaker

Table 9.5

	Comparison operators (see Figure 9.31)		
SYMBOL	NAME	DEFINITION	EXAMPLES
=	Equal to	True when both items are equal	4=5 returns False 4=4 returns True
≠ or <>	Not equal to	True when the items are not equal	4≠5 returns True 4≠4 returns False
>	Greater than	True when value on left exceeds value on right	4>5 returns False 5>4 returns True
<	Less than	True when value on left is less than value on right	4<5 returns True 5<4 returns False
≥ or >=	Greater than or equal to	True when value on left is greater than or equal to value on right	5≥4 returns False 5≥5 returns True
≤ or <=	Less than or equal to	True when value on left is less than or equal to value on right	5≤4 returns False 4≤4 returns True

Table 9.6

	Logical operators (see Figure 9.31)	
SYMBOL	DEFINITION	EXAMPLES
AND	True only when both values are true: True when true AND true False when true AND false False when false AND false	Cost per square foot <200 AND Bedrooms≥2
OR	True when either value is true: True when true OR true True when true OR false False when false OR false	Cost per square foot <200 OR Bedrooms≥2
XOR	True when either, but not both, of values is true: False when true AND true True when false AND true False when false AND false	Cost per square foot <200 XOR Bedrooms≥2
NOT	Changes value within parentheses from false to true, or true to false: False when NOT (true) True when NOT(false)	NOT Cost per square foot >200

UNDERSTANDING FORMULAS

Using predefined formulas (functions)

A function is simply a *predefined* formula with a set name, such as TextToDate. Functions perform a particular calculation and return a single value. FileMaker comes with more than 150 functions, all of which are listed in Appendix E on page 287. All those functions are available via the right-hand list within the Specify Calculation dialog box, but scrolling through the whole list for one function would be a bother. Instead, use the top-right pop-up menu to display handier portions of the list (**Figure 9.32**). By toggling among the options, you can zero in on the function you need (**Figure 9.33**).

Functions have three parts: the predefined function, the parameters used by the function, and a set of parentheses enclosing the parameter. In almost all cases, FileMaker functions follow this syntax, or order:

Function name(*parameter*)

For example: TextToDate(*time*) or Average(*field*)

The parameter (the value within the parentheses) can be a field reference, a constant, an expression, or another function. Sometimes a function needs more than a one parameter, in which case separate each parameter from the next parameter with a comma or semicolon:

Average (*field1, field2, field3*). In this example, field1, field 2, and field3 are just placeholders for the actual field reference you'd place into the formula.

Calculation Results: Once the formula runs, it displays the calculation as a result. The result can take several forms—text, number, date, time, or container—which you control via the Specify Calculation dialog box. For more information, see "To change the display of calculation results" on page 112.

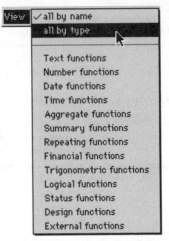

Figure 9.32 Use the Specify Calculation dialog box's upper-right pop-up menu to fine tune your view of FileMaker's 150+ built-in functions.

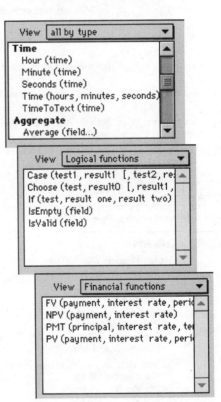

Figure 9.33 Use the View pop-up menu to quickly find the function you need.

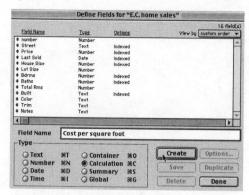

Figure 9.34 Once you create a new field, select the Calculation radio button within the Type area and click Create.

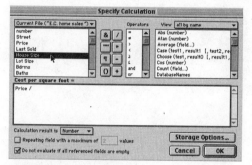

Figure 9.35 Use the Specify Calculation dialog box to create your formula, then click OK.

Figure 9.36 The Specify Calculation dialog box's formula operators are controlled by the the keypad (left) and the scrolling window (right).

Using calculation and summary fields

You cannot enter anything directly into a calculation or summary field. Instead, the fields store and display the results of calculations you build via the Specify Calculation dialog box or the Options for Summary Field dialog box.

Formulas used to define a calculation field can be as basic or as complex as you need, and will seldom use every tool available in the Specify Calculation dialog box. Our first example walks through a very simple formula.

To define a calculation field

1. To create a calculation field, click Define in the File menu and select Fields. Or use your keyboard: Ctrl Shift D (Windows) or Shift ⌘ D (Mac).

2. When the Define Fields dialog box appears, type into the Field Name text box the name of your field.

3. Select the Calculation radio button within the Type area of the dialog box, then click Create (**Figure 9.34**).

4. The Specify Calculation dialog box, where you define a formula for the selected field, appears (**Figure 9.35**). The simple "Cost per square foot" example uses just two field references and a single symbol: (Price/House Size).

   Add the Price field reference by double-clicking its name within the left-side list, click the division symbol (/) in the symbols keypad (**Figure 9.36**), then double-click the House Size field reference in the left-side list. (For information on using the Storage Options button in the lower right of the Specify Calculation dialog box, see "To store calculation results" on page 113.)

   (continued)

5. Once you're finished building the formula, click OK. The Define Fields dialog box will reappear.

6. Click Done.

✔ Tips

- Instead of mouse-clicking on the symbols keypad within the Specify Calculation dialog box, you can use their equivalents on your keyboard.

- Selecting the "Do not evaluate if all referenced fields are empty" checkbox will keep FileMaker from performing a calculation unless the field referenced by the formula has a value—saving some otherwise wasted time.

To edit a formula

1. To reach the Specify Calculation dialog box and edit a formula, click Define in the File menu and select Fields. Or use your keyboard: `Ctrl` `Shift` `D` (Windows) or `Shift` `⌘` `D` (Mac). When the Define Fields dialog box appears, double-click on the name of the calculation field you want.

2. The Specify Calculation dialog box will show the formula in the center box. If you want to start fresh, double-click on the formula, then press `Delete` or simply click on the first piece of the new formula (usually a field reference).

   To edit individual parts of the formula, highlight that piece, and then click the replacement field reference, operator, or function.

3. When you've finished editing the formula, click OK, then click Done when the Define Fields dialog box reappears.

✔ Tip

■ If you ever change the name of a field, you don't need to manually edit the formulas that reference that field. FileMaker automatically updates the field references in formulas to reflect any field name changes.

EDITING FORMULAS

To change the display of calculation results

1. First create a calculation field and build a formula for it. (See "To define a calculation field" on page 109.) While the formula for your calculation field still appears within the Specify Calculation dialog box, click on the lower left pop-up menu labeled "Calculation result is" (**Figure 9.37**).

   By default, FileMaker displays the results of a calculation as a number, which is what's needed in most cases. However, there are formulas that may need to be displayed as text, a time, or even a container. Make your selection among the five choices and release the cursor.

2. Click OK. When the Define Fields dialog box reappears, click Done.

To repeat a calculation field

1. Use the Define Field keyboard command to reach the Specify Calculation dialog box—[Ctrl][Shift][D] (Windows) or [Shift][⌘][D] (Mac)—where you create a repeating calculation field

2. Within the Define Fields dialog box, double-click on the name of the calculation field you want to repeat. When the Specify Calculation dialog box appears, click the checkbox in the lower left labeled "Repeating field with a maximum of __ repetitions." Fill in the blank with the number of repetitions you want. Click OK.

3. When the Define Fields dialog box reappears, click Done. Remember: The appearance of a repeating field doesn't change until you format it. See "To format a repeating field" on page 103.

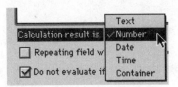

Figure 9.37 Use the lower-left pop-up menu "Calculation result is" within the Specify Calculation dialog box to control how the results are displayed.

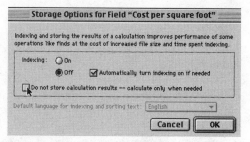

Figure 9.38 Use the Storage Options dialog box to control whether to store a calculation result or calculate it only when needed.

Storing calculation results

Storing calculation results carries the same tradeoffs as indexing any other field: It speeds finding records but also increases your database's size. FileMaker offers a decent compromise, however, by giving you the option of only performing a calculation (and, so, storing the result) when it's needed, such as when you're printing or browsing that particular field and record.

Unless you tell it otherwise, FileMaker automatically stores calculations except those from summary and global fields, as well as those that depend on another calculation already marked as unstored.

To store calculation results

1. First create a calculation field and build a formula for it. (See "To define a calculation field" on page 109.) If you already have a calculation field defined, use the Define Field keyboard command to reach it: Ctrl Shift D (Windows) or Shift ⌘ D (Mac).

2. When the Define Fields dialog box appears, double-click on the name of the calculation field whose results you want to store or index. The Specify Calculation dialog box will appear with the formula in the center box. Click the lower right button "Storage Options."

3. The Storage Options dialog box will appear (**Figure 9.38**). To keep a result from being stored, select the "Do not store calculation results—calculate only when needed" checkbox.

4. Click OK. When the Define Fields dialog box reappears, click Done.

To define a summary field

1. Click Define in the File menu and select Fields. Or use your keyboard: [Ctrl][Shift][D] (Windows) or [Shift][⌘][D] (Mac).

2. When the Define Fields dialog box appears, type into the Field Name text box the name of your summary field. Select Summary within the Type panel in the lower-left section of the dialog box. Click the Create button (**Figure 9.39**).

3. When the Options for Summary Field dialog box appears, choose which type of summary you want performed from the left-hand list, and select which field you want summarized from the scrolling list in the center (**Figure 9.40**, **Table 9.7**). You can also modify several of the summary types by selecting the checkbox just below the scrolling list, whose function varies in response to which type you've chosen. For more information, see **Table 9.7**, "Summary field types," below.

4. Click OK. When the Define Fields dialog box reappears, click Done.

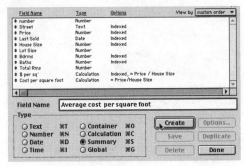

Figure 9.39 To define a Summary field, click that choice in the Type area of the Define Fields dialog box, then click Create.

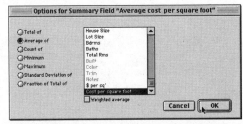

Figure 9.40 Use the Options for Summary Field dialog box to select a summary action. The checkbox just below the center window modifies many of the left-hand options.

✔ Tip

■ Formatting summary fields varies depending on which summary part you use to display them. See Chapter 10, "Creating Layouts" on page 115.

Table 9.7

Summary field types (see Figure 9.40)			
NAME	**DEFINITION**	**OPTION VIA CHECKBOX**	**TO FINE TUNE OPTION:**
Total of	Totals values in selected field	Running total	
Average of	Averages values in selected field	Weighted average	Pick a field for averaged values
Count of	Counts how many records contain a value for field	Running total	
Minimum	Finds lowest number, or earliest time or date, for field	none	
Maximum	Finds highest number, or latest time or date, for field	none	
Standard Deviation of	Calculates standard deviation from mean of values in field	by population	
Fraction of Total of	Calculates the ratio of field's value to total for all values in field	Subtotaled	Pick a field for subtotaled values

CREATING LAYOUTS

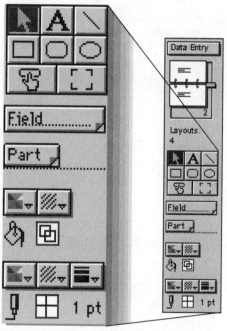

Figure 10.1 All the tools for creating layouts reside in the left-hand status area whenever you're in Layout mode.

FileMaker's layouts allow you to vary the *appearance* of your data without changing the data itself. This gives you the freedom to create layouts tailored to specific tasks and users. Workers entering orders into a database, for example, probably will find it easier to use a layout that mirrors the sequence of information they get from customers. Sales managers, on the other hand, may need layouts that help them spot what's selling well. Day-to-day tasks need a different layout than big-picture analysis demands. Remember: You need not show all of a database in a layout. In fact, the more you can pare down a layout to just the essential information, the easier it will be to use.

The Layout status area (**Figure 10.1**), runs down the left side of your screen when you're in Layout mode. The status area includes all the tools you'll need for adding text, graphics, fields, and parts to a layout and then applying colors, patterns, and lines to make them attractive.

You don't necessarily need to start from scratch in creating layouts: FileMaker includes dozens of built-in templates. Some you may want to use as is, others may provide a starting point for creating your own custom layouts. For more information, see Chapter 12, "Using Templates and Scripts," on page 179.

Choosing a layout type

When you first define fields in a database, FileMaker by default generates a *standard* layout, which lists the fields and their labels in the order they were created (**Figure 10.2**). You're free to modify that default layout anyway you like. Or you may save yourself some trouble in generating a new layout by choosing from the predefined layout types built into FileMaker.

Use the New Layout command for creating standard, columnar, extended columnar, single page, and blank layouts. For information on label and envelope layouts, see "To create a label layout" on page 125 and "To create an envelope layout" on page 127.

Here's a quick comparison of each layout type:

Standard: Nothing fancy here. This layout displays all the database's fields in the order they were created. The field labels for each field appear just *left* of the fields (**Figure 10.2**). It includes a blank header and footer.

Columnar report: This layout places the database's fields in a row across a single page. The labels for the fields appear in the header *above* the body of the record (**Figure 10.3**). (The footer is blank.) You determine the order of the fields when creating the layout or you can go back and rearrange them any time. Columnar reports make it easier to compare one record to another or to squeeze multiple records onto the same screen.

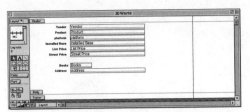

Figure 10.2 When you first define fields, FileMaker by default generates a *standard* layout with fields and labels listed in the order they were created.

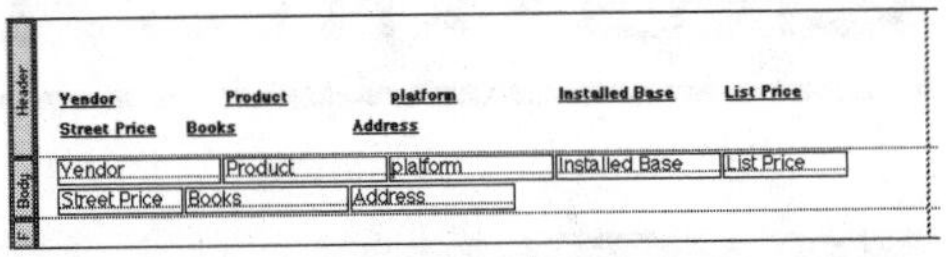

Figure 10.3 The *columnar* layout arranges fields across a single page, creating a second row if needed. The fields' labels appear in a single header *above* the body of the record.

Extended columnar: This layout is similar to the columnar report except that the row of fields extends beyond the width of a single page (**Figure 10.4**). It's best used for onscreen work to squeeze as many records into view as possible. Be aware that any fields extending beyond the end of the page will not print.

Single-page form: This layout is nearly identical to the standard layout, except it has no header or footer. By default, it's the same size as a single page.

Labels: Use this layout only for labels: you can't enter data into it directly. The Label Setup dialog box lets you choose from dozens of pre-set Avery label styles. For more information, see "To create a label layout" on page 125.

Envelope: This layout is tailored for printing on regular business envelopes and includes main and return address areas. Like the labels layout, it's not used for entering data. It includes a header and body but no footer. For more information, see "To create an envelope layout" on page 127.

Blank: This layout is entirely blank—nothing appears in the header, body, or footer. If you want to start with a clean slate and only add fields as you're ready, this is the layout for you.

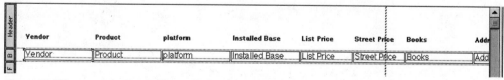

Figure 10.4 The *extended columnar* layout is best used onscreen only since fields extending beyond the paper's edge (marked by the vertical hash) won't print.

Working with layouts

To create a new layout

1. Switch to Layout mode by clicking on the Mode menu and selecting Layout. Or use your keyboard: Ctrl L (Windows) or ⌘ L (Mac).

2. Select New Layout (Ctrl N for Windows/ ⌘ N on the Mac) from the Mode menu (**Figure 10.5**).

3. When the New Layout dialog box appears, type a name into the Layout Name text box (**Figure 10.6**). By default, FileMaker assigns each new layout a generic name (e.g., Layout #3), but it's best to give it an easy to recognize name within the Layout Name text box. Choose one of the seven radio buttons within the Type panel.

   By default, FileMaker also selects the "Include in layouts menu" checkbox just below the Layout Name text box. Leave it checked to ensure that this layout appears in your layouts pop-down menu.

   When you're done, click OK.

Figure 10.5 The New Layout command can be found within the Mode menu. The command also is used to *add* a layout.

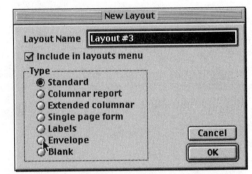

Figure 10.6 In the New Layout dialog box, give your layout a name, choose one of seven types, and click OK.

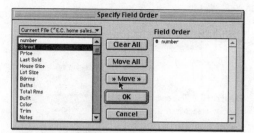

Figure 10.7 Use the Specify Field Order dialog box to choose which fields appear in a new layout—and their order.

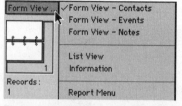

Figure 10.8 To switch to another layout, click on the pop-down menu above the flipbook.

4. When the Specify Field Order dialog box appears (**Figure 10.7**), highlight the fields in the left-hand list that you want to appear in the layout and use the Move or Move All buttons to place them in the right-hand list. Or double-click on fields in the left list and they will automatically appear in the right list. When you're done, click OK.

FileMaker will remain in Layout mode and the new layout will appear on your screen. If you're happy with the layout, switch to Browse ((Ctrl)(B) for Windows/ (⌘)(B) on the Mac) and begin entering data. More likely, however, you'll want to further format the layout. For more information, see "Formatting fields or objects" on page 162.

✔ Tip

- As you create more layouts, click on the pop-down menu above the flipbook icon to quickly switch to the layout you need to use (**Figure 10.8**).

To rename a layout

1. Make sure you're in Layout mode (Ctrl L for Windows/⌘ L on the Mac). Select the layout you want to rename by clicking on it in the pop-down menu just above the flipbook icon (**Figure 10.9**).

2. Select Layout Setup from the Mode menu (**Figure 10.10**).

3. When the Layout Setup dialog box appears, type in the new name and click OK (**Figure 10.11**). The layout pop-down menu now displays the renamed layout (**Figure 10.12**).

To delete a layout

1. Make sure you're in Layout mode (Ctrl L for Windows/⌘ L on the Mac). Select the layout you want to delete by clicking on it within the pop-down menu just above the flipbook icon.

2. Once the layout appears onscreen, select the Delete Layout command from the Mode menu (**Figure 10.13**) or use your keyboard: (Ctrl E for Windows/⌘ E on the Mac).

3. A warning dialog box will appear. If you're sure, click Delete (**Figure 10.14**). The layout will disappear onscreen, replaced by the next layout listed in the pop-down menu.

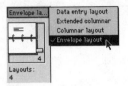

Figure 10.9 To rename a layout, select it in the pop-down menu above the flipbook icon...

Figure 10.10 ...and choose the Layout Setup command from the Mode menu.

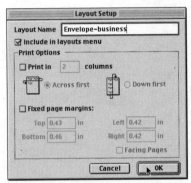

Figure 10.11 Type the new layout name inside the Layout Name text box and click OK.

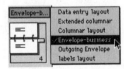

Figure 10.12 The new name will appear in the pop-down menu of available layouts.

Figure 10.13 Use the Delete Layout command in the Mode menu (Ctrl E for Windows/⌘ E on the Mac) to eliminate the layout on your screen.

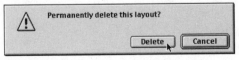

Figure 10.14 Still sure you want to get rid of the layout? Then click Delete.

RENAMING AND DELETING LAYOUTS

Figure 10.15 Use the Duplicate Layout command in the Mode menu to copy an existing layout.

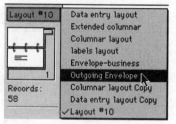

Figure 10.16 To choose among your existing layouts, use the pop-down menu just above the flipbook icon.

Duplicating a layout

This procedure will save you some time if you need to design a new layout based on an existing layout.

To duplicate a layout

1. Make sure you're in Layout mode ([Ctrl][L] for Windows/[⌘][L] on the Mac). Select the layout you want to duplicate by clicking on it in the pop-down menu just above the flipbook icon.

2. Select Duplicate Layout from the Mode menu (**Figure 10.15**). Sorry, there's no keyboard equivalent. The duplicate layout will appear onscreen and will be listed in the layout pop-down menu as a copy of the layout you'd selected. If you want to give the duplicate layout a more distinctive name, see "To rename a layout" on the previous page.

To choose a layout view

1. Make sure you're in Layout mode ([Ctrl][L] for Windows/[⌘][L] on the Mac). Click on the pop-down menu just above the left-hand flipbook and release your cursor on the layout of your choice (**Figure 10.16**).

DUPLICATING LAYOUTS

To reorder the layout pop-down menu

1. Make sure you're in Layout mode (Ctrl L for Windows/⌘ L on the Mac). Select Set Layout Order from the Mode menu (**Figure 10.17**).

2. When the Set Layout Order dialog box appears, click on the layout name you want to reorder. Keep your cursor down and a double arrow will appear (**Figure 10.18**). Holding down the cursor, drag the layout name to the place you want it listed in the order. Release the cursor. Repeat this step to further rearrange the layout order.

3. Once you're satisfied with the order, click OK. The layout pop-down menu will now reflect the new order.

✔ Tip

■ If you've set up a database for multiple users, only the host will be able to reorder the list—and only when filesharing for the database is turned off. For more information, see Chapter 15, "Networking," on page 211.

Figure 10.17 Use the Set Layout Order command from the Mode menu to reorder the pop-down menu of layouts.

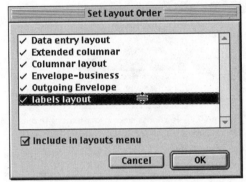

Figure 10.18 Click and drag to reorder layouts listed within the Set Layout Order dialog box.

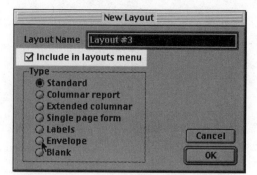

Figure 10.19 So easy to miss: The "Include in layouts menu" checkbox within the New Layout dialog box determines which layouts *initially* appear in the pop-down menu.

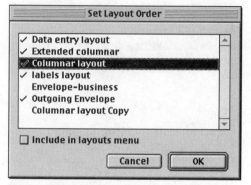

Figure 10.20 Use your cursor to control which layouts appear in the revised pop-down menu of layouts. Checked layouts will appear; unchecked will not.

Putting layouts in the pop-down menu

FileMaker's default is to automatically include layouts in the pop-down menu via the checkbox within the New Layout dialog box (**Figure 10.19**). If you want to tidy up the list by excluding some layouts—or you mistakenly excluded a layout from the list—the steps are the same.

To exclude or include layouts in the pop-down menu

1. Make sure you're in Layout mode ([Ctrl][L] for Windows/[⌘][L] on the Mac). Select Set Layout Order from the Mode menu.

2. When the Set Layout Order dialog box appears, there will be a column of checkmarks just left of the list of layouts. To *exclude* a layout from the pop-down menu, move your cursor over the layout item's checkmark and click. The checkmark will disappear. To *include* a layout, move your cursor to the blank area just left of the layout's name and click the cursor. A checkmark will appear (**Figure 10.20**).

3. When you're satisfied, click OK.

Changing the layout setup

Use this to change how layout columns print and to change a layout's page margins.

To change the layout setup

1. Pick the layout you want to change by selecting it via the pop-down menu just above the left-hand flipbook.

2. Choose Layout Setup from the Mode menu (**Figure 10.21**).

3. Within the Layout Setup dialog box (**Figure 10.22**), you have three options for controlling how the layout prints out:

   ■ You can have your layout print in columns—even if it's not a columnar-type layout—if it's narrow enough for more than one record to fit on the page. Select the "Print in" checkbox, then fill in how many columns you want. The "Across first" option works well for mailing labels; use "Down first" for directory-style printouts.

   ■ Use the "Fixed page margins" check-box and the four number-entry boxes if you want to use different margins from your printer's default settings.

   ■ Use the "Facing Pages" checkbox if you'll be printing on both sides of the page. This will place the narrower, inside margin on the left of odd-numbered pages and on the right of even-numbered pages.

4. When you're done, click OK.

Figure 10.21 Choose Layout Setup under the Mode menu to reach the Layout Setup dialog box.

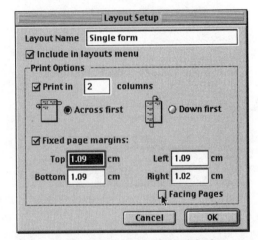

Figure 10.22 Within the Layout Setup dialog box you can set how the layout prints (across or down the page), its page margins, and whether it accommodates facing pages.

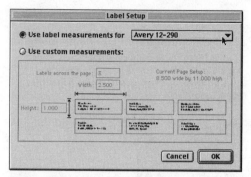

Figure 10.23 Use the Label Setup dialog box to choose a preset Avery-based label size or create a custom size.

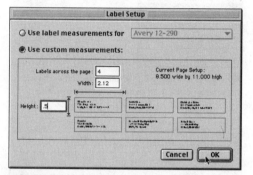

Figure 10.24 Choosing the "Use custom measurements" button lets you adjust the label's width and height, along with setting how many labels fit across the page.

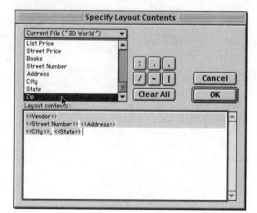

Figure 10.25 Use the Specify Layout Contents dialog box to choose the fields you want displayed. The top-center keypad lets you place punctuation between selected fields, which appear in the lower window within « » brackets.

Using label and envelope layouts

To create a label layout

1. Switch to Layout mode (⟨Ctrl⟩⟨L⟩ for Windows/⟨⌘⟩⟨L⟩ on the Mac), then select the New Layout command from the Mode menu (⟨Ctrl⟩⟨N⟩ for Windows/⟨⌘⟩⟨N⟩ on the Mac).

2. When the New Layout dialog box appears, type a name into the Layout Name text box. Choose the Labels radio button within the Type panel and click OK.

3. The Label Setup dialog box appears, giving you the choice of using one of several dozen preset Avery-based label sizes or creating a custom-size label (**Figure 10.23**).

   To use an Avery-based label, leave the top radio button selected. Use the pop-down menu to choose the appropriate Avery size based on the labels you're using. By the way, even non-Avery label packages usually list an Avery-equivalent stock number.

   To create a custom size, select the Use custom measurements radio button, then use the "Labels across the page," "Width," and "Height" boxes to configure your label's size (**Figure 10.24**).

4. Click OK.

5. When the Specify Layout Contents dialog box appears (**Figure 10.25**), double-click on the fields you want displayed within the upper-left list. Selected fields will appear in the lower window surrounded by « » brackets. The brackets act as placeholders for data and, for that reason, you use a slightly different approach for formatting the areas between each field.

   To place a field on a new line, press ⟨Enter⟩ (Windows) or ⟨Return⟩ (Mac). Use the

   (continued)

dialog box's keypad to insert any of six punctuation marks between the fields you've selected. Use the spacebar to insert blank spaces between selected fields.

To remove a mistake, select the entry in the lower box and press Delete. To start over, click on the dialog box's Clear All button. To further format the layout, see "Formatting fields or objects" on page 162.

6. When you're done, click OK. The labels layout will appear showing how the labels will be arranged across the page (**Figure 10.26**).

7. To adjust the width of the labels, click on the vertical mark between each label and drag it left (narrower) or right (wider). Or choose Layout Setup from the Mode menu (**Figure 10.27**). When the Layout Setup dialog box appears, select the "Fixed page margins" checkbox and then use the Top, Bottom, Left, and Right boxes to make your adjustments (**Figure 10.28**). For information on printing labels, see Chapter 14, "Printing," on page 207.

Figure 10.26 The layout for the label appears once you close the Specify Layout Contents dialog box. Click on and drag the vertical marker to adjust the label's width.

Figure 10.27 The Layout Setup command in the Mode menu also can be used to adjust the size of a label.

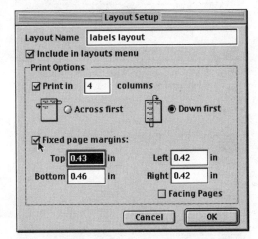

Figure 10.28 To change a label's margins, check "Fixed page margins" and make your changes in the four number-entry boxes.

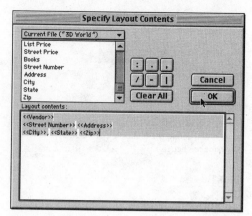

Figure 10.29 Within the Specify Layout Contents dialog box, double-click in the upper-left list on the fields you want displayed.

To create an envelope layout

1. Switch to Layout mode (Ctrl L for Windows/⌘L on the Mac), then select the New Layout command from the Mode menu (Ctrl N for Windows/⌘N on the Mac).

2. When the New Layout dialog box appears, type a name into the Layout Name text box. Choose the Envelope radio button within the Type panel and click OK.

3. In the Specify Layout Contents dialog box that appears (**Figure 10.29**), double-click within the upper-left list on the fields you want displayed. Selected fields will appear in the lower window surrounded by « » brackets. The brackets act as placeholders for data and, for that reason, you use a slightly different approach for formatting the areas between each field.

   To place a field on a new line, press Enter (Windows) or Return (Mac). Use the dialog box's keypad to insert any of six punctuation marks between the fields you've selected. Use the spacebar to insert blank spaces between selected fields.

   To remove a mistake, select the entry in the lower box and press Delete. To start over, click on the dialog box's Clear All button. To further format the layout, see "Formatting fields or objects" on page 162.

4. When you're done, click OK. For more information on printing, see Chapter 14, "Printing," on page 207.

To create an envelope return address

1. Once you've created an envelope layout, be sure you're still in Layout mode. Select the layout using the pop-down menu just above the flipbook icon (**Figure 10.30**).

2. Select the Type tool from within the Layout mode's status area, then click within the envelope layout's *header*.

3. Type in the return address, using the text options under the Format menu. For more on formatting *individual* blocks of text, see "Formatting fields or objects" on page 162. For more on *database-wide* text defaults, see "To set formatting defaults" on page 160.

4. Click on and drag the double arrow between the header and footer to close up the empty space around the return address (**Figure 10.31**).

5. Choose Preview from the Mode menu ([Ctrl] [U] for Windows/[⌘] [U] on the Mac) to double-check your envelope layout before you print it (**Figure 10.32**).

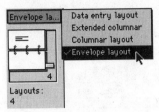

Figure 10.30 While still in Layout mode, use the pop-down menu above the flipbook icon to select the layout you want to change.

Figure 10.31 After creating a return address for an envelope, drag the double arrow to close up empty space around the return address.

Figure 10.32 Use the Preview command ([Ctrl] [U] for Windows/[⌘][U] on the Mac) to double-check the envelope's appearance before printing.

Creating form letter layouts

Form letters—standard letters containing bits of customized information—are easy to create using FileMaker's merge fields. By creating a layout that's mostly text with a few judiciously placed merge fields, you can create a customized letter for your customers:

Dear Mr. Jones,

The new millenium is right around the corner! Like most of us, you've probably got big plans for that big day. We can help. Because of your outstanding credit, stellar social skills, and stunning wardrobe, you and your dog Binx are eligible for more debt than even the federal government can handle.

Call today and we'll get you in hock for tomorrow—and beyond!

Sincerely,

James Smith

In FileMaker, which uses << and >> to mark merge fields, the letter looks like this:

Dear <<Mr.>> <<Jones>>,

The new millenium is right around the corner! Like most of us, you've probably got big plans for that big day. We can help. Because of your outstanding credit, stellar social skills, and stunning wardrobe, you and your <<dog>> <<Binx>> are eligible for more debt than even the federal government can handle.

Call today and we'll get you in hock for tomorrow—and beyond!

Sincerely,

<<James>> <<Smith>>

If you resist the urge to drown customers with frequent mailings, form letters with merge fields can be a powerful tool.

To create a form letter with merge fields

1. Open the database from which the data will be drawn and switch to Layout mode by clicking on the Mode menu and selecting Layout. Or use your keyboard: Ctrl L (Windows) or ⌘ L (Mac).

2. Select New Layout (Ctrl L for Windows/⌘ L on the Mac) from the Mode menu. When the New Layout dialog box appears, type a name into the Layout Name text box, choose Single page form within the Type area, and click OK (**Figure 10.33**).

3. A new layout will automatically contain *every* field you've defined for this database. For a form letter, however, you'll want to start with a clean slate, so select all the fields (Ctrl A in Windows/⌘ A on the Mac) and click Delete.

4. Select the Type tool from the left-hand Layout status area and begin typing in your letter. When you reach the spot where you want the first merge field to appear (**Figure 10.34**), choose Paste Special from the Edit menu, then select Merge Field near the bottom of the drop-down menu (**Figure 10.35**). Or use your keyboard: Ctrl M for Windows/⌘ M on the Mac.

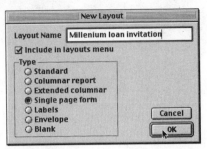

Figure 10.33 To create a form letter, choose the Single page form when selecting a new layout.

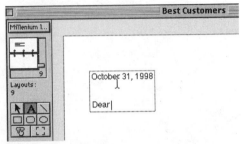

Figure 10.34 When you reach the spot for a merge field, choose Paste Special from the Edit menu and select Merge Field.

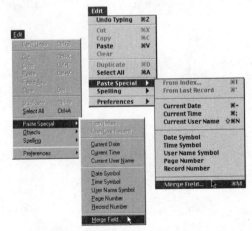

Figure 10.35 The Merge Field command can be found within the Edit Menu under the Paste Specials.

Figure 10.36 When the Specify Field dialog box appears, double-click on the field you want as a merge field.

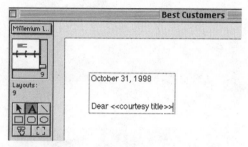

Figure 10.37 Once you place a merge field in a layout, a pair of << >> will mark its boundaries.

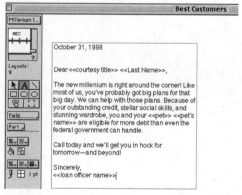

Figure 10.38 The final form letter shows where each merge field's contents will be inserted once you switch to Browse mode.

5. When the Specify Field dialog box appears, double-click on the field you want to appear in the letter (**Figure 10.36**). A merge field will appear within the form letter layout (**Figure 10.37**). Continue typing the letter, adding additional merge fields as you need them until you're done (**Figure 10.38**). To see what the form letter will look like, switch to Browse mode. To format the letter's fonts and other text attributes, see "Formatting fields or objects" on page 162. To set the letter's margins and prepare it for printing, see Chapter 14, "Printing," on page 207.

Using Paste Specials

FileMaker includes a great time-saving feature called Paste Special. The use of Paste Specials is not confined to Layout mode, but I've included it here because they're so often used in form letters. There are two types of Paste Specials: fixed and variable. Fixed Paste Specials—Current Date, Current Time, and Current User Name—paste information that is current *at the time they are entered*. Once pasted into a file, the data remains fixed and is not updated. In contrast, variable Paste Specials—Date Symbol, Time Symbol, User Name Symbol, Page Number, and Record Number—are updated for *when the file is viewed or printed*.

Variable Paste Specials are particularly handy for form letters because a letter can be prepared in advance, yet contain the dates and times reflecting the time when it's actually printed out. This trick, by the way, need not be confined to form letters. Use it in any layout where you need updated information to appear—including onscreen forms.

Fixed Paste Specials also can be used in Browse and Find modes. In Browse mode, use a fixed Paste Special to instantly enter a date, time, or user name. In Find mode, you can use fixed Paste Specials to quickly construct a search request. For more information, see "Doing a simple search" on page 42.

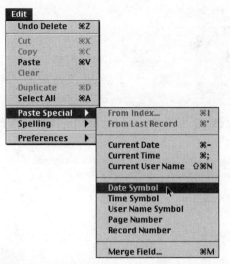

Figure 10.39 Variable Paste Specials (Date, Time, User Name, Page, and Record) are found in the third grouping under Paste Special.

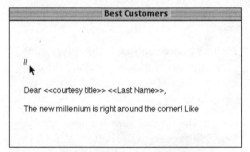

Figure 10.40 When you select the Date Symbol from the variable Paste Specials, a double forward slash (//) acts as a placeholder within the layout.

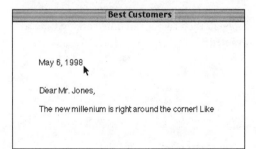

Figure 10.41 When you switch from Layout to Browse mode, the date symbol is replaced by the *current* date, which will be continually updated.

To create a variable Paste Special

1. Select the field and layout where you want the Paste Special to appear. Choose Paste Special from the Edit menu and then select the *variable* Paste Special you want: Date Symbol, Time Symbol, User Name Symbol, Page Number, or Record Number (**Figure 10.39**). Release your cursor and a placeholder symbol will be inserted (**Figure 10.40**).

2. Return to Browse mode and the place-holder is updated to reflect the most current data (**Figure 10.41**).

✔ Tip

■ The formatting for dates, times, and numbers inserted with Paste Special is controlled like any other date, time, or number field. For example, you can have dates appear as 5/6/98 or May 6, 1998. For more information, see Chapter 11, "Formatting and Graphics in Layouts," on page 157.

Working with parts

In most cases, the function of the various layout parts are obvious from their names: header, body, and footer. Summary parts work a bit differently than other layout parts. Since summary fields gather information from across several records, they cannot appear within the body of an individual record. That's where the various kinds of summary parts come in by providing a way to display this cross-record data. *Grand summary* parts summarize information for all the records being browsed. *Subsummary* parts do the same for a group of records, based on the break field you designate within the Part Definition dialog box.

Title header: This special type of header appears only at the top of the page or first screen. It can also be used as a title page. Each layout can only contain one title header.

Header: Use for field titles or column headings in columnar and extended columnar layouts (**Figure 10.42**). It appears at the top of every page or screen. Each layout can only contain one header.

Leading grand summary: Use this type of summary part to display summary information at the *beginning* of the group of the records being browsed.

Body: Use for the bulk of your data, including graphics. The body will appear for each record in the database. Each layout can only contain one body.

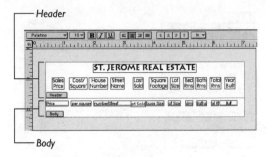

Figure 10.42 Used in a columnar or extended columnar layout, a header part enables you to run field titles across the top for more than one row of records.

Subsummary: Use this type of summary part to display summary information for the group of the records specified by the break field.

Trailing grand summary: Use this type of summary part to display summary information at the *end* of the group of the records being browsed.

Footer: Use for dates or page numbers. The footer will appear at the bottom of each page or screen. Each layout can contain only one footer.

Title footer: This special type of footer appears only at the bottom of the first page or screen. Each layout can only contain one title footer.

Figure 10.43 Add a part to your layout by selecting Part Setup from the Mode menu.

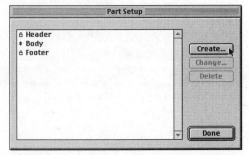

Figure 10.44 Click Create when the Part Setup dialog box appears.

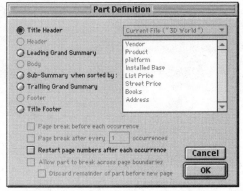

Figure 10.45 The Part Definition dialog box offers eight part type choices.

To add a layout part

1. Make sure you're in Layout mode ([Ctrl][L] for Windows/[⌘][L] on the Mac). Select Part Setup from the Mode menu (**Figure 10.43**).

2. When the Part Setup dialog box appears, click Create (**Figure 10.44**).

3. Within the Part Definition dialog box, select the type of part you want to create from the eight choices (**Figure 10.45**).

4. If you're creating a subsummary part, you'll also need to select from the right-hand list which field (also known as a break field) you'd like the records to sort by.

5. The Part Definition dialog box also allows you to control where and how pages will break. Check the appropriate box or boxes.

6. Click OK. The new part appears in the layout.

✔ Tip

■ If you're clear about the purpose and placement of layout parts, you can add a part directly by clicking on the Part button in the left-hand Layout status area and dragging the resulting part to where you want it (**Figure 10.46**).

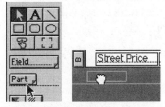

Figure 10.46 The Part button within the Layout status area lets you add a part by clicking and dragging directly within the layout.

To delete a part

1. Make sure you're in Layout mode
   ([Ctrl] [L] for Windows/[⌘] [L] on the Mac).
   Select Part Setup from the Mode menu.

2. Within the Part Setup dialog box, select
   the part you want eliminated and press
   [Delete]. If you've selected a part that contains objects, you'll get a warning dialog
   box. If you're sure, click Delete.

To reorder parts

1. Make sure you're in Layout mode
   ([Ctrl] [L] for Windows/[⌘] [L] on the Mac).
   Select Part Setup from the Mode menu.

2. Click on the part you want to move, hold
   the cursor down, and drag the part to a
   new position in the order (**Figure 10.47**).

3. Click Done. The part appears in the new
   position.

To resize a part

1. Make sure you're in Layout mode
   ([Ctrl] [L] for Windows/[⌘] [L] on the Mac).
   Click on the dotted line separating one
   part from another and drag it to make the
   part larger or smaller (**Figure 10.48**).

✔ Tip

■ Resizing one part doesn't change the size
  of any other parts in the layout. Instead,
  the size of the entire layout will grow or
  shrink accordingly.

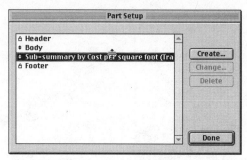

Figure 10.47 Reorder parts by clicking and dragging them within the Part Setup dialog box.

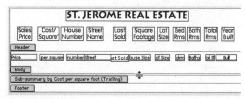

Figure 10.48 To resize a part, click and drag on the dotted line separating one part from another.

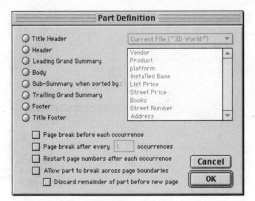

Figure 10.49 The Part Definition dialog box lets you change a part's type, plus control page breaks and numbering related to that part.

Table 10.1

Page break and numbering options	
IN THE PART DEFINITION DIALOG BOX	
CHOOSE	FOR USE WITH THESE LAYOUT PARTS
Page break before each occurrence	Subsummary (if sorted by body) Trailing subsummary Trailing grand summary
Page break after every x occurrences	Leading grand summary Subsummary (if sorted by body) Trailing grand summary
Restart page numbers after each occurrence	Title header Header Leading grand summary Subsummary (if sorted by body) Footer
Allow part to break across page boundaries	Leading grand summary · Subsummary (if sorted by body) Trailing grand summary
Discard remainder of part before new page	Leading grand summary Subsummary (if sorted by body) Trailing grand summary

Changing a part's type and options

FileMaker's Part Definition dialog box (**Figure 10.49**) does more than simply let you change a part's type. It also gives you control over where a page breaks in relation to a particular part and whether the pages are renumbered after that part. The page break and renumbering options are particularly useful when creating forms from which you may want to print out one record per page (**Table 10.1**). Here's a quick rundown of these options:

Page break before each occurrence: Choosing this checkbox will place a page break right *before* the selected part. Examples might include using it for a Trailing Grand Summary, Title Header, Header, or Body.

Page break after every __ occurrences: Choosing this checkbox will place a page break *after* x instances of the selected header. You set the number of instances. Examples might include selecting a body or footer part where you've created a layout in which x records will fit on a page.

Restart page numbers after each occurrence: Use this checkbox if, for example, you want to group a subsummary of records together and restart the page numbers after each subsummary.

Allow part to break across page boundaries: By default, FileMaker will try to keep a part on a single page. Use this checkbox if you do not want to keep a part on the same page or when the body is simply too large to fit on a single page.

Discard remainder of part before new page: This option can only be used if you've also checked "Allow part to break across page boundaries."

To change a part type or break field

1. Make sure you're in Layout mode ((Ctrl)(L) for Windows/(⌘)(L) on the Mac). Double-click on the label of the part you want to change.

2. When the Part Definition dialog box appears, make your new part type choice from the eight left-side choices.

   If you want to change the field used by a subsummary part (called a break field by FileMaker), click the "Sub-Summary when sorted by" button and then make a new field selection in the right-hand list (**Figure 10.50**).

3. Click OK. The part type will now change.

To paginate layout parts

1. Make sure you're in Layout mode ((Ctrl)(L) for Windows/(⌘)(L) on the Mac). Double-click on the label of the part you want to change.

2. When the Part Definition dialog box appears, select the appropriate checkbox among the five in the lower part of the dialog box. See **Table 10.1** for more information on which page breaks and numbering schemes work best with various layout parts.

3. When you're done making your changes, click OK.

4. If you chose a summary part, a dialog box may appear asking whether you want the part printed above or below the records it's summarizing (**Figure 10.51**). Click on your choice.

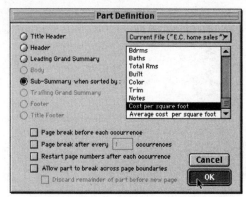

Figure 10.50 If you create a subsummary part, use the right-hand list to pick a field.

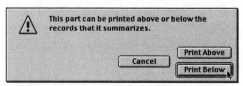

Figure 10.51 You can elect to have the subsummary part printed above or below the records it summarizes.

Working with fields in layouts

When you're working with layouts remember: *Adding* a field to a *layout* isn't the same thing as *creating* a field for the *database*. Layouts are simply differing views of the same data. Add a layout or delete a layout—either way the database itself isn't changed. The same notion applies when adding a field to a layout: It's just a view of a field that's already been created within the database.

For information on how to create a brand new field, see "To define a field" on page 88 in Chapter 9. Once you've created a field, however, you can easily add it to a new layout directly without having to define it again. In fact, it's common while designing a layout to discover that you need to define a new field. Just keep straight the difference between defining fields for the database versus adding a field to a layout and you'll be fine.

To add a field to a layout

1. To add *already defined* fields to a layout, click on the Field button in the left-hand Layout status area and drag the resulting field where you want it within the layout (**Figure 10.52**).

2. When the Specify Field dialog box appears, click on a name for the new field (**Figure 10.53**). You can add a field defined in another database by clicking on the Current File pop-down menu above the field list and navigating to the desired field.

3. If you want a field label to appear in the layout, also check the "Create field label" box below the list.

4. Click OK. The layout will reappear with the added field. If you want to further format the field, see "Formatting fields or objects" on page 162.

✔ Tip

■ If you want to redefine the just-added field, stay in Layout mode and just double-click on the field. The Specify Field dialog box will reappear, allowing you to pick another field definition.

To delete a field from a layout

1. Make sure you're in Layout mode (Ctrl L for Windows/⌘ L on the Mac). Select the field you want to delete by clicking on it.

2. Press Delete.

✔ Tip

■ Remember: Deleting a field from a layout merely removes it from that layout. The data and field still exist in the *database* and, so, can be used in other layouts as you need them.

Figure 10.52 To add an already defined field to a layout, click on the status area's Field button and drag the resulting field to where you want it.

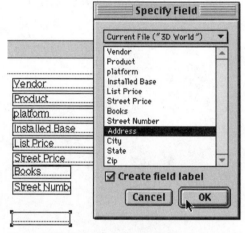

Figure 10.53 Selecting the Field button will open the Specify Field dialog box, allowing you to select a field definition (and add its name if you leave the bottom box checked).

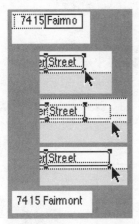

Figure 10.54 To resize a field in Layout mode, click on the field and drag a corner. Once back to Browse mode (bottom), the field's text is no longer cut off.

Resizing fields

Sometimes you create a field and only later realize that it is small for the intended text. (**Figure 10.54**). In that case, the text will be cut off. Resizing solves the problem.

To resize a field

1. Switch to Layout mode ((Ctrl)(L) for Windows/(⌘)(L) on the Mac).

2. Click on the field you want to resize and hold down your cursor. The corners of the field will become small black boxes, known as handles.

3. Drag the handles to make the field larger or smaller. When it reaches the size you want, release the cursor.

4. Switch back to Browse mode ((Ctrl)(B) for Windows/(⌘)(B) on the Mac) and you'll see that all the field's text now shows. Getting the field big enough may require some toggling between Layout and Browse modes to check your progress.

✔ Tip

■ To cleanly enlarge a field horizontally or vertically, click on the field and press (Shift) just before you drag the handle. The field will then only expand in the direction you first drag it, whether it's horizontal or vertical.

Adding scroll bars to large text fields

Sometimes enlarging a field isn't practical, either because your layout doesn't have the room or because the field has so much text that it would overwhelm the rest of the layout (**Figure 10.55**). In such cases, adding a scroll bar to the text field is the best approach.

To add a scroll bar

1. Switch to Layout mode ([Ctrl][L] for Windows/[⌘][L] on the Mac) and click on the field to select it (**Figure 10.56**).

2. Choose Field Format from the Format menu (**Figure 10.57**). The Field Format dialog box will appear.

3. Inside the Field Format dialog box, choose the "Standard field" radio button, and then check "Include vertical scroll bar." Click OK (**Figure 10.58**).

4. Back in Layout mode, the field now has a scroll bar. Switch to Browse mode and you'll see that the scroll bar not only allows you to scroll through all the text but also offers an immediate visual cue that there's more text than what shows (**Figure 10.59**).

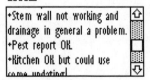

Figure 10.59 Back in Browse mode, the field's newly added scroll bar signals there's more text than meets the eye.

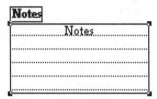

Figure 10.55 Consider adding a scroll bar when a field has too much text to fit within your layout.

Figure 10.56 Switch to Layout mode, then click on the field to select it.

Figure 10.57 Choose Field Format from the Format menu to open the Field Format dialog box.

Figure 10.58 Within the Field Format dialog box, choose the "Standard field" radio button, check "Include vertical scroll bar," and click OK.

Figure 10.60 To change the entry order for your fields, choose Set Tab Order from the Mode menu.

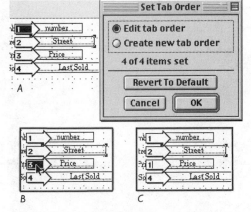

Figure 10.61 To slightly alter the existing tab order (A), click on the arrow you want to change (B), and type in the new number (C).

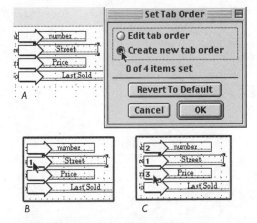

Figure 10.62 To completely change the tab order, click on the "Create new tab order" radio button, which will erase all the previous numbers (A). Then click on the arrows in the order you want the tab order set (B, C).

To set the field tab order

1. Switch to Layout mode ([Ctrl][L] for Windows/[⌘][L] on the Mac), then choose Set Tab Order from the Mode menu (**Figure 10.60**).

2. The Set Tab Order dialog box appears, along with a series of numbered arrows indicating the current tab order for your fields.

   If you want to just slightly alter the order, click on the tab number you want to change and type it in. If you assign No. 1 to an arrow, you'll also need to renumber the original No. 1 arrow (**Figure 10.61**).

   If you want to completely change the order, click on the "Create new tab order" radio button in the dialog box, which will eliminate all the tab numbers. Then just click on the arrows in the order you want the tab order set (**Figure 10.62**).

3. When you're done, click OK. The new tab order is now set.

✔ Tip

- Each layout can have its own Tab Order, allowing you to customize each layout for its intended users.

Arranging objects

Whether it's text, a field, a field name, or a graphic, FileMaker treats them all as separate *objects* that can be selected, moved, rearranged and grouped. Most of these functions reside under the Arrange menu, which appears only when you're in Layout mode. These objects also can be graphically embellished with shading, borders, and fills via the tools in the Layout status area. For more information on using graphics with objects, see "Working with graphics" on page 170.

While FileMaker makes it easy to move individual objects around a layout, it also allows you to *group* objects and then treat them as a single object. By creating groups of groups, you can organize pieces of a layout into units that speed your work.

By default, FileMaker displays objects in the order they were created, with the most recent atop (or in front of) the earlier objects. Sometimes in designing a layout, it's useful to stack objects atop each other to create a special effect, such as the appearance of a three-dimensional object. While each object remains a separate object, rearranging the stack order changes the overall appearance.

To make it easier to build layouts, FileMaker comes with built-in rulers, T-squares, and grids. For more information, see "Using layout guides," on page 152.

ARRANGING OBJECTS

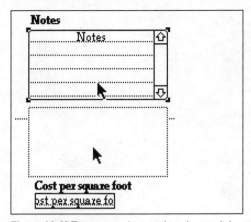

Figure 10.63 To move an object within a layout, click on it and drag it. A dotted outline of the object appears as you move the object.

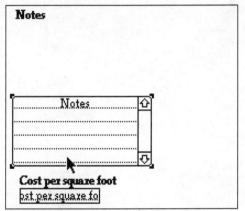

Figure 10.64 Once you've dragged an object to where you want it, release the cursor.

To move an object within the same layout

1. Switch to Layout mode (Ctrl L for Windows/⌘ L on the Mac), then select the object by clicking on it with your cursor. Keep pressing your cursor and drag the object to its new location in the layout. A set of dotted lines mark the object's position as you drag it (**Figure 10.63**).

   If you want to ensure that the object only moves horizontally (or vertically), hold down Shift as you drag it.

2. Once you put the object where you want it, release the cursor (**Figure 10.64**). The object will now appear in the new location within the layout.

✔ Tip

- While the field moved in the above example, the "Notes" field label did not. That's because the label is a separate object. While you can move more than one object at a time by Shift-clicking on several before dragging them, grouping such objects often makes more sense because things like field labels automatically tag along when you move a field. See "To group objects" on page 147.

To move an object to another layout

1. Switch to Layout mode (Ctrl L for Windows/⌘L on the Mac), then select the object by clicking on it with your cursor.

2. Choose Cut from the Edit menu or use your keyboard: (Ctrl X for Windows/⌘X on the Mac).

3. Switch to the other layout and choose Paste from the Edit menu. Or use your keyboard: (Ctrl V for Windows/⌘V on the Mac).

4. Once the object appears in the layout, use your cursor to move it exactly where you want it.

To copy an object

1. Switch to Layout mode (Ctrl L for Windows/⌘L on the Mac), then select the object by clicking on it with your cursor.

2. Choose Duplicate from the Edit menu. Or use your keyboard: (Ctrl D for Windows/⌘D on the Mac).

3. Use your cursor to move the duplicated object to where you want it.

To delete an object

1. Switch to Layout mode (Ctrl L for Windows/⌘L on the Mac), then select the object by clicking on it with your cursor.

2. Press Del. If you deleted the wrong object, choose Undo from the top of the Edit menu. Or use your keyboard: (Ctrl Z for Windows/⌘Z on the Mac).

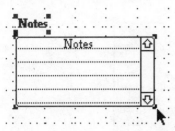

Figure 10.65 To select a field and its label for grouping, press (Shift) and click on both objects.

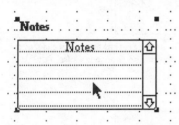

Figure 10.66 After you've selected several objects, choose Group from the Arrange menu.

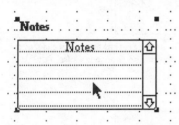

Figure 10.67 Once they're grouped, the field and its label become one object, as indicated by the single set of handles at the object's corners.

Grouping objects

By default, FileMaker treats each item added to a layout as a separate object. But sometimes there can be great advantage to having multiple objects treated as a single object (grouping). For example, if you use labels for fields, grouping the label with the field ensures that they stay together when you move a field within a layout. Similarly, it can speed up your layout work to group related topic fields and then move them to a new spot with a single click-and-drag.

To group objects

1. Switch to Layout mode ((Ctrl)(L) for Windows/⌘(L) on the Mac), then select the first object by clicking on it with your cursor.

2. Hold down (Shift) while you continue clicking on the objects you want to group together (**Figure 10.65**).

3. Choose Group from the Arrange menu or use your keyboard: (Ctrl)(G) in Windows, ⌘(G) on the Mac (**Figure 10.66**). The previously individual objects now become a single object (**Figure 10.67**).

✔ Tip

■ You can create subgroups within larger groupings. For example, create a group of just two objects (a field label with its field) before grouping that field with other fields. That way, if you later decide to ungroup the fields, you'll still have the field name grouped with its field.

To ungroup objects

1. Make sure you're in Layout mode ([Ctrl] [L] for Windows/[⌘] [L] on the Mac), then select the objects you no longer want grouped by clicking on each as you hold [Shift].

2. Choose Ungroup from the Arrange menu (**Figure 10.68**) or use your keyboard: [Ctrl] [Shift] [G] in Windows, [Shift] [⌘] [G] on the Mac. The selected objects will no longer be grouped (see Tip for exceptions).

✔ Tip

■ If you have created subgroups within a group, you'll have to repeat the Ungroup command at each level to fully break up those groupings.

To lock layout objects

1. Make sure you're in Layout mode ([Ctrl] [L] for Windows/[⌘] [L] on the Mac), then select the pieces of the layout you want to protect from accidental changes by holding down [Shift] as you click on each object.

2. Choose Lock from the Arrange menu (**Figure 10.69**) or use your keyboard: [Ctrl] [H] in Windows, [⌘] [H] on the Mac.

To unlock layout objects

1. Make sure you're in Layout mode ([Ctrl] [L] for Windows/[⌘] [L] on the Mac), then hold down [Shift] as you click on the objects you want to unlock.

2. Choose Unlock from the Arrange menu (**Figure 10.70**) or use your keyboard: [Ctrl] [Shift] [H] in Windows, [Shift] [⌘] [H] on the Mac.

✔ Tip

■ When creating groups, if one object is locked, all the grouped objects will become locked as well.

Figure 10.68 To break a grouped object back into individual objects, select it and choose Ungroup from the Arrange menu.

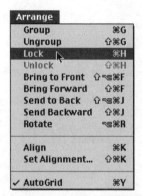

Figure 10.69 To protect against accidental changes to a layout, select objects and choose Lock from the Arrange menu.

Figure 10.70 To unlock a layout object—enabling others to easily change it—choose Unlock from the Arrange menu.

UNGROUPING, LOCKING, UNLOCKING OBJECTS

1.

2.

3.

4.

5.

Figure 10.71 1. Initially, the black square lies in the middle of the stack order. **2.** Brought to the front. **3.** Brought forward one layer from its initial position. **4.** Sent to the back. **5.** Sent back one layer from its initial position.

To change the stack order of objects

1. Switch to Layout mode (Ctrl L for Windows/⌘ L on the Mac), then select the object you want to move by clicking on it with your cursor.

2. From the Arrange menu, choose one of four commands: Bring to Front, Bring Forward, Send to Back, or Send Backward. The closer an object lies to the front (or top) of the stack, the more of it will be visible. By selecting and moving various objects, you can manipulate the arrangement to your satisfaction (**Figure 10.71**).

Bring to Front (no Windows keyboard equivalent, Shift Option ⌘ F on the Mac): Use this command to bring the selected object to the very front (or top) of the stack.

Bring Forward (Ctrl Shift F in Windows, Shift ⌘ F on the Mac): Use this command to bring the selected object forward one layer.

Send to Back (no Windows keyboard equivalent, Shift Option ⌘ J on the Mac): Use this command to send the selected object to the very back (or bottom) of the stack.

Send Backward (Ctrl Shift J in Windows, Shift ⌘ J on the Mac): Use this command to send the selected object back one layer.

CHANGING OBJECTS' STACK ORDER

Rotating objects

Because every field, label, and graphic within FileMaker is treated as an object, you're free to rotate them to make a layout more compact, less cluttered, or just more eye-grabbing. FileMaker limits you to rotating objects in 90-degree increments. If you need more precise control, create the object within a true graphics program and then import it into FileMaker.

To rotate an object

1. Switch to Layout mode (Ctrl L for Windows/⌘ L on the Mac), then select the object you want to rotate by clicking on it with your cursor (**Figure 10.72**).

2. Choose Rotate from the Arrange menu (**Figure 10.73**) or use your keyboard: (no Windows keyboard equivalent, Option ⌘ R on the Mac). The Rotate command moves an object 90 degrees clockwise (**Figure 10.74**).

✔ Tips

■ Repeat the Rotate command to continue spinning an object in 90-degree increments until it reaches the position you want.

■ If you prefer, press and hold your cursor on the selected object's "handles"—the small black squares on its periphery—then rotate it directly.

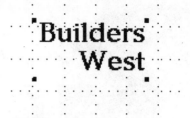

Figure 10.72 To rotate an object, first select it while in Layout mode.

Figure 10.73 Choose Rotate from the Arrange menu.

Figure 10.74 The Rotate command spins the object clockwise in 90-degree increments. Repeat the command to spin the object 180 and 270 degrees.

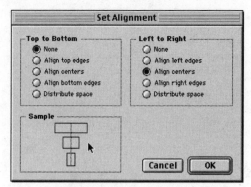

Figure 10.75 Use the Set Alignment dialog box to control the top-to-bottom and left-to-right relationships among several selected objects. The lower-left panel displays a sample of the chosen setting.

Aligning objects

Your layout will be easier to read and look more professional if you vertically or horizontally align fields, labels, and groups of fields as much as possible.

To align objects

1. Switch to Layout mode ([Ctrl][L] for Windows/[⌘][L] on the Mac), then select the objects you want to align by holding down [Shift] and clicking on them with your cursor.

2. Choose Set Alignment from the Arrange menu or use your keyboard: [Ctrl][Shift][K] for Windows/[Shift][⌘][K] on the Mac.

3. When the Set Alignment dialog box appears, you can control the top-to-bottom and the left-to-right alignment of the selected objects (**Figure 10.75**). The Sample area in the window's lower-left corner lets you see the effect of each combination.

4. When you're satisfied with the alignment, click OK.

✔ Tip

■ If you're happy with the choices you've made in the Set Alignment dialog box, you can apply them to any selected objects without having to reopen the window simply by using the align command: [Ctrl][K] for Windows/[⌘][K] on the Mac.

ALIGNING OBJECTS

Using layout guides

FileMaker's various layout guides are strictly optional but you'll find that they make it much easier and quicker to create professional layouts. You can use them while you're creating a layout or to go back and tidy up previous work. Here's a quick rundown on how each guide functions:

Text Ruler: Besides providing a horizontal measure in inches, pixels, or centimeters, the ruler also includes tools for choosing the font, font size, font style, text alignment, and tabs (**Figure 10.76**).

Graphic Rulers: Provides horizontal and vertical rulers in inches, pixels, or centimeters (**Figure 10.77**).

Ruler Lines: Provides a matrix of horizontal and vertical dotted lines to help position layout objects. The matrix can be set in inches, pixels, or centimeters (**Figure 10.78**).

T-Squares: Provides an intersecting horizontal line and vertical line, which can be moved to guide the positioning of layout objects (**Figure 10.79**).

AutoGrid: Provides an invisible grid whose measurement units can be adjusted. When AutoGrid is on, layout objects "snap" to the nearest grid line.

Size Palette: Provides a set of number entry boxes that help you precisely position layout objects (**Figure 10.80**).

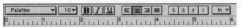

Figure 10.76 The Text Ruler lets you choose your measurement units and includes icons for choosing fonts, alignments, and tabs.

Figure 10.77 The measurement units for Graphics Rulers, which aid horizontal and vertical placement of the selected object, can be changed via the Mode menu.

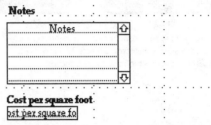

Figure 10.78 The Ruler Lines provide a visible matrix to help position layout objects.

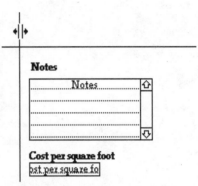

Figure 10.79 The T-Squares option provides a horizontal and vertical line that extends across the entire layout—easing alignment of multiple objects.

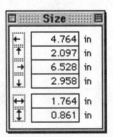

Figure 10.80 The Size palette allows you to precisely position layout objects via the numeric entry boxes.

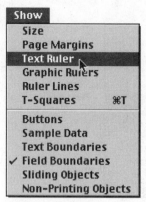

Figure 10.81 If you're in Layout mode, you can turn on the Text ruler via the Show menu.

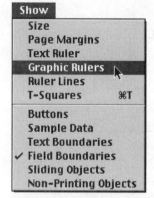

Figure 10.82 Once you're in Layout mode, you can turn on the Graphic Rulers via the Show menu.

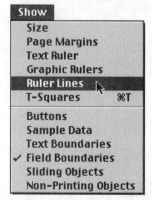

Figure 10.83 Turn on the Ruler Lines via the Show menu while in Layout mode.

To use the text ruler

1. Make sure you're in Layout mode (Ctrl L for Windows/⌘ L on the Mac), then choose Text Ruler from the Show menu (**Figure 10.81**).

2. Use the ruler or the various text icons to adjust selected text as you desire. For more information on text formats, see "Formatting fields and objects," on page 162. You can adjust the measurement units via the ruler's far-right pop-down menu.

3. To hide the ruler, choose Text Ruler from the Show menu.

To use graphic rulers

1. Make sure you're in Layout mode (Ctrl L for Windows/⌘ L on the Mac), then choose Graphic Rulers from the Show menu (**Figure 10.82**). To adjust the measurement units used, see "To change ruler and grid units" on page 156.

2. To hide the graphic rules, choose Graphic Rulers from the Show menu.

To use ruler lines

1. Make sure you're in Layout mode (Ctrl L for Windows/⌘ L on the Mac), then choose Ruler Lines from the Show menu (**Figure 10.83**). To adjust the measurement units used, see "To change ruler and grid units" on page 156.

2. To hide the rulers, choose Ruler Lines from the Show menu.

USING LAYOUT RULERS

To use T-Squares

1. Make sure you're in Layout mode
   (Ctrl L for Windows/⌘ L on the Mac),
   then choose T-Squares from the Show
   menu (**Figure 10.84**). To adjust the placement of the T-Square lines, click and hold
   your cursor, then drag the line where you
   want it (**Figure 10.85**).

2. To hide the T-Squares, choose T-Squares
   from the Show menu.

To use AutoGrid

1. Make sure you're in Layout mode
   (Ctrl L for Windows/⌘ L on the Mac),
   then choose AutoGrid from the Arrange
   menu. There's no Windows keyboard
   equivalent; use ⌘ Y on the Mac (**Figure
   10.86**). To adjust the measurement units
   used and the fineness of the grid, see "To
   change ruler and grid units" on page 156.

2. To turn off AutoGrid, choose AutoGrid
   from the Arrange menu.

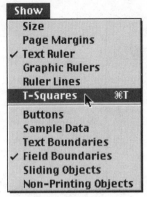

Figure 10.84 Turn on the T-Squares via the Show
menu while in Layout mode.

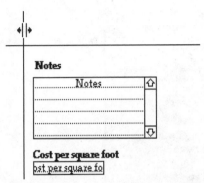

Figure 10.85 Adjust the placement of the T-Square
lines by clicking on a line and dragging it

Figure 10.86 Choosing AutoGrid from the Arrange
menu turns on an invisible set of lines to which new
layout objects will "snap."

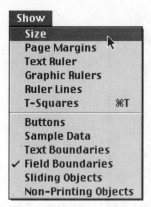

Show
Size
Page Margins
Text Ruler
Graphic Rulers
Ruler Lines
T-Squares   ⌘T

Buttons
Sample Data
Text Boundaries
✓ Field Boundaries
Sliding Objects
Non-Printing Objects

Figure 10.87 While in Layout mode, choose Size under the Show menu to reach the Size palette.

To use the Size palette

1. Make sure you're in Layout mode (Ctrl L for Windows/⌘ L on the Mac), then select the object you want to position by clicking on it with your cursor.

2. Choose Size from the Show menu (**Figure 10.87**).

3. Once the Size palette appears (**Figure 10.88**), make sure you're working in the measurement units you prefer: inches, pixels, or centimeters. To adjust the palette's measurement units, see "To change ruler and grid units" on page 156.

4. Type in the measurements you want in the Size palette's number entry boxes. When you're done, press Enter in Windows/Return on the Mac. The object will be resized based on your entry.

✔ Tip

■ Use the Size palette while click-dragging an object to position a layout object *exactly* where you want it. Just select your object, open the Size palette, and click-drag the object while keeping an eye on the palette's measurements.

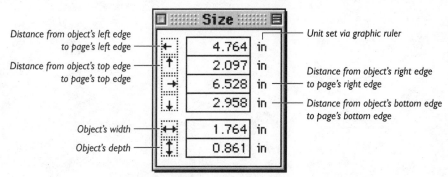

Distance from object's left edge to page's left edge — 4.764 in — Unit set via graphic ruler

Distance from object's top edge to page's top edge — 2.097 in

6.528 in — Distance from object's right edge to page's right edge

2.958 in — Distance from object's bottom edge to page's bottom edge

Object's width — 1.764 in

Object's depth — 0.861 in

Figure 10.88 The Size palette provides details on the position—and dimensions—of a selected object.

Changing ruler and grid units

FileMaker lets you set the ruler and grid to measure the layout and its items in inches, pixels, or centimeters.

To change ruler and grid units

1. To change the units, choose Set Rulers from the Mode menu (**Figure 10.89**).

2. The Set Rulers dialog box includes two pop-down menus (**Figure 10.90**). The top one sets the units used by the Graphic rulers, Ruler lines, the AutoGrid, and the Size Palette. The second pop-down menu, Grid Spacing, controls the fineness of the AutoGrid's mesh of horizontal and vertical lines. Make your adjustments to one or both pop-down menus and click OK.

Figure 10.89 Choose Set Rulers under the Mode menu to adjust the measurement units of Graphic rulers, Ruler lines, the AutoGrid, and the Size Palette.

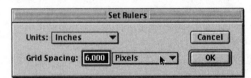

Figure 10.90 The Set Rulers dialog box includes two pop-down menus: one for ruler measure units and one for controlling the fineness of the AutoGrid.

FORMATTING AND GRAPHICS IN LAYOUTS

Once you've done the basic construction for a layout—the parts, fields, and objects covered in Chapter 10—you're ready to start the formatting and graphics detailing that will make your database visually inviting. Whether it's choosing suitable fonts or adding a color graphic, this often time-consuming work can spell the difference between a so-so database that's little used or a professional-grade product with immediate appeal.

Working with text

Quite often you'll find yourself working with text in a two-step process: You'll add text for the information it provides and then later go back to style the text by choosing special fonts or colors. This section deals with the first step. For information on styling *individual* blocks of text, see "Formatting fields or objects" on page 162. To set *database-wide* text defaults, see "To set formatting defaults" on page 160.

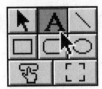

Figure 11.1 Click on the Text tool in the Layout status area to add text.

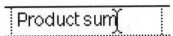

Figure 11.2 An I-beam cursor marks your text-insertion spot.

To add text to a layout

1. Make sure you're in Layout mode (Ctrl L for Windows/⌘ L on the Mac), then click the Text tool in the left-hand status area (**Figure 11.1**).

2. Click in the layout where you want the text and start typing. An I-beam cursor marks your progress (**Figure 11.2**).

✔ Tip

- Because creating a text label for a field has no effect on the actual field name, you can create different labels in different layouts for the same field. The sales force, for example, may have an in-house name for something that the accounting folks call something else entirely. By creating a sales layout and an accounting layout—each with its own labels—everyone's happy, even though the field's *actual* name remains the same.

To select text

1. In either Layout mode (Ctrl L for Windows/⌘ L on the Mac) or Browse mode (Ctrl B for Windows/⌘ B on the Mac), click on the text you want to select. If you want to select an entire word, double-click. To select a full line of text, triple-click on it.

2. Once you've selected the text, you can:

   ■ Delete it (press Del).

   ■ Cut it for pasting elsewhere (Ctrl X for Windows/⌘ X on the Mac).

   ■ Replace it with other text (type in the new text or paste selected text from elsewhere).

   ■ Change its attributes, such as its font, size, or style (see following pages).

SELECTING TEXT

Setting format defaults

Default formats apply to fields and objects across the *entire* database. (To set attributes for *individual* fields and objects, see "Formatting fields or objects," on page 162.) At times, you may want to set format defaults up front to save you the bother of formatting each time you create a new field. Other times, setting formats field by field may be exactly what you want to do. FileMaker, as usual, lets you do either.

Setting some basic *database-wide* defaults early on, however, gives you a foundation to build on. As you work along and find you want to change the format for an *individual* field or object differently, you can then use specific choices within the Format menu (**Figure 11.3**).

To set formatting defaults

1. Make sure you're in Layout mode (⌃Ctrl L for Windows/⌘ L on the Mac) with *nothing* selected (otherwise some of the Format menu's choices will be unavailable, signified by them being grayed out).

2. Under the Format menu, choose any of the five middle items (Text, Number, Date, Time, Graphic) to set the default formatting. Examples of each of your selections will appear in that dialog box's sample area. (For information on the Portal and Button, see Chapters 12 and 13.) Here's the rundown on each:

   Text Format: With this dialog box (**Figure 11.4**), you can set the default font, text size, color, and style. By clicking on the lower-left Paragraph button, you'll reach the Paragraph dialog box (**Figure 11.5**) where you can set the default alignment, indents, and line spacing for text. Finally, by clicking on the Tabs button, you'll reach the Tabs dialog box. See "To set text tabs" on page 163.

Figure 11.3 Depending on what you've selected, you can use the Format menu to set individual fields or database-wide defaults.

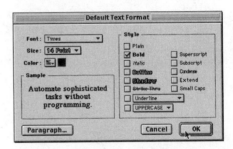

Figure 11.4 Use the Text Format dialog box to set the font, text size, color, and style. Click the Paragraph button to set text alignment, indents, and line spacing.

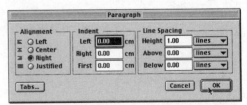

Figure 11.5 The Paragraph dialog box, reached via the Text Format dialog box, lets you set text alignment, indents, and line spacing.

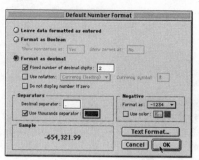

Figure 11.6 Use the Number Format dialog box to control the appearance of field numbers.

Figure 11.7 Use the Date Format dialog box to choose five standard options or click Custom for even more choices.

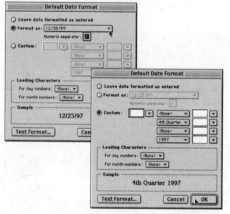

Figure 11.8 Custom date formats include fiscal-year quarters.

Figure 11.9 Use the Time Format dialog box to select from a myriad of options.

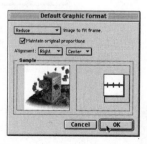

Number Format: Within this dialog box (**Figure 11.6**), you can set the default to Boolean (Yes-No, True-False) format, control how many decimals you want showing, set a currency symbol to precede numbers (an unlikely database-wide choice unless every number field in the database deals with money), what sort of decimal separator you want (if any), and how negative numbers are displayed. The lower-right Text Format button, by the way, takes you back to the Text Format dialog box. Sorry, you can't use it to set a different font for numbers only: If you go back and change the text settings, they'll change in all default fields.

Date Format: Within this dialog box (**Figure 11.7**), you can choose five different date formatting options—or click the Custom radio button and get still more choices (**Figure 11.8**).

Time Format: Within this dialog box (**Figure 11.9**), you've got another zillion choices on time formats. Who knew there were so many?

Graphic Format: Within this dialog box (**Figure 11.10**), you can control how graphics are cropped and fitted within your field's frame. Use the Sample window to see how the various options are displayed.

3. When you're done making your default choices, click OK. Repeat to set other format defaults.

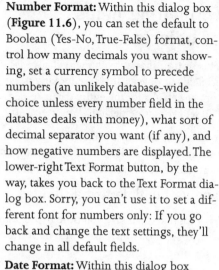

Figure 11.10 Use the Graphic Format dialog box to control cropping and fitting. The sample window previews the options.

SETTING FORMAT DEFAULTS

Formatting fields or objects

This section shows you how to change individual fields or objects. If you're looking to set format defaults for the entire database, see "To set formatting defaults," on page 160.)

You can, by the way, format several fields at the same time—as long as you're setting the same attribute in each field, for example, text.

Setting multiple text attributes

This approach can save you time if you want to change, say, a font's size and style at the same time.

To set several text attributes at once

1. Select your text and choose Text from the Format menu (**Figure 11.11**).

2. When the Text Format dialog box appears (**Figure 11.12**), use the pop-down menus to select the font, size, color, and style of your text. To set the alignment, indentation, or line spacing of text, click the Paragraph button in the lower left.

3. Once the Paragraph dialog box appears (**Figure 11.13**), you can set those three text attributes.

4. When you're done, click OK.

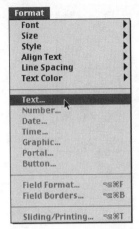

Figure 11.11 Choose Text from the Format menu to reach the Text Format dialog box.

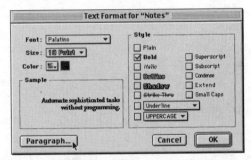

Figure 11.12 The Text Format dialog box lets you set multiple text attributes, including paragraph formatting via the lower-left button.

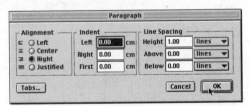

Figure 11.13 The Paragraph dialog box lets you set text alignment, indentation, and line spacing.

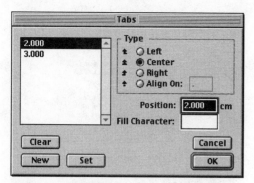

Figure 11.14 The Tabs dialog box lets you change existing tabs or create new ones.

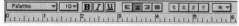

Figure 11.15 For easy access to text controls, use the Text Ruler, which is reached via the Show menu.

To set text tabs

1. Select the text for which you want to set tabs and choose Text from the Format menu (**Figure 11.11**).

2. When the Text Format dialog box appears (**Figure 11.12**), click the Paragraph button in the lower left. When the Paragraph dialog box appears (**Figure 11.13**), click the Tabs button. The Tabs dialog box appears.

3. Within the Tabs dialog box (**Figure 11.14**), the current tab settings appear in the upper-left window. To change them, select one with your cursor and type in a new position number, and click Set.

   To create a new tab, select the type in the upper-right panel, type in the position number, and click New.

   To start over, click Clear.

   To set a decimal tab, click Align On. If you want to use something other than a period, type it into the adjacent entry box.

   Fill characters appear between tabbed items (usually dashes or periods). Type in your choice.

4. When you're done, click OK.

✔ Tip

- It's much quicker to set tabs via the Text Ruler. Just choose Text Ruler from the Show menu (**Figure 11.15**), then double-click on any one of the ruler's four tab markers. Better still, if you frequently format text, just leave the Text Ruler showing and you'll be one click away from tabs and most other text settings.

To choose a font

1. Select the text to which you want to apply another font. To select multiple fields or objects, just press (Shift) as you click on each field or object.

2. Choose Font from the Format menu (**Figure 11.16**). When the pop-down menu of fonts appears, drag your cursor to the font you want and release the cursor. The selected text will change to the newly selected font.

To choose a text size

1. Select the text or field containing text you want to change. To select multiple fields or objects, just press (Shift) as you click on each field or object.

2. Choose Size from the Format menu (**Figure 11.17**). When the pop-down menu of text sizes appears, drag your cursor to the size you want and release the cursor. The selected text will change size.

To choose a text style

1. Select the text or field containing text you want to change. To select multiple fields or objects, just press (Shift) as you click on each field or object.

2. Choose Style from the Format menu (**Figure 11.18**). When the pop-down menu of text styles appears, drag your cursor to the style you want and release the cursor. Since text can have multiple styles (bold with italic with underline), continue using the pop-down menu until you've applied all the desired styles.

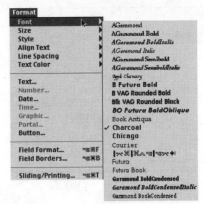

Figure 11.16 Use the Font command within the Format menu to quickly apply any font to your selected text.

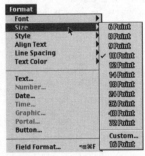

Figure 11.17 The Size command within the Format menu gives you quick access to all the point sizes in the current font.

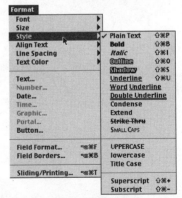

Figure 11.18 Use the Style command within the Format menu to change text you've selected.

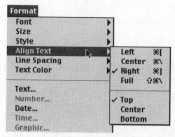

Figure 11.19 The Align Text command within the Format menu gives you quick access to alignment options without having to open a dialog box.

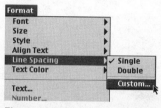

Figure 11.20 The Line Spacing command within the Format menu lets you choose single, double, or custom spacing.

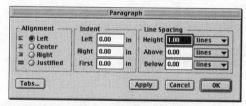

Figure 11.21 Custom line spacing is handled within the Paragraph dialog box.

To align text

1. Select the text or field containing text you want to change. To select multiple fields or objects, just press (Shift) as you click on each field or object.

2. Choose Align Text from the Format menu (**Figure 11.19**). When the pop-down menu of alignment choices appears, drag your cursor to the alignment you want and release the cursor. The alignment of the selected text will reflect your new choice.

To choose line spacing

1. Select the text or field containing text you want to change. To select multiple fields or objects, just press (Shift) as you click on each field or object.

2. Choose Line Spacing from the Format menu (**Figure 11.20**). When the pop-down menu of spacing choices appears, drag your cursor to the one you want and release the cursor.

   If single or double line spacing won't do, choose Custom, which opens the Paragraph settings dialog box (**Figure 11.21**).

3. Use the far-right column to set your line height and the spacing above and below the line. The pop-down menus for each allow you to make your spacings based on the number of lines, inches, pixels, or centimeters.

4. Once you're ready, click Apply, then click OK.

To choose a text color

1. Select the text or field containing text you want to change. To select multiple fields or objects, just press [Shift] as you click on each field or object.

2. Choose Text Color from the Format menu (**Figure 11.22**). When the pop-down menu of colors appears, drag your cursor to the one you want and release the cursor. The text will change to the color you've chosen.

To format a number field

1. Make sure the field you want to format is, in fact, a number-type field. (You can check via the Define Fields dialog box: [Ctrl][Shift][D] in Windows/[Shift][⌘][D] on the Mac.)

2. Choose Number from the Format menu (**Figure 11.23**), which will open the Number Format dialog box (**Figure 11.24**).

3. Make your choices (for specifics on the dialog box, see step 2 of "To set formatting defaults," on page 160). Click OK.

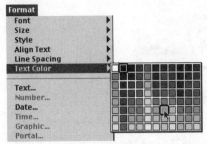

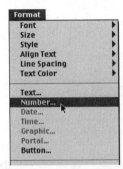

Figure 11.22 Use the Text Color command within the Format menu to quickly apply color to selected text.

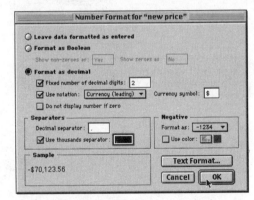

Figure 11.23 To format a number-type field only, choose Number from the Format menu.

Figure 11.24 The Number Format dialog box's settings are applied to number fields you've selected or used to set *default* number settings if no field's selected.

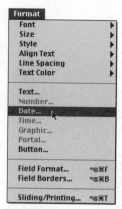

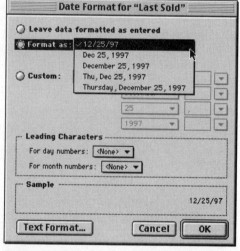

Figure 11.25 To format a date-type field only, choose Date from the Format menu.

Figure 11.26 The Date Format dialog box's settings are applied to selected date fields or used to set *default* date settings if no field's selected.

To format a date field

1. Make sure the field you want to format is a date-type field. You can do this by checking the Define Fields dialog box: Ctrl Shift D in Windows/Shift ⌘ D on the Mac.

2. Choose Date from the Format menu (**Figure 11.25**), which will open the Date Format dialog box (**Figure 11.26**).

3. Make your choices (for specifics on the dialog box, see step 2 of "To set formatting defaults," on page 160). Click OK.

FORMATTING DATE FIELDS

To format a time field

1. Make sure the field you want to format is a time-type field. You can do this by checking the Define Fields dialog box: [Ctrl][Shift][D] in Windows/[Shift][⌘][D] on the Mac.

2. Choose Time from the Format menu (**Figure 11.27**), which will open the Time Format dialog box (**Figure 11.28**).

3. Make your choices (for specifics on the dialog box, see step 2 of "To set formatting defaults," on page 160). Click OK.

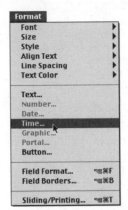

Figure 11.27 To format a time-type field only, choose Time from the Format menu.

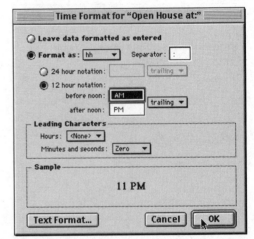

Figure 11.28 The Time Format dialog box's settings are applied to selected time fields or used to set *default* time settings if no field's selected.

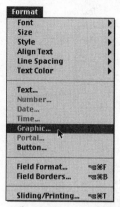

Figure 11.29 To format a container-type field only, choose Graphic from the Format menu.

Figure 11.30 The Graphic Format dialog box's settings are applied to selected graphics or used to set *default* graphic settings if no field's selected.

To format a graphic field

1. Make sure the field you want to format is a container-type field. You can do this by checking the Define Fields dialog box: (Ctrl)(Shift)(D) in Windows/(Shift)(⌘)(D) on the Mac.

2. Choose Graphic from the Format menu (**Figure 11.29**), which will open the Graphic Format dialog box (**Figure 11.30**).

3. Make your choices (for specifics on the dialog box, see step 2 of "To set formatting defaults," on page 160). Click OK.

Working with graphics

The Layout status area includes a powerful collection of tools for adding graphic interest and emphasis to your layouts (**Figure 11.31**).

Pointer Tool: Use this tool to select or resize fields and objects.

Text Tool: Though it's nestled amid the draw tools, this tool's really for, well, text. See "Working with text" on page 158 for more information.

Line Tool: Use this tool with the Pen Tools to create lines of varying width, color, and pattern.

Shape Tools (rectangle, rounded rectangle, oval): Use the three tools with the Fill Tools to create shapes of varying colors and patterns. Also see "To change the stack order of objects" on page 149 for information on how to arrange overlapping shapes.

Button, Portal Tools: Buttons are used to trigger scripts and, so, are covered in Chapter 12, "Using Templates and Scripts," on page 179. Portals are views of data from other databases and, so, are covered in Chapter 13, "Creating Relational Databases," on page 191.

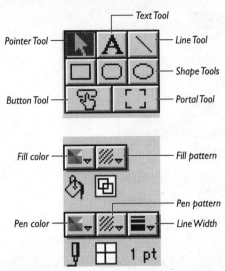

Figure 11.31 The Layout mode's status area contains drawing, fill, and pen tools for adding graphic impact to your layouts.

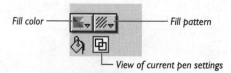

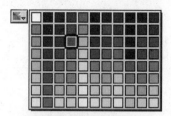

Figure 11.32 The Fill Tools control colors and patterns for shapes.

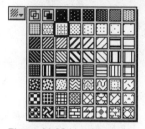

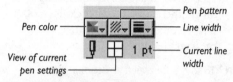

Fill Tools (color, pattern): Use this pair of tools (**Figure 11.32**) with the Shape Tools. Both tools offer a variety of choices via their pop-down menus (**Figure 11.33**).

Pen Tools (color, pattern, line width): Use this trio of tools (**Figure 11.34**) with the Line Tool. Like the Fill Tools, these three tools operate via pop-down menus (**Figure 11.35**).

Figure 11.34 The Pen Tools control line colors, patterns, and widths.

Figure 11.33 Use the pop-down menus to reach the fill colors and patterns.

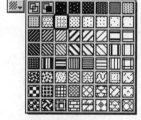

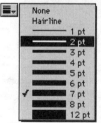

Figure 11.35 Use the pop-down menus to choose line colors, patterns, and widths.

WORKING WITH GRAPHICS

To select a drawing tool

1. Switch to Layout mode (Ctrl L for Windows/⌘ L on the Mac), then click on the tool of your choice. When it's active, it will become gray (left in **Figure 11.36**).

✔ Tips

■ It's easy to accidentally unselect a tool. To keep it selected until you deliberately click on another tool, double-click the tool. It will become black to indicate it's locked on (right in **Figure 11.36**).

■ To toggle between any tool and the Pointer tool, press Enter (the one by the numeric keypad).

To draw an object

1. Switch to Layout mode (Ctrl L for Windows/⌘ L on the Mac), then click on the drawing tool of your choice: Line, Rectangle, Rounded Rectangle, or Oval.

2. Click with your cursor where you want the shape to begin and drag the cursor to where you want the shape to end. See **Table 11.2**, "FileMaker's Object Drawing Tools," for more details.

Figure 11.36 When a tool's selected it becomes gray (left); when it's selected and locked it becomes black (right).

Table 11.2

FileMaker's Object Drawing Tools		
TOOL ICON	**SHAPE**	**ACTION**
Line	Line	Select Line Tool, click on start point, and press cursor until end point reached.
	Horizontal, vertical, or 45-degree line	Select Line Tool. Press Alt (Windows) or Option (Mac) while clicking on start point, and dragging cursor until end point reached.
Rectangle	Rectangle	Select Rectangle Tool. Click on start point and drag cursor until rectangle is the size you want.
	Square	Select Rectangle Tool. Press Alt (Windows) or Option (Mac) while clicking on start point, and dragging cursor until square is the size you want.
Rounded rectangle	Rounded rectangle	Select Rounded Rectangle Tool. Click on start point and drag cursor until rectangle is the size you want.
Oval	Oval	Select Oval Tool. Click on start point and drag cursor until oval is the size you want.
	Circle	Select Oval Tool. Press Alt (Windows) or Option (Mac) while clicking on start point, and dragging cursor until circle is the size you want.

Figure 11.37 To move an object, click on it with the Pointer Tool and drag it. A dotted outline marks your progress.

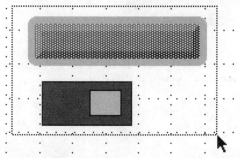

Figure 11.38 Click and drag the Pointer Tool to select multiple objects.

To select and move an object

1. Make sure you're in Layout mode (Ctrl L for Windows/⌘ L on the Mac), then click on the object. To select multiple objects, just press and hold down Shift before clicking on the objects.

2. Small squares will appear on each corner of the object to let you know it's been selected. Continue holding down your cursor and drag the object where you want it. A dotted outline of the object will mark your movement until you release the cursor (**Figure 11.37**).

✔ Tips

■ You also can select multiple objects with the Pointer Tool by pressing and holding down the cursor, then dragging the resulting square to include the objects (**Figure 11.38**).

■ To select everything in a layout, use the Select All keyboard command (Ctrl A in Windows/⌘ A on the Mac).

SELECTING AND MOVING OBJECTS

To deselect an object

1. Simply click your cursor anywhere within the layout or select a tool other than the Pointer Tool within the tool palette.

To resize an object

1. Select the Pointer Tool, then click on the object.

2. Handles (small black squares) will appear at the object's corners. Click on any handle and drag it to reshape the object. A dotted outline of the object's new shape will mark your movement until you release the cursor (**Figure 11.39**).

✔ Tip

■ If you want more precision in resizing an object (such as making its size identical to other objects), use the Size Palette: Click on the object, then choose Size from the Show menu, and use the palette to enter measurements for the object. When done, press ⁅Enter⁆ in Windows/⁅Return⁆ on the Mac. The selected object will assume the sizing you entered.

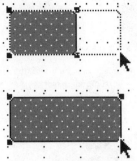

Figure 11.39 To resize an object, grab on the corner handles and drag until it reaches the size you want. A dotted outline marks your progress.

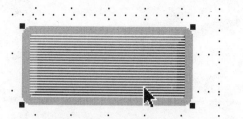

Figure 11.40 To change an object's pattern, first select it with the Pointer Tool.

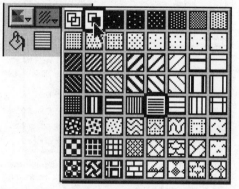

Figure 11.41 Use the Fill Tool's pattern pop-down menu to select a new pattern. The arrow marks the new solid choice; the dark box marks the previous pattern.

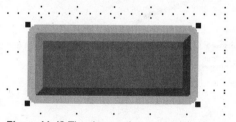

Figure 11.42 The object with its new solid pattern.

Changing fill colors and patterns

Setting a fill color or pattern is like setting a default: You start by making sure nothing is selected.

To set or change an object's fill color or pattern

1. To change an object's *existing* fill color or pattern, select the object using the Pointer Tool (**Figure 11.40**).

2. Now click on either of the Fill tools to select a color or pattern (**Figure 11.41**).

3. When the tool's pop-down menu appears, drag your cursor to the choice you want and release the cursor (**Figure 11.42**).

✔ Tip

■ If you want to start all over on the pattern, select the object and then click the transparent pattern, found in the upper-left corner of the pop-down choices.

Changing lines

Setting the pen color, pattern, or width is like setting a default: You start by making sure nothing is selected.

To set or change line color, pattern, or width

1. To change an *existing* line, select it using the Pointer Tool (**Figure 11.43**).

2. Now click on any of the Pen tools that control color, pattern, or line width (**Figure 11.44**).

3. When the tool's pop-down menu appears, drag your cursor to the line style choice you want and release the cursor (**Figure 11.45**). The selected line will change to reflect your choice.

✔ Tip

■ Use the pen color to change the border color of *objects* (fields use a separate process, see "To change field borders, fills, and baselines" on page 177). Just select the object and click the pen color pop-down menu to make your choice.

Figure 11.43 To change a line's width, first select it with the Pointer Tool.

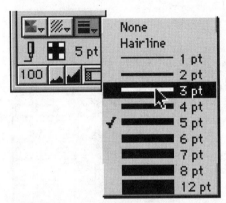

Figure 11.44 Use the Pen Tool's line-width pop-down menu to select a new line width. The check marks the previous line width.

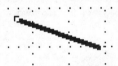

Figure 11.45 After using the pop-down menu, the line assumes its new, sleek look.

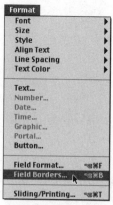

Figure 11.46 The Field Borders command under the Format menu is only available for fields, not objects.

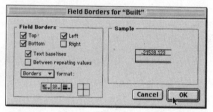

Figure 11.47 When the Field Borders dialog box first opens, the lower-left pop-down menu is already set to Borders.

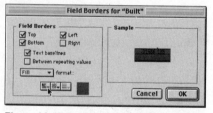

Figure 11.48 Choose Fill from the Field Borders dialog box's pop-down menu to control field color and pattern.

Figure 11.49 Choose Baselines from the Field Borders dialog box's pop-down menu to control the baseline pattern and weight.

Changing borders, fills, and baselines

To set the *defaults* for field borders, fills, or baselines, first make sure *nothing* is selected.

To set or change field borders, fills, and baselines

1. To change an *existing* field's borders, fills, or baselines, first select it using the Pointer Tool. This procedure applies to fields only, not other objects.

2. Choose Field Borders from the Format menu (**Figure 11.46**).

3. When the Field Borders dialog box appears (**Figure 11.47**), use the lower-left pop-down menu to set the borders, fill, or baselines.

   In setting field borders, the four upper-left boxes control the boundary around the field. The results of your choices appear in the upper-right Sample area. Checking "Text baselines" will place horizontal lines within fields containing multiple lines of text. Checking "Between repeating values" will separate repeating field entries with lines.

   In setting field fills (**Figure 11.48**), the action is down at the bottom left where two pop-down menus let you set the color and the pattern. In our example, we've selected a dark color, which is shown in the Sample area.

   In setting field baselines (**Figure 11.49**), your choices are confined to the three bottom pop-down menus: color, pattern, and line weight. In our example, we've made the baseline thin and dashed, as shown in the Sample area.

4. When you've made your choices, click OK.

USING TEMPLATES AND SCRIPTS

Why reinvent the wheel when FileMaker has rounded up a terrific collection of templates and predefined scripts for you? Templates can give you a quick start in creating records, fields, and layouts. Scripts take things another step by helping you automate many parts of the database process, from record entry to finding and sorting records, from dialing a modem to greeting users with personalized messages. Even if you choose to work from scratch, these templates and scripts contain a trove of ideas and inspiration.

Working with templates

FileMaker comes with 44 templates in three categories: Business, Education, and Home. The layouts run the gamut: business cards, expense reports, purchase orders, field trip forms, memos, family medical records, music lists—the list goes on.

If that's not easy enough, FileMaker comes with its own database, "Template Information," which contains brief descriptions of all the templates and how to best customize them for your own purposes (**Figure 12.1**). To open it, follow the directions below.

To copy a template

1. Choose New from the File menu. The New Database dialog box appears (**Figure 12.2**).

2. At the lower left you'll see the "Template Info" button. To open the Template Information database, click the button.

   To go straight to creating a new file, click "Create a new file using a template."

3. Choose among the three categories (Business, Education, Home) using the right-side pop-up menu.

4. Select a template from the right-side list and double-click it to open it.

5. Give your copy of the template a new name within the text box. By default, FileMaker gives it the same name as the original template but it'll be less confusing if you use a distinctive name (**Figure 12.3**). Click Save and the copy of the template appears (**Figure 12.4**).

✔ Tip

- Once you copy a template, just treat it like any other file and use the book's various chapters—particularly Chapter 10, "Creating Layouts," and Chapter 11, "Formatting and Graphics in Layouts"— to further customize the template.

Figure 12.1 FileMaker includes a database describing how to use and customize 44 built-in templates.

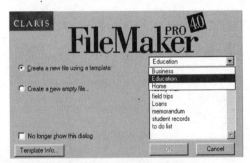

Figure 12.2 Use the pop-up menu in the New Database dialog box to choose from three categories of templates: Business, Education, or Home.

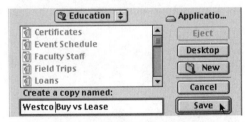

Figure 12.3 Rename the template copy and click Save.

Figure 12.4 Once you've copied one of FileMaker's templates, you can change it to suit your needs.

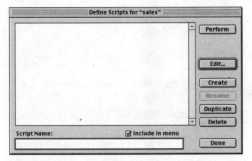

Figure 12.5 Use the Define Scripts dialog box to create, rename, edit, duplicate, delete, and perform (test) scripts.

Working with scripts

Creating a script is a lot like designing a database: The more you plan it out in advance, the smoother the actual construction will go.

Running a script simply triggers a series of automatic commands that you've strung together. A script can be a one-step task such as opening a record, or it can involve a cascade of actions that would take a person much longer to do manually. By automating certain tasks, scripts can reduce the chance of data-entry errors and ease the demands on those less comfortable with databases in general. To make scripts even easier to use, you can link them to buttons placed within different layouts (see "Using buttons with scripts" on page 188).

In planning a script, break the task you want to perform into the smallest pieces possible. These pieces, what FileMaker calls *steps*, are easier to build than a long, single script. With this modular approach, you can recombine the steps into other scripts later on. Many of the steps have been already defined within FileMaker, reducing the need for you to generate a step from scratch. Take a look at the complete list of FileMaker's scripting steps in Appendix F, "Script Commands," on page 295.

Remember as well that a script need not be entirely automatic. For example, inserting pauses into a script can let users enter data at particular points and resume the script when they're ready.

Most of FileMaker's scripting steps are put to use within just two dialog boxes. The Define Scripts dialog box is where you create (name), rename, edit, duplicate, and delete scripts, as well as test them (**Figure 12.5**).

All available script steps are listed within
the Script Definition dialog box, which is
where you build a script once you name it
(**Figure 12.6**).

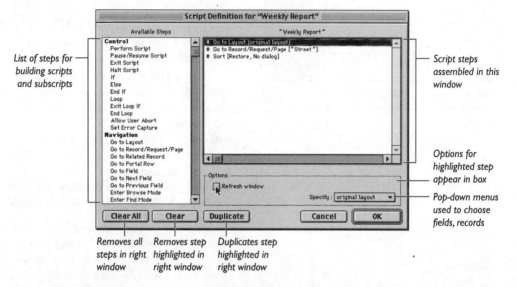

*List of steps for
building scripts
and subscripts*

*Script steps
assembled in this
window*

*Options for
highlighted step
appear in box*

*Pop-down menus
used to choose
fields, records*

*Removes all
steps in right
window*   *Removes step
highlighted in
right window*   *Duplicates step
highlighted in
right window*

Figure 12.6 Use the Script Definition dialog box to build scripts using the
Available Steps list and the Options panel.

Pre-script settings

When you begin defining a script, you'll
find that FileMaker has saved some of your
database's current settings, if they exist, and
included them in the Script Definition dialog
box. For that reason, it's best to prepare and
store such settings *before* you define the script.
Mind you, you don't have to do this but it
can save you some scripting work. These settings can include the layout you'll be using
in the script, along with the mode, find
request, sort order, print setup and options,
and import/export order.

To store pre-script settings

1. To set your script settings:

Layout: Use the layout pop-up window above the flipbook to choose which layout you'll be using in the script.

Mode: Use the Mode menu to place your database in the mode you'll be using in the script.

Find Request: If you'll be building a script that needs to use a particular found set of records, go ahead and set up the appropriate Find Request (Ctrl F in Windows/⌘ F on the Mac). You need not actually run Find, just specify the Find Request. For more information, see Chapter 5, "Finding and Sorting Records," on page 39.

Sort Order: If your script will depend on a particular sort, switch to Browse and set up the sort (Ctrl S in Windows/⌘ S on the Mac). You don't need to run the sort, just set it up. For more information, see "To run a simple sort" on page 56.

Print/Page Setup and Print Options: If your script will depend on specific print settings, choose Print Setup from the File menu. You need not actually print, just specify the setup. Choose Print from the File menu (Ctrl P in Windows/⌘ P on the Mac) to specify any print options such as number of copies.

Import/Export Order: If your script involves either importing or exporting data, you'll want to set the order of the fields. Choose Import/Export from the File menu and make your choices in the related Field Mapping and Field Order dialog boxes. For more information, see Chapter 7, "Converting Files" on page 67.

2. When you're done making the various settings, choose ScriptMaker from the Script menu. You are now ready to define a script.

STORING PRE-SCRIPT SETTINGS

To define a script

1. While in any mode, choose ScriptMaker from the Script menu (**Figure 12.7**).

2. When the Define Scripts dialog box appears, type in a name for your new script and click Create (**Figure 12.8**).

3. The Script Definition dialog box appears with all the stored settings for the database already listed in the right-side window (**Figure 12.9**). Keep the settings you'll need for the script and delete the rest by highlighting each and then clicking Clear.

4. Find the first step you want to add from the left-side Available Steps list, highlight it, and click Move. Options, if any, for Available Steps appear in the lower-right Options panel (**Figure 12.10**). For a complete list of script steps and their use, see Appendix F, "Script Commands," on page 295.

5. If you need to reorder a step within the right-side list, highlight it and use the double-arrow just to the left of the script name to drag the step to its new position in the order.

6. When you're done, click OK.

Figure 12.7 The first step for any script: Choosing ScriptMaker from the Script menu.

Figure 12.8 When the Define Scripts dialog box appears, give your planned script a distinctive name and click Create.

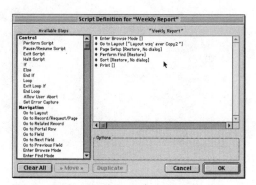

Figure 12.9 The Script Definition dialog box with predefined settings on the right side.

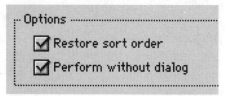

Figure 12.10 If an available step has options, use the Option panel's checkboxes to make your choices.

Figure 12.11 If your script changes predefined settings, a dialog will ask whether to keep or replace them.

Figure 12.12 Unless you choose otherwise, new scripts appear within the Script menu.

7. If you included any pre-script settings in your script—and have since changed those settings—a dialog box will appear asking whether you want to keep the original setting or replace it with the setting now in use (**Figure 12.11**). Make your choice among the radio buttons and click OK.

8. The script is now listed in the Define Scripts dialog box. If you want to test whether your new script runs correctly, click Perform and see if the scripting actions play out as you desire. If you're happy with it, click Done. If your script needs more work, click Edit and see "To change a script," on page 186.

Once you click Done, your new script is available under the Script menu (**Figure 12.12**).

To change/copy a script

1. Choose ScriptMaker from the Script menu.

2. Within the Define Scripts dialog box, highlight the existing script you want to change or duplicate by clicking on it in the right-side window.

3. To change the script, click Edit. To copy it, click Duplicate.

4. Type in a distinctive name for the changed or duplicated script and click Create.

5. The Script Definition dialog box will reappear, in which you can change and substitute script steps. When you're satisfied, click OK. Your changed script now is available under the Script menu.

To delete a script

1. Choose ScriptMaker from the Script menu.

2. Within the Define Scripts dialog box, highlight the existing script you want to delete and click Delete.

3. A warning dialog box will appear. If you're sure you want to delete the script, click OK.

Script
ScriptMaker™...
Weekly Report ⌘1
Monthly Report ⌘2
Quarterly Report ⌘3
Regional comparison ⌘4

Figure 12.13 Up to 10 scripts listed within the Script menu can be assigned keyboard shortcuts.

Reordering script shortcuts

The first 10 scripts listed under the Scripts menu automatically receive keyboard shortcuts ([Ctrl] 1–10 in Windows/⌘ 1–10 on the Mac) (**Figure 12.13**).

To reorder or change the script menu list

1. To reassign script shortcuts, choose ScriptMaker from the Script menu.

2. Within the Script Definition dialog box, drag the listed scripts up or down in the order by click-dragging the double-arrows just left of each script.

   You also can shorten the Script menu list by highlighting a less-used script in the right-side list. Uncheck the "Include in menu" box, which sits just above the Script Name entry box.

3. Once you've fully ordered the list, click Done.

Using buttons with scripts

Some folks find the whole notion of scripts intimidating. But put a clearly labeled, script-linked button in a layout and the message is clear: "Click me."

To define a button

1. Once you've defined a script, switch to Layout mode (Ctrl L in Windows/ ⌘ L on the Mac) and select a layout via the pop-up menu just above the flip-book icon.

2. Click the Button Tool within the Layout status area (**Figure 12.14**), then use your cursor to draw a button within the layout. Release the cursor when the button reaches the size you want.

3. When the Specify Button dialog appears, select a step from the list and set its options, if any, in the Options panel. Use the second pop-up menu as appropriate to control the state of your script (Halt, Exit, Resume, or Pause). Not every step will offer the same options, and steps grayed out in the list don't apply to your particular button.

   If you want to use a step of your own that you've already defined, select "Perform Script" from the Control portion of the listed steps. Then use the Specify pop-up menu in the Options panel to select your step (**Figure 12.15**).

4. Click OK.

5. When the layout reappears with the new button, type a name for it at the I-beam cursor. When you're done, press Enter on the numeric keypad.

6. Switch to Browse mode (Ctrl B in Windows/⌘ B on the Mac) and your button's ready for action.

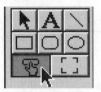

Figure 12.14 Click the Button Tool to add a script-linked button to a layout.

Figure 12.15 Use the Specify Button dialog box to select a script step and to control its options.

✔ Tips

- The difference between Halt versus Pause in controlling a script is small but crucial. Halt stops *all* scripts, no matter what level they're running at. Pause only pauses the specific script containing that step, which means if it's inside a subscript, the higher-level scripts continue to run.

- Generally, you don't want buttons to appear on printouts, so switch to Layout mode and select the button. Choose Sliding/Printing from the Format menu. In the Set Sliding/Printing dialog box, check "Do not print the selected objects" and click OK (**Figure 12.16**).

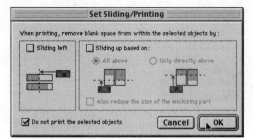

Figure 12.16 Use the checkbox in the Set Sliding/Printing dialog box to keep buttons from cluttering up printouts.

Copying or deleting a button

Copying a button duplicates not just the graphic but the linked script as well.

To copy or delete a button

1. Switch to Layout mode ([Ctrl][L] in Windows/[⌘][L] on the Mac) and click on the button with the Pointer Tool to select it.

2. To copy the button, use the Copy command ([Ctrl][C] in Windows/[⌘][C] on the Mac), move to the layout where you want the button to appear, and paste it in place ([Ctrl][V] in Windows/[⌘][V] on the Mac). To delete the button, simply press [Del] or [Backspace].

✔ Tip

- You can even copy a button into another database, though you'll probably need to edit the script to reflect the new field names and layouts.

To resize or move a button

1. Switch to Layout mode ([Ctrl][L] in Windows/[⌘][L] on the Mac) and click on the button with the Pointer Tool.

2. To resize the button, simply hold down the cursor and drag one of the button's corner handles to the size you want.

   To move the button, click on its center and drag the button where you want it.

To change a button's definition

1. Switch to Layout mode ([Ctrl][L] in Windows/[⌘][L] on the Mac) and double-click on the button.

2. When the Specify Button dialog box appears, change the steps or option choices as desired. (To change a step itself, see "To change/copy a script" on page 186.)

To change a button's appearance

1. Switch to Layout mode ([Ctrl][L] in Windows/[⌘][L] on the Mac) and click on the button with the Pointer Tool.

2. To change the button's background color or pattern, select one of the Fill Tools (color or pattern) from the status area and use the related pop-up menu to change the button as desired.

   To change the button's border color, pattern or width, select one of the Pen Tools (color, pattern, or line width) from the status area and use the related pop-up menu to change the button as desired.

   To change the button's font, text size, or text color (**Figure 12.17**), go to the Format menu and select the appropriate option in the menu's top half.

✔ Tip

■ For more information on formatting and styling objects such as buttons, see Chapter 11, "Formatting and Graphics in Layouts," on page 157.

Figure 12.17 Before and after: The default script button (top) and its fully styled cousin (bottom).

CREATING RELATIONAL DATABASES

As you build databases, sooner or later you want to go relational, that is, to connect one database to another. Relational databases offer a way to make that connection—without slowing performance or requiring gigabytes of extra storage—by sharing data rather than duplicating it.

Instead of creating one big database packed with everything you might ever need to know about a subject, it makes far more sense to create a number of much smaller relational databases. Not only will relational databases help you focus on what's key to each database—contacts in one database, products in another, invoices in still another—they take up far less space. All your product data, for example, stays in the product database. If you need the price of a product while generating an invoice, the relational link lets you "see" the price data without actually copying it into your invoice database. That way you get speed—without the bulk of FileMaker's original "flat file" design, which required that each database contain *all* the data it needed. One final advantage of relational databases: Different users can update or redesign one of the databases without forcing everyone else to stop using the related databases.

Despite the obvious advantages of relational databases, building them can quickly become a chicken-and-egg problem of which database comes first and which does what. It's easy to become overwhelmed by the possible options. Start small and simple. You can always go back and create more lookups and relationships as you need them. To keep focused, approach the process in six sequential steps:

Step 1 Plan, plan, plan: Take a big-picture look at what you want to accomplish and sketch out the *overall* connections: what kinds of data you want to track and how many databases that might take. Then consider the connections needed between various files and fields. It's common to revise your notions of what information should go where as your plans progress, so don't use the computer just yet. Rely instead on paper, pencil, and eraser—especially the eraser—to draw boxes, arrows, or whatever it takes to identify the best way to organize the data.

Step 2 Define the fields: From the big picture, narrow down to the details of defining exactly what fields need to be in each database. Try to avoid duplicating fields and data from database to database. Instead think about ways the data can be shared.

Step 3 Define the relational links: Thinking of how to share data leads naturally to defining the relationships between various files. As the link between databases, the relationship is simply a formula that names two databases and a field that contains matching data in both databases. The relational link triggers an action, but defining exactly what that action should be comes in the next step.

Step 4 Put the links to use: The actions triggered by a relationship—what FileMaker calls lookups and portals—can be limited to one field or involve the whole database. See "Lookups versus portals" on page 196 to better understand the pros and cons of both.

Step 5 Create layouts: Only after the first four steps should you actually begin creating layouts for your lookups and portals. Aim for layouts that present the related information as clearly as possible by using portals, buttons, and scripts to tuck the relational "wiring" out of sight.

Step 6 Enter the data: Now that you've built destinations for your data, you can start importing existing files or entering information record by record as you use your new relational system.

A jargon jump-start

Each relationship in FileMaker includes only one master (destination) file and one related (source) file. But you can create multiple relationships, which means the same file can be the destination (master file) for some data and the source (related file) of other data. Whether you're dealing with a file, a record, or a field, just keep straight where the data's coming from (the source) versus where it's eventually going to (the destination). For a bit of lingo help, see **Table 13.1**, "Too Many Terms for Two Simple Ideas."

The examples in this chapter are based on three database files: 3D, which lists products from 3D software companies; 3D vendor addresses, which lists all the contact information for each company; and 3D Books, which lists information about books that explain how to use the software program (**Figure 13.1**). To put all the information in a single database file would be unwieldy. By dividing it into three files, each database remains focused and simple to use, which is what relational databases are all about. As you read the rest of the chapter, refer back to **Figure 13.1** to see how these three relational files put relationships, match fields, lookups, and portals to use.

Table 13.1

Too Many Terms for Two Simple Ideas	
FILEMAKER TERM	WHAT IT MEANS
master file, record, or field *destination* *target* *current*	The file, record, or field you copy data *to*
related *source* *originating*	The file, record, or field you copy data *from*

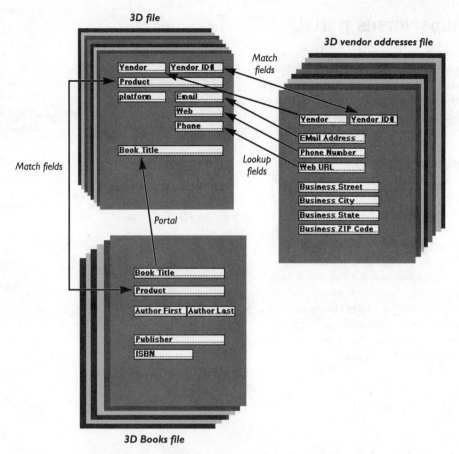

Figure 13.1 How three files connect: The "Vendor ID#" match fields link the files "3D" to "3D vendor addresses," allowing the separately defined lookup fields to be copied to "3D." The "Product" match fields link "3D" and "3D Books," making the multiple-record portal appear within "3D."

UNDERSTANDING RELATIONAL JARGON

Lookups versus portals

Lookup fields *copy* data from one database into another, where it remains unchanged unless you update it manually. A lookup can contain only one record from the related file, whereas a portal can display any number of records from the related file. The portal does not copy the files into the master file, but simply *displays* them via a window (hence the name, portal) back to where the data resides in the related file. For that reason, portals require less storage space since the data remains in just one file. The portal is also "live" in that any change in the linked data is automatically reflected in the portal. There are times, however, when you don't want a live connection. Take, for example, an invoice where you want to preserve the cost of an item at the time of the sale. A portal to item costs would reflect the current price, not the sale price. In that case, a lookup would be better.

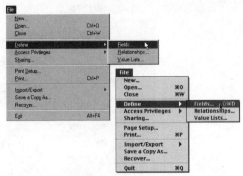

Figure 13.2 To create a lookup field, choose Define from the File menu and select Fields from the submenu.

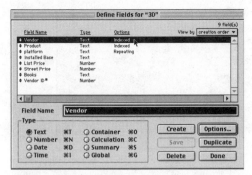

Figure 13.3 Pick a *destination* field—the one you want data copied *to*—in the Define Fields dialog box.

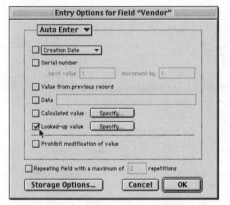

Figure 13.4 Checking "Looked-up value" in the Entry Options dialog box will open the Lookup dialog box.

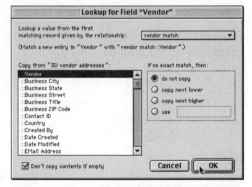

Figure 13.5 Use the Lookup dialog box to pick a field (Vendor) from the source file (3D vendor addresses) that you want to copy into the destination file (3D).

To define a lookup

1. Open the database you want to be the master (destination) file. In either Browse or Layout mode, choose Define from the File menu and select Fields from the submenu (**Figure 13.2**).

2. When the Define Fields dialog box appears (**Figure 13.3**), double-click on what you want to be the *destination* field— the one data will be copied *to*—and the Entry Options dialog box will open.

3. When the Entry Options dialog box appears (**Figure 13.4**), check "Looked-up value," which will open the Lookup dialog box.

4. Within the Lookup dialog box, use the pop-up menu to choose a relationship (**Figure 13.5**). (If no relationships have been defined, choose Define within the Edit menu and select Relationships from the submenu and see Step 2 of "To define relationships" on page 200.) In this example, two databases, 3D and 3D vendor addresses, have been linked by matching the Vendor ID# field.

   Once you define and choose a relationship from the pop-up menu, pick within the left-side list a *source* field, which is the field you want to copy data *from*.

5. Pick a match option from the "If no exact match, then" panel. Generally you'll use the default "do not copy" but you have the option of using the next lower or higher value, or even using a custom value. Also, leave "Don't copy contents if empty" checked to keep from generating empty lookup fields in your master file. Once you've made your choices, click OK.

6. The Entry Options dialog box reappears. Click OK again. Finally, the Define Fields dialog box reappears. Click Done—and now you really are done.

Creating multiple lookups

Once you've defined a relationship, you can link it to any number of lookup fields.

To create multiple lookups from one relationship

1. As you did in defining your first lookup, open the database containing the *master* (destination) file and choose Define from the File menu and select Fields from the submenu (**Figure 13.2**). The Define Fields dialog box appears.

2. Within the Define Fields dialog box, double-click on a *new* field into which you want data copied.

3. When the Entry Options dialog box appears, check "Looked-up value."

4. When the Lookup dialog box appears, use the pop-up menu to pick the *same* relationship you previously defined linking this master file with a particular related file (e.g., "vendor field lookup for ID# match").

5. Unlike the first time you used this box, now pick *another* field from the related file. In our example, since we're defining a lookup for the master 3D file's Phone field, the related file's Phone Number field has been selected (**Figure 13.6**). Set your options as needed, and click OK.

6. Click OK again when the Entry Options dialog box reappears, and click Done when the Define Fields dialog box reappears. You can continue repeating Steps 1–5 to hook even more lookups to the same relationship (**Figure 13.7**). As an example of how this works once you're done, see **Figure 13.8**: When you enter an ID number in the *master* file, FileMaker will see that it matches the ID number in the *related* file, and automatically fill in the Vendor, Phone, Email, and Web fields within the 3D file.

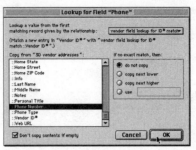

Figure 13.6 Once you've defined a relationship linking a destination and source file, you can use it to lookup data from other fields (e.g., Phone Number) in the source file (3D vendor addresses).

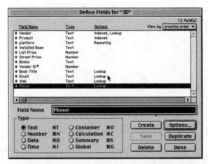

Figure 13.7 It's easy to create multiple lookup fields (e.g., Vendor, Email, Web, and Phone) once you've defined a relationship between two files.

Figure 13.8 The lookup in action: Enter a number into the (3D) ID# field that matches a number in the related database (3D vendor addresses) and data from that same record will be copied back to the lookup fields (Vendor, Phone, Email, and Web).

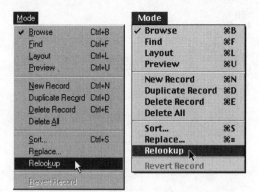

Figure 13.9 To update a lookup field, open the master file and choose Relookup from the Mode menu.

Updating lookups

Lookup fields must be manually updated—unless you create a script to do it. For information on scripting, see Chapter 12, "Using Templates and Scripts," on page 179 and Appendix F, "Script Commands," on page 295.

To update a lookup

1. Open the master (destination) database and use the Find, Sort, and Omit commands to select only the records needing updating.

2. Make sure you're in Browse mode ([Ctrl][B] in Windows/[⌘][B] on the Mac) and select the lookup (destination) field.

3. Choose Relookup from the Mode menu (**Figure 13.9**). When the alert dialog box appears, click OK. The selected records will now contain the latest data from the related file.

To define relationships

1. Open the database you want to be the master (destination) file. In either Browse or Layout mode, choose Define from the File menu and select Relationships from the submenu (**Figure 13.10**).

2. When the Define Relationships dialog box appears, click New (**Figure 13.11**).

3. When the Open File dialog box appears, navigate to the *related* (source) file and open it (**Figure 13.12**).

4. When the Edit Relationship dialog box appears, FileMaker will automatically fill in the Relationship Name text box with the name of the related file. If you like, rename it (**Figure 13.13**).

5. Select a field from the master file's fields (listed on the left side of the Edit Relationship dialog box) and a field from the related file's fields (listed on the right) that *match*—that is, have the *same* name (**Figure 13.13**). For details on the three options at the bottom of the dialog box, see **Table 13.2**, "Edit Relationship Options." This step can be a conceptual stumbling block: Just remember that you're creating a relationship, which is what links the two databases together. Picking fields from one database to show in the other comes later.

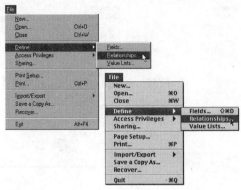

Figure 13.10 Link two databases by choosing Define from the File menu and selecting Relationships from the submenu.

Figure 13.11 To create a relationship between two files, click New in the Define Relationships dialog box.

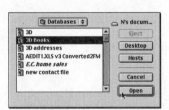

Figure 13.12 Use the Open File dialog box to find the related (source) file you want to link to the master (destination) file.

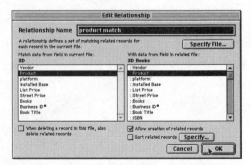

Figure 13.13 It's simple: create a relationship by picking two fields that *match exactly*. Choosing other fields activated by this link comes later.

DEFINING RELATIONSHIPS

Table 13.2

Edit Relationship Options*

CHECK BOX NAMED	TO
When deleting record in this file, also delete related records	Automatically delete records in *related* file when you delete data in *master* file's portal or related field that meets match field criteria. Press Tab to activate.
Allow creation of related records	Automatically create a record in the *related* file if you enter data in *master* file's portal or related field that meets match field criteria. Press Tab to activate.
Sort related records	Sort related records *before* they're displayed in master file. Press Specify to set Sort order.

*Options set in Edit Relationship dialog box. Options activated only if using *master* file in Browse mode.

Figure 13.14 Use the Define Relationships dialog box to create new relationships or to edit, duplicate, and delete them. When you're finished, click Done.

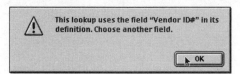

Figure 13.15 FileMaker won't let you define a relationship using a field that you've also included as the match field in the definition.

6. Click OK, which will take you back to the Define Relationships dialog box where you can create another relationship. When you've finished defining your relationships, click Done (**Figure 13.14**). To now define how these new relationships will be used, see "To define a lookup" on page 197, "To create multiple lookups from one relationship" on page 198, or "To create a portal for multiple related fields" on page 203.

✔ Tips

- You cannot use as a match field the very field for which you're defining a relationship. Otherwise, FileMaker will stop and tell you to pick another field (**Figure 13.15**). Go back and redefine the relationship to use a different field for the lookup (or use a different match field).

- Match fields don't have to be identically *named*, but they must *contain* the very same data.

To change or edit relationships

1. Choose Define from the File menu and select Relationships.

2. The Define Relationships dialog box will appear. Select a relationship and then click Edit, Duplicate, or Delete.

3. If you choose Edit, the Edit Relationship dialog box will appear where you can rename the relationship, specify another database file to use in the relationship, and pick other source and destination fields. When you're done, click OK.

✔ Tip

■ The Duplicate and Delete choices within the Define Relationships dialog box work similarly to duplicating or deleting layouts or scripts: Duplicate a relationship to save yourself time in creating a variation of an existing relationship; delete relationships you no longer need.

Figures 13.16–13.17 Click the Portal Tool (left) ... and drag the pointer in the layout to set the portal's size (right).

Figure 13.18 By picking "product match" as the relationship for the portal...

Figure 13.19 ...the Product field in the 3D Books file will be linked to the portal within the 3D file.

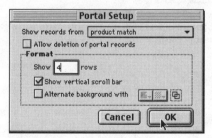

Figure 13.20 Use the Format panel to how many rows are in portal and if it has scroll bar or contrasting background.

Creating a portal for multiple fields

Once you've defined a relationship, you can use portals if your layout needs to show *more than one* record from a related file. To show a *single* record, see "To define a lookup" on page 197.

To create a portal for multiple related fields

1. Open the database you want to be the *master* (destination) file.

2. Make sure you're in Layout mode ([Ctrl][L] in Windows/[⌘][L] on the Mac) and click the Portal Tool (**Figure 13.16**).

3. Click in the layout and drag the pointer until the portal reaches the shape and size you want (**Figure 13.17**). Release the cursor.

4. When the Portal Setup dialog box appears, use the pop-up menu to choose the relationship you want to use in the portal (**Figure 13.18**). In the example, two databases, 3D and 3D Books, have been linked by matching the Product field (**Figure 13.19**). If the relationship hasn't been created yet, choose Define from the File menu and select Relationships and see Step 2 of "To define relationships" on page 200.

5. Use the checkboxes in the Format panel of the Portal Setup dialog box to choose how many rows (record listings from the related file) you want to appear in the portal, whether it should have a scroll bar, and whether you want it to have a different color or pattern to stand out from the rest of the layout. You can change these Format options later if need be. When you're done, click OK (**Figure 13.20**).

(continued)

6. The portal appears in the layout with a label for which relationship it uses (**Figure 13.21**). However, you still need to place your related fields into the portal.

7. Remain in Layout mode (Ctrl L in Windows/⌘ L on the Mac), press the Field Tool, and drag it into the first row of the portal (**Figure 13.22**). When you release the cursor, the Specify Field dialog box will appear (**Figure 13.23**). The top pop-up menu, by default, will be set to the related (source) database you picked in the Portal Setup dialog box in Step 4. The list shows all the fields within the source database. Select a field whose data you want to appear in the *destination* database. To reduce any cross-database confusion, leave "Create field label" checked. Click OK.

8. The source field will appear *inside* the portal (**Figure 13.24**). You can style and format this field as you would any other. When you switch to Browse mode, related data from multiple records within the 3D Books database appears inside the 3D database's portal (**Figure 13.25**).

Figure 13.21 Halfway there: The portal appears in the layout with a label for which relationship it uses.

Figure 13.22 Use the Field Tool to drag a field into the portal.

Figure 13.23 The Specify Field dialog box lets you choose which field from the *source* database will appear in the *destination* database's portal.

Figure 13.25 It's magic: The portal within the 3D database displays multiple records (book titles) from the related 3D book database.

Figure 13.24 Once the field appears within the portal, you can style or format it as you would any other field.

PART IV

PRINTING & NETWORKING WITH FILEMAKER

PRINTING

Figure 14.1 To change your Windows printer, choose Print Setup from the File menu.

Figure 14.2 The pop-up menu within the Print Setup dialog box lets you select a new Windows printer.

Figure 14.3 To change your Mac printer, use the Chooser dialog box.

In general, printing in FileMaker is not too different from your other applications. But there are a few twists worth considering, so read on.

To select a printer

1. Unless you change it, FileMaker will use your regular printer and its default settings. If you want to use a *different* printer for FileMaker files than your regular printer, do this:

Win In Windows, choose Print Setup from the File menu (**Figure 14.1**). When the Print Setup dialog box appears, select a new printer with the pop-up menu (**Figure 14.2**). Make sure your page margins are correct by checking the Paper and Orientation panels at the bottom of the dialog box. Click OK.

Mac On the Mac, select Chooser from the Apple menu. When the Chooser dialog box appears, make your new selection (**Figure 14.3**). Click the close box in the upper-left corner of the title bar.

To show page margins

1. Switch to Layout mode ([Ctrl] [L] in Windows/[⌘][L] on the Mac), and choose Page Margins from the Show menu (**Figure 14.4**). The page margin is marked by a gray boundary, while the edge of the paper is marked by a darker boundary (**Figure 14.5**).

To set page margins

1. First, make sure you've got the right paper size selected by choosing Print Setup (Windows) or Page Setup (Mac) under the File menu and selecting your paper as necessary using the pop-up menus.

2. Switch to Layout mode ([Ctrl] [L] in Windows/[⌘][L] on the Mac), and choose Layout Setup from the Mode menu (**Figure 14.6**).

3. When the Layout Setup dialog box appears (**Figure 14.7**), select the "Fixed page margins" checkbox and use the four number-entry boxes to adjust your top, bottom, left, and right margins. Check "Facing Pages" if you'll be printing on both sides of the paper to account for a narrower inside margin.

4. Click OK.

Figure 14.4 Check your margins by switching to Layout mode and choosing Page Margins from the Show menu.

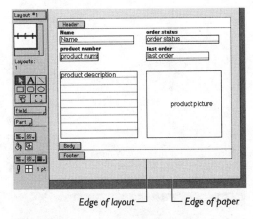

Figure 14.5 A gray boundary marks the layout's edge; a darker boundary the paper's edge.

Figure 14.6 To change your margins, choose Layout Setup from the Mode menu.

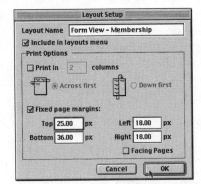

Figure 14.7 Within the Layout Setup dialog box, select "Fixed page margins" and enter new numbers to adjust your top, bottom, left, and right margins.

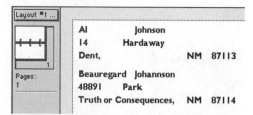

Figure 14.8 The problem with fixed field size printouts: Giving Beauregard enough room makes Al space out.

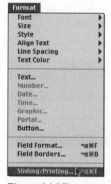

Figure 14.9 To remove unwanted space in fields or parts, choose Sliding/Printing from the Format menu.

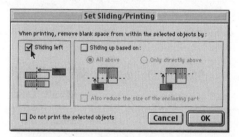

Figure 14.10 Within the Set Sliding/Printing dialog box, check "Sliding left" to close horizontal gaps or "Sliding up based on" to close vertical gaps in fields or parts.

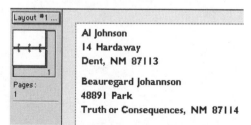

Figure 14.11 With sliding activated, the field size printouts match their entries.

Removing unwanted space

Data varies: some runs long, some short (**Figure 14.8**). To eliminate wasted field space, create a neater printout—and keep Al and Beauregard happy—you want to use a feature FileMaker calls "sliding." With this feature, FileMaker automatically closes up unused space either to the left or above any fields you select. The great thing about sliding is that FileMaker only applies it when necessary. If you have a field with a long text entry, it gets the room it needs.

To remove unwanted spaces

1. Switch to Layout mode (Ctrl L in Windows/⌘ L on the Mac).

2. Use the Pointer Tool to select all the fields you want to make sure are closed up properly. Choose Sliding/Printing from the Format menu (Option ⌘ T on the Mac, no Windows equivalent) (**Figure 14.9**).

3. When the Set Sliding/Printing dialog box appears, check the "Sliding left" box (**Figure 14.10**). (Check "Sliding up based on" to control vertical spacing in a layout, especially within layout *parts.*) Click OK.

4. Switch to Preview mode (Ctrl U in Windows/⌘ U on the Mac) to see the change (**Figure 14.11**).

✔ Tips

- Sliding can be applied to objects, along with layout items that aren't in a field, such as lines you've placed in a layout for visual effect. In both cases, just select the item and apply sliding via the Format menu.

- Sliding only works on the body; headers and footers won't slide. Instead, see "To resize a part" on page 136.

To preview a printout

1. Choose Preview from the Mode menu ([Ctrl][U] in Windows/[⌘][U] on the Mac) to see if your printout will be just as you want it (**Figure 14.12**).

To print

1. Switch to the layout you want to print from and run any needed Find Requests or Sorts. Choose Print from the File menu ([Ctrl][P] in Windows/[⌘][P] on the Mac).

2. When the Print dialog box appears:

Win In Windows, use the pop-down list (**Figure 14.13**) to determine whether you print all the records being browsed (the found set), only the current record, a blank record with the fields showing, a list of field definitions, or the script definitions for the current layout.

Mac On the Mac, use the lower portion of the Print dialog box (**Figure 14.14**) to determine whether you print all the records being browsed (the found set), only the current record, a blank record with the fields showing, the script definitions for the current layout, or a list of field definitions. A pop-up menu for the blank record option lets you choose whether you want fields in blank records printed as formatted, with boxes, or with underlines.

3. Once you've set your other choices (print range and number of copies), click OK (Windows) or Print (Mac).

✔ Tips

■ Change your paper orientation to horizontal when printing extended columnar layouts—otherwise the right edge will be cut off. Use Preview to be sure.

■ Printing out a script can be a terrific way to troubleshoot any problems that you can't quite find. Sometimes you see on paper what you can't see on the screen.

Figure 14.12 Before printing, you can choose Preview from the Mode menu or use your keyboard: [Ctrl][U] (Windows) or [⌘][U] (Mac).

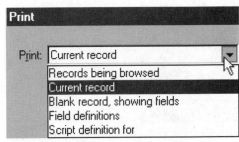

Figure 14.13 In Windows, a pop-down list lets you choose which FileMaker records you print.

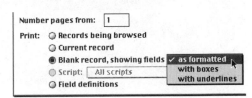

Figure 14.14 On the Mac, the lower portion of the Print dialog box contains radio buttons for controlling which FileMaker records print.

NETWORKING

FileMaker's networking abilities make it easy for PCs and Macs to share the same FileMaker database file. Inevitably, layouts will not look exactly the same on each platform. And since the Windows and Mac operating systems use different default fonts, text may also appear a bit differently. But, overall, the FileMaker match across platforms is pretty close.

To *host* a file simply means being the first user to open a shared FileMaker file. Anyone opening the file after the host is considered a *guest*. The host can set access rights and make file changes that guests cannot. For details, see **Table 15.1**, "Network Rights: Host vs. Guests," on page 213. FileMaker's network access privileges, by the way, are not the same as the access rights set by Windows 95, Windows NT, or the Mac OS. For information on setting Web access to FileMaker, see Chapter 16, "Preparing for Web Publishing," on page 225.

File sharing is set file by file. When a file needs to be shared, it must be set to Multi-User. By default, all FileMaker databases begin as Single User files. When a host needs to make substantial changes to a file, the file must be set back to Single User (see **Table 15.1**, "Network Rights: Hosts vs. Guests") and guest users temporarily denied access to the file. Once the host finishes the modifications, the file can again be set to Multi-User.

To turn on file sharing

1. Open the file you want to share: Ctrl O in Windows/⌘ O on the Mac.

2. Choose Sharing from the File menu (**Figure 15.1**). When the Sharing dialog box appears, click Multi-User, then click OK (**Figure 15.2**).

To turn off file sharing

1. If you're hosting the file, close it: Ctrl W in Windows/⌘ W on the Mac.

2. A dialog box will appear listing other users of the file. Click Ask and they will be alerted to close the file as well. If they don't respond, FileMaker automatically closes the file in 30 seconds.

3. Choose Sharing from the File menu (**Figure 15.1**). When the Sharing dialog box appears, click Single User, then click OK (**Figure 15.3**). The file will remain set to Single User until you turn file sharing back on, so it's best to make any changes promptly and return the file to its original Multi-User setting.

Figure 15.1 To turn FileMaker file sharing on or off, choose Sharing from the File menu.

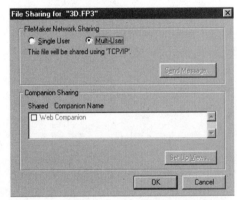

Figure 15.2 To share a file, click Multi-User within the File Sharing dialog box.

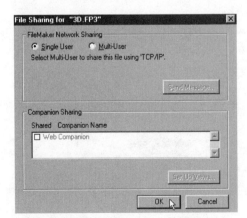

Figure 15.3 To stop sharing a file, click Single User within the File Sharing dialog box.

Table 15.1

Network Rights: Host vs. Guests

PARTY	HAS RIGHT TO
Host Only (File must be set to Single User. Guests must close file.)	Change file to single-user status or close shared file Define, delete, change access rights or groups Define fields or change field definitions Save file copies (With Save a Copy command) Reorder layouts
Any User (One at a time)	Edit record or layout Define, change value lists Define, change own passwords Define, change relationships Open ScriptMaker dialog box
Any User (Any time)	Find, sort, browse records Export, import records Choose a page setup and print Switch layout view or mode Check spelling

To open a database as the host

1. Choose Open from the File menu or use your keyboard: [Ctrl][O] in Windows/[⌘][O] on the Mac.

2. When the Open dialog box appears, choose a file and click Open.

3. Choose Sharing from the File menu (**Figure 15.1**). Within the File Sharing dialog box, make sure Multi-User is selected. If the button is dimmed, a message will appear in the middle of your screen explaining why.

4. Click OK.

HOSTING A DATABASE

To open a database as a guest

1. Choose Open from the File menu or use your keyboard: [Ctrl][O] in Windows/[⌘][O] on the Mac.

2. When the Open File dialog box appears, click Hosts (**Figure 15.4**). The appearance of the Hosts dialog box—and your choices—will vary depending on your network setup.

3. If you're using IPX/SPX, MacIPX, or AppleTalk with no server zones, select a file in the Host dialog box and click Open.

   If you're using AppleTalk with several server zones, pick a zone in the box's lower-left panel, then select a file and click Open (**Figure 15.5**).

   If you're using TCP/IP on a local area network, click Local Hosts in the box's lower-left panel(**Figure 15.6**), then select a file and click Open.

   If you're using TCP/IP and want to pick a host outside your local area network, click Specify Host (**Figure 15.6**). Within the Specify Host dialog box, enter a host name or IP address (**Figure 15.7**). Click OK.

✔ Tip

■ If you frequently use a host outside your local area network, click "Permanently add entry to Hosts list" within the Specify Host dialog box.

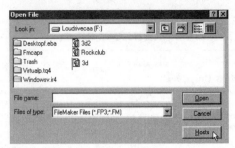

Figure 15.4 To open a shared FileMaker file as a guest, click Hosts in the Open File dialog box.

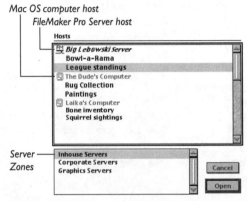

Figure 15.5 If you're using AppleTalk with several server zones, pick a zone from the lower list and a file on that server in the upper list.

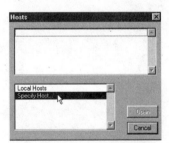

Figure 15.6 To find a FileMaker host outside your local area network, click Specify Host.

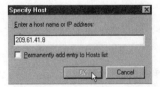

Figure 15.7 Enter the host's name or IP address in the Specify Host dialog box.

Table 15.2

Password Access Privileges	
CHECK	TO LET USERS
Access the entire file	Do any task via a master password. Only choice that grants right to define, change, or delete passwords. Also grants right to change field or group definitions, and document preferences.
Browse records	View record data
Print records	Print any records
Export records	Export any records, copy a found set, enable Web Companion sharing
Override data entry warnings	Enter data even if it doesn't match preset entry options
Design layouts	Create and change layouts
Edit scripts	Create and change scripts
Define value lists	Create and change value lists
Create records	Create new records and enter data
Edit records	Change data in records
Delete records	Delete any records

Controlling file access

By giving you the options to set a mix of passwords and group definitions, FileMaker lets you precisely control who can access files on your network. Be careful to not overdo security, however. The first time users can't get to something they need because of a password restriction, you'll hear about it and they won't be happy. Obviously you may need to control access to sensitive records, such as personnel and cost data. But in general, it's better to add passwords as you need them than to set up a security maze from the start. If you're the only one using a database or you're working in a very small group, you may not even need to set passwords.

Passwords should be relatively easy to remember but not so obvious that people outside the group can easily figure them out. The most secure passwords are a random mix of letters and numbers, but these passwords can be very hard to remember. Ultimately, security versus ease of use requires a balancing act determined by your group's particular needs.

Group and password definitions are so interrelated it can get confusing as to which controls what. Remember: Groups control *access* or what users can *see*; passwords control *actions* or what users can *do*. In practical terms that means only the members of a group can see a particular layout or field, while passwords determine what they can do with the data once they reach it.

The first step in creating passwords is defining what FileMaker calls a master password, which grants access to everything in the database. Only then can you begin creating passwords for individual users. Aside from the master password, passwords are set based on the level of access needed. Password access privileges can run the gamut. For details, see **Table 15.2**, "Password Access Privileges."

(continued)

CONTROLLING FILE ACCESS

(continued from previous page)

The first step in creating groups is defining them. Only then do you set a group's access privileges. Once passwords have been set and groups linked to them, FileMaker controls all users' access and their layout and field views of the database.

To set a master password

1. Open the file for which you want to set a password ([Ctrl][O] in Windows/[⌘][O] on the Mac).

2. Turn off File Sharing (see page 212).

3. Choose Access Privileges from the File menu and select Define Passwords from the submenu (**Figure 15.8**).

4. Within the Define Passwords dialog box, type in a password (**Figure 15.9**). It can include up to 31 characters and can include spaces. Capitalization within passwords is ignored.

5. Check "Access the entire file" at the top of the Privileges panel.

6. Click Create, then click Done.

7. When the Confirm dialog box appears, type in the master password and click OK (**Figure 15.10**). Remember to turn file sharing back on.

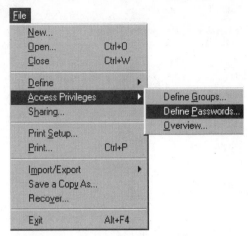

Figure 15.8 To work with FileMaker passwords, choose Access Privileges from the File menu and select Define Passwords.

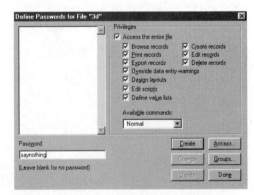

Figure 15.9 Within the Define Passwords dialog box, create a master password by checking "Access the entire file."

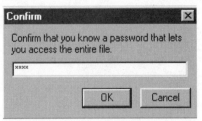

Figure 15.10 Any time you define other users' passwords, you'll need to confirm that you know the master password.

SETTING A MASTER PASSWORD

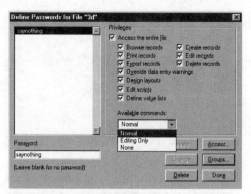

Figure 15.11 Control which FileMaker menu commands are linked to a password with the Available commands pop-up menu within the Define Passwords dialog box.

Defining passwords

Only users who know the master password can change a password other than their own.

To define user passwords

1. Open the file for which you want to set a password (Ctrl O in Windows/⌘ O on the Mac).

2. Turn off File Sharing (see page 212).

3. Choose Access Privileges from the File menu and select Define Passwords from the submenu (**Figure 15.8**).

4. Within the Password text box, type in a password.

5. Check the appropriate access boxes within the Privileges panel. (See **Table 15.2**, "Password Access Privileges.")

6. To grant access to all the FileMaker *menu commands* associated with the privilege boxes you've checked, leave the Available commands pop-up menu set to Normal (**Figure 15.11**). If you want to enable only commands associated with simple data entry, choose Editing Only. To block use of any menu commands, choose None.

7. Click Create.

8. Repeat the process for as many passwords as you need to define. To associate passwords with existing groups, see "To define groups," on page 220.

9. Click Done.

10. When the Confirm dialog box appears, type in the *master* password and click OK (**Figure 15.10**).

✔ Tip

■ A file can have more than one password with each offering a different degree of access.

To create a blank password

1. For users who only need limited access and can't be bothered with remembering a password, follow Steps 1–3 of "To define user passwords."

2. When the Define Passwords dialog box appears, leave the Password text entry box entirely blank, but go ahead and define a limited set of access options within the Privileges panel (top in **Figure 15.12**). Click Create.

3. A [no password] password now appears within the left-side list (bottom in **Figure 15.12**). Click Done.

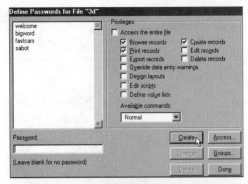

Figure 15.12 Top: Create a blank password by leaving the name window empty but give it limited access privileges. Bottom: Once created, a blank password appears in the list as [no password].

Changing or deleting passwords

Only users who know the master password can change or delete passwords other than their own.

To change or delete passwords

1. Choose Access Privileges from the File menu and select Define Passwords from the submenu (**Figure 15.8**).

2. When the Define Passwords dialog box appears (**Figure 15.9**), select the password within the left-side list.

3. Type a new password in the text entry box and make any changes in Privileges. Click Change. The new password is now active. To delete the password, click Delete.

4. Click Done.

5. When the Confirm dialog box appears, type in the *master* password and click OK. Be sure to alert other users affected by the password changes.

Changing your own password

Even if you don't know the master password, you can change your individual password (if you have one).

To change your own password

1. Choose Change Password from the File menu.

2. When the Change Password dialog box appears, type in your old password once and your new password twice.

3. Click OK.

To define groups

1. Open the file for which you want to set group access (Ctrl O in Windows/⌘ O on the Mac). If you've already created passwords for the file, FileMaker will ask you to enter the master password.

2. Turn off File Sharing (see page 212).

3. Choose Access Privileges from the File menu and select Define Groups from the submenu (**Figure 15.13**).

4. When the Define Groups dialog box appears, type in the new group name and click Create (**Figure 15.14**).

5. Make sure the new group name remains highlighted in the left-side list, then click Access (**Figure 15.15**). The Access Privileges dialog box appears, showing groups, passwords, layouts, and fields for the file you're working in.

6. Select the group in the far-left column by clicking on it. In **Figure 15.16**, the print vendor group is associated with three passwords, all marked by solid bullets: welcome, fastcars, and bigword. (As the master password, bigword is linked to *every* group; the password sabot is dimmed because it is *not* linked to the print vendor group.) For the access level signified by different bullets, see **Table 15.3**, "Access Symbols."

Table 15.3

Access Symbols	
THIS BULLET	MEANS THE LAYOUT OR FIELD
● Solid bullet	Can be read and edited by selected group
○ Hollow bullet	Can only be read by selected group
● Dimmed bullet	Cannot be seen by selected group

Figure 15.13 To create groups with varying rights, choose Access Privileges from the File menu and select Define Groups.

Figure 15.14 Type in a new group's name and click Create.

Figure 15.15 Once a group has been created, click Access to set its rights to the file.

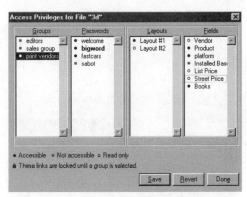

Figure 15.16 Select a group in the left column of the Access Privileges dialog box to see the passwords, layouts, and fields associated with the group.

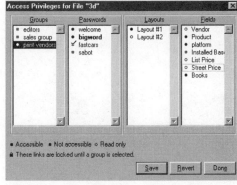

Figure 15.17 To change the passwords, layouts, and fields associated with a group, select the group's name in the left column and then click the bullets next to items in the other columns.

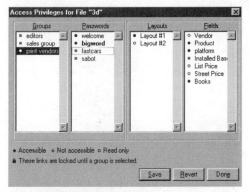

Figure 15.18 The dimmed bullet of the fastcars password means it's no longer associated with the printer vendors group.

7. To change passwords linked to a group, keep the group selected in the far-left column and click the bullet next to a password you no longer want linked to the group (**Figure 15.17**). In the example, the bullet next to fastcars has changed to gray (**Figure 15.18**). To relink a password, click the bullet again.

8. The print vendors group in **Figure 15.18** can see Layout #1 and six fields within it. Of those fields, group members can edit just three: Product, platform, and Books. To change layout and field access, just click on the adjacent bullet.

9. Click Save. If you want to make other changes, repeat the process, clicking Save after each round. If you change your mind mid-way through a round of changes, click Revert to go back to the version last saved. When you're satisfied, click Done twice.

Changing group definitions

To change group definitions, you must host the file, know the master password, and first turn off file sharing.

To change a group definition

1. Choose Access Privileges from the File menu and select Overview from the sub-menu (**Figure 15.19**).

2. Within the Access Privileges dialog box, select a group in the left column and click the bullets in the other three columns (passwords, layouts, and fields) to change the group's definition.

3. Click Save, and then click Done.

Deleting group definitions

To delete any group definitions, you must host the file, know the master password, and first turn off file sharing.

To delete a group definition

1. Choose Access Privileges from the File menu and select Define Groups from the submenu.

2. When the Define Groups dialog box appears, select a group name in the left-side list and click Delete.

3. When the warning dialog appears, click Delete again. Click Done.

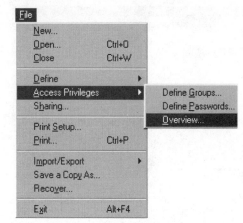

Figure 15.19 The host can control group and password settings by choosing Access Privileges from the File menu and selecting Overview.

PART V

WEB PUBLISHING WITH FILEMAKER

PREPARING FOR WEB PUBLISHING

This whole last section covers FileMaker 4's biggest improvement: database publishing with its new Web Companion. By necessity, we hit mostly highlights. If you want to learn more once you're done here, get a copy of Maria Langer's *Database Publishing with FileMaker Pro on the Web*, also from Peachpit Press.

In the past, only FileMaker users could work *directly* with a FileMaker database. Thanks to FileMaker's Web Companion, however, any computer with a Web browser can view and even edit FileMaker data. Don't worry—Web Companion includes security options to let you precisely control who sees your data and what they can do with it. For now, consider the advantages: Your company's sales force can place orders from the road, outside vendors can check delivery dates, and you can check the latest product deadlines from home.

In fact, timeliness is one of the best things about Web database publishing. Much of the Web uses static pages, which look the same every time you visit them. In contrast, Web Companion's dynamic pages change constantly because they are directly linked to the FileMaker data used to create the page.

How it works and what you'll need

FileMaker's Web Companion acts like a Web server by handling the file requests placed by Web browsers visiting your database. It does this by interpreting the HTTP (HyperText Transfer Protocol) commands from the browser, along with operating as a de facto CGI (Common Gateway Interface) application between FileMaker and visiting Web browsers. Best of all, Web Companion handles all this in the background so you don't have to deal with it.

Inside the FileMaker Pro 4 folder installed on your computer, there should be these three folders: Web, Web Security, and Web Tools. If they aren't there, go back and install them. Besides FileMaker and Web Companion, you'll need a PC with at least an Intel-compatible 486/33 chip or any Mac to publish on the Web. It's also best to have a full-time Internet connection (dial-up, ISDN, T1, T2, or T3). In theory, you could publish a Web database via a part-time dial-up connection, but no one could use the database unless you were online at the very same time. The IP address for most part-time connections also changes from session to session, which would make it all but impossible for users to keep track of your databases's latest location.

What if you're just running a small business and don't have the dough to install a Web server, a T1 line, and a closet of cables? Not to worry—you can still publish FileMaker databases on the Web. Many of the same Internet Service Providers who offer dial-up connections can host your FileMaker database on one of their Internet-linked computers for a small monthly fee. FileMaker offers a partial list of such ISPs at: www.filemaker.com/products/isp.html

Figure 16.1 With Instant Web Publishing, Web Companion uses a built-in home page that automatically links to your databases.

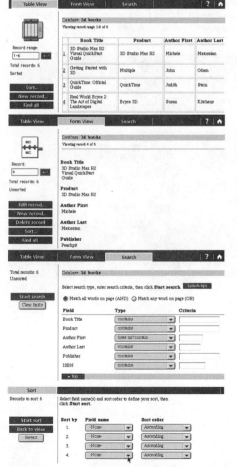

Figure 16.2 Instant Web Publishing presents your data in one of four standard page types: Table, Form, Search, or Sort (top to bottom).

Instant versus Custom Web Publishing

FileMaker's Web Companion offers you two routes to the Web: Instant Web Publishing and Custom Web Publishing. Each has its advantages and disadvantages. Instant is quick and easy, but limited. Custom takes more time but has much more flexibility. Keep these points in mind when making your choice:

Instant Web Publishing: With Instant Web Publishing, you don't need to know HTML (HyperText Markup Language), which is used to format Web pages. Instead, Web Companion uses a built-in home page that automatically links to your databases (**Figure 16.1**). And Web Companion formats each database for you, using its built-in standard page types (**Figure 16.2**). Those standard page types—Table, Form, Search, and Sort—also underscore Instant Web Publishing's main disadvantage: You can't change how your pages look. Another potentially major limitation is that Instant Web Publishing cannot run any of your FileMaker scripts. You can run a script *before* you publish a page to the Web, though that won't help much if you need dynamic scripts.

Custom Web Publishing: Not only do you need to generate the HTML for your Web pages but you also need to learn and use FileMaker's CDML (Claris Dynamic Markup Language) as well. But if you've got the time, Custom Web Publishing gives you tremendous control over the appearance of your Web pages. Custom Web Publishing also lets you use scripts and buttons on the Web just as you do in regular FileMaker layouts.

A compromise: Use Instant Web Publishing to get your data up on the Web now, then use Custom Web Publishing to gradually customize pages as you get the time and experience. In most organizations, the advantages of getting shared data up on the Web quickly probably outweigh waiting until everything's just-so.

INSTANT VERSUS CUSTOM WEB PUBLISHING

Preparing files for the Web

Aside from enabling Web Companion and possibly configuring Web Companion, which we'll get to in a moment, there are only a few extra steps required for getting your FileMaker database ready for the Web.

Instant Web Publishing: If you're using Instant Web Publishing, Web Companion will display every field in your designated layout—even if you've used passwords and group definitions to block certain fields. The solution: Create a Web-only layout that contains only those fields that you don't mind every Web user seeing. By the way, don't bother making your Web-only layout particularly fancy because Instant Web Publishing's four page types won't recognize text styles, colors, or custom backgrounds. Instant Web Publishing, however, will use any text and number formats you've selected in creating a layout.

Custom Web Publishing: If you're using Custom Web Publishing, you need to put all your finished Web pages in the Web folder, which resides inside the FileMaker Pro 4 folder. One caution: *Any* file within the Web folder potentially can be read, replaced, or deleted by Web miscreants. They'd have to be *skilled* miscreants, but don't put company secrets in the Web folder.

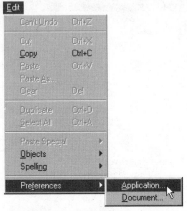

Figure 16.3 To set general options for Web Companion, choose Preferences from the Edit menu and select Application from the submenu.

Figure 16.4 Within the Application Preferences dialog box, choose Plug-Ins and then enable Web Companion by selecting the checkbox.

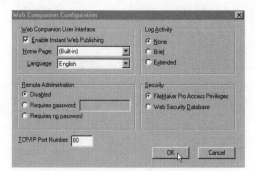

Figure 16.5 The Web Companion's default settings don't need to be changed—at least until you're farther along in the process.

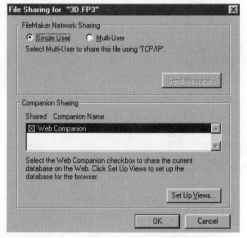

Figure 16.6 To share a file over the Web, check Web Companion in the lower portion of the File Sharing dialog box. The upper portion's settings do not affect Web sharing.

Setting up Web Companion

Generally, you'll only need to set up Web Companion once. Selecting which FileMaker files will be published on the Web, however, must be done file by file using the File Sharing dialog box.

To set up Web Companion

1. Choose Preferences from the Edit menu and select Application from the submenu (**Figure 16.3**). The Application Preferences dialog box appears (**Figure 16.4**).

2. Choose the Plug-Ins tab (Windows) or use the pop-up menu (Mac).

3. Check the Web Companion box and—just to get a quick sense of what's going on behind the scenes—click Configure (**Figure 16.4**). Most of the default settings within the Web Companion Configuration dialog box can remain unchanged for now, so click OK (**Figure 16.5**). For details, see "To configure Web Companion," on page 231.

4. Click Done.

To share a file over the Web

1. Open the file you want to share: Ctrl O in Windows/⌘ O on the Mac.

2. Choose Sharing from the File menu, which will open the File Sharing dialog box.

3. Ignore the upper half of the dialog box. It concerns network sharing, which is different from Web sharing. Instead, look within the lower Companion Sharing panel and check Web Companion (**Figure 16.6**).

4. Click OK. Once you also configure Web Companion, the file will be shared over the Web. Repeat the steps for each file you want to share.

Configuring Web Companion

The Web Companion Configuration dialog box (**Figure 16.7**) controls the user interface, log activities, remote administration, and security. Here's a quick rundown of each:

Enable Instant Web Publishing: Go ahead and check it. Even if you plan on using Custom Web Publishing for most of your pages, inevitably you'll find the Instant Web Publishing option will be fine for certain pages.

Home Page: Web Companion comes with a built-in home page. If you've created your own home page—as you will with Web Companion's Custom Web Publishing—put it in the FileMaker Pro 4 folder and then use the pop-up menu to select it.

Language: This only affects the Instant Web Publishing interface and its built-in Help feature—not your data or layouts. Use the pop-up menu to select one of seven languages.

Log Activity: Web Companion can automatically record visits to your Web database, though its detail is limited at best. The Web.log text file is stored in the FileMaker Pro 4 folder (Windows) or the Control Panels folder (Mac). Check "None" if you don't want a log or if you already have another application logging your activity. "Brief" will note the time and date for which files were requested. "Extended" will include the server's response to requests.

Figure 16.7 The Web Companion Configuration dialog box controls the user interface, log activities, remote administration, and security.

Remote Administration: This allows you to upload and download Web Companion files if they reside on an offsite server, a handy feature if you depend on an Internet Service Provider for hosting your FileMaker database. You can leave this option off or enable it. If you choose to use remote administration, always check the password requirement as well. For more details, see "Web Security" on the next page.

Security: This option lets you choose between two levels of security: FileMaker Pro Access Privileges, which are set file by file using passwords and groups as explained in Chapter 15, "Networking," on page 211, or the Web Security Database, which is explained on page 233.

TCP/IP Port Number: Unless you've already got a Web server connected to your computer, the default setting of 80 is fine. Otherwise, you'll have to set it to 591 and users visiting your Web site will have to add ":591" to the end of your normal IP address (e.g., 146.98.21:591).

To configure Web Companion

1. To reach the Web Companion Configuration dialog box, follow Steps 1, 2, and 3 of "To set up Web Companion" on page 229.

2. The default settings are: Instant Web Publishing enabled, using the built-in home page, using English, and a port number of 80. To change any of the settings as explained in detail on pages 230–231, check the boxes and buttons you want.

3. Check OK.

Web Security

In many cases, FileMaker's standard access privileges, which will remain in effect even when the file moves to the Web, are all the security you'll need. Web users browsing the data will encounter a dialog box where they'll still need to enter their name and password. For more information on using passwords and group definitions to control access, see Chapter 15, "Networking," on page 211.

Use the Web Security database that comes with FileMaker's Web Companion if you want to add another layer of security. The security database lets you control whether Web users of your database can work with certain fields, and whether they can search, update, add, or delete records. It can also block the use of scripts even if you're using Custom Web Publishing. Using the security database also gives you the option of remotely administering access via the Web. As always, resist the temptation to create a complicated set of overlapping privileges and passwords that will only confuse and frustrate the very people you want to see your data.

To enable Web security and remote administration

1. Be sure that the database's Web Companion is configured for Web Security and remote administration, as described on page 231. Choose Preferences from the Edit menu and select Web Companion (**Figure 16.8**).

2. When the Web Companion View Setup dialog box appears, click Configure. When the Web Companion Configuration dialog box (**Figure 16.9**) appears:

3. Click "Requires password" in the Remote Administration panel (and enter a password if you haven't done so previously).

4. Click "Web Security Database" within the Security panel.

5. Click OK, and then click Done.

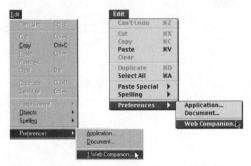

Figure 16.8 Once its plug-in has been enabled, Web Companion can be reached directly via Preferences in the Edit Menu.

Figure 16.9 Click "Requires password" and "Web Security Database" to configure Web Companion for remote administration and limited Web access.

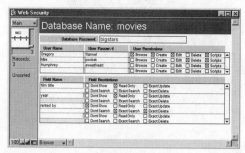

Figure 16.10 Within the Web Security database, enter the name of a file for which you want to set passwords and field restrictions.

Table 16.1

Web user permissions	
CHECK	TO LET USERS
Browse	View records
Create	Add new records
Edit	Change records
Delete	Delete records
Scripts	Use the database's scripts

Table 16.2

Web field and record restrictions	
CHECK	TO BLOCK
DontShow	View of named *field*
DontSearch	Search of named *field*
ReadOnly	Changes in named *field*
ExactSearch*	Retrieval of any *record* unless value in named field exactly matches criteria
ExactUpdate*	Changes of *record* unless value in named field exactly matches criteria
ExactDelete*	Deletion of *record* unless value in named field exactly matches criteria
*Used only with Custom Web Publishing	

To use the Web Security database

1. Once Web Security is enabled, choose Open from the File menu (Ctrl O in Windows/⌘ O on the Mac) and click your way to: FileMaker Pro 4\Web Security\Databases\Web Security.

2. Once the Web Security database opens, choose New Record from the Mode menu (Ctrl N in Windows/⌘ N on the Mac).

3. Type in the name of the database to which you want to limit Web access and make your access choices (**Figure 16.10**). If you've already set a password for the database using FileMaker's regular access privileges, type it into the Database Password field.

4. Set your user permissions and field/record restrictions using the check boxes. See **Table 16.1**, "Web user permissions," and **Table 16.2**, "Web field and record restrictions," for details on each option. Continue creating new records for each Web database you're publishing. When you're done, close the database (Ctrl W in Windows/⌘ W on the Mac). Web access privileges for the databases you selected are now set.

✔ Tips

- You can create a Web password that applies to all Web users by typing "All Users" into the User Name field. But be careful what permissions you grant under that password since it will override other access restrictions.

- No matter what Web privileges you set, they will never override those already set through FileMaker's non-Web password privileges. (For more information on setting non-Web privileges, see Chapter 15, "Networking," on page 211.)

USING THE WEB SECURITY DATABASE

To remotely administer passwords

1. Once Web Security and Remote Administration are enabled, open the Web Security folder, which is inside the FileMaker Pro 4 folder.

2. Now *copy* the Security folder into the Web folder, which resides up a level but still within the FileMaker Pro 4 folder (**Figure 16.11**).

3. Open your Web browser and type in the IP address of your Web database server (which will be different from the IP number shown below), adding /Security/default.htm at the end, like so:

   146.98.21/Security/default.htm

4. On the Web Companion Security Administration page that appears, type in the name of the Web database whose access rights you want to change (**Figure 16.12**). Click the Add Database link.

5. If you configured Remote Administration to require a password—and you're living fast and dangerous if you didn't—type in your name and the password when the dialog box appears.

6. When the Add Web Database page appears, type in the new name, password, and user permissions as you need to (**Figure 16.13**). Click the Add Database button and reconfirm your changes.

Figure 16.11 To remotely administer passwords, *copy* the Security folder into the Web folder.

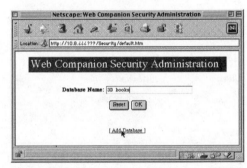

Figure 16.12 Type into the text box the name of the Web database whose access rights you want to change remotely.

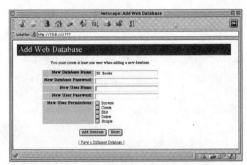

Figure 16.13 Make remote changes to names, passwords, and permissions on the Add Web Database page.

Once you're open for business

Once you're up, you'll need to let users know how to reach your new Web database so they can put it to work. Typically these first users will be customers or co-workers. There are a couple of ways to point them your way.

You can simply tell them the IP address for the computer hosting the Web database, which they can type directly into their Web browser's location window. If you've used Web Companion's default setting, this address will be something like: **146.98.21**

If you changed the port setting while configuring Web Companion, then the IP would be: **146.98.21:591**

Tell visitors to bookmark your database's page in their browsers once they reach the page, and they'll never have to key in that pesky number again.

If you know how to use HTML, you can avoid the whole "What's an IP address?" issue with users by putting a Web link to it on some other Web page that they already visit. That way, they only have to point and click. If you want to learn HTML, there's no better book than Liz Castro's HTML for the World Wide Web: Visual QuickStart Guide.

USING INSTANT WEB PUBLISHING

Figure 17.1 Table View uses a standard tabular form with a record per row.

Figure 17.2 Form View is similar to the standard Single Page layout.

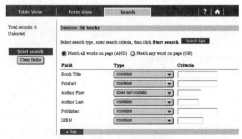

Figure 17.3 The Search page is set up like a FileMaker Find Request.

Instant Web Publishing lets Web users see your database in four different page types: Table, Form, Search, and Sort. You control which of the four are available to users. Here's a quick rundown on each:

Table View: This page type uses a standard tabular form displaying a record per row and the fields arranged in columns (**Figure 17.1**).

Form View: This page type looks similar to FileMaker's standard Single Page layout with one record per screen (**Figure 17.2**).

Search: This page type, set up like a Find Request, offers Web users a limited set of the search capabilities you use in FileMaker's non-Web pages (**Figure 17.3**).

Sort: This page type allows users to select fields to sort and the sort order type (**Figure 17.4**).

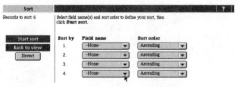

Figure 17.4 The Sort page simply adds a Sort button to the Table and Form views.

To set view options

1. Assuming you've already enabled Web Companion (see Chapter 16, "Preparing for Web Publishing" on page 225), choose Preferences from the Edit menu and select Web Companion from the submenu (**Figure 17.5**).

2. When the Web Companion View Setup dialog box appears, choose one of the four page types with the tabs (Windows) or the pop-up menu (Mac) (**Figure 17.6**).

3. Choose one of your file's layouts with the pop-up in the middle of the dialog box (**Figure 17.7**). Your regular FileMaker layout will not appear—just its fields. Remember, the page type is built drawing on *every* field within the layout. For that reason, it's sometimes best to create a Web-only layout with a limited set of fields.

4. Click Done. Repeat the steps for each database you'll be putting on the Web with Instant Web Publishing.

✔ Tip

- Be careful which layouts you use with Instant Publishing. If you select a layout that includes related fields, those fields will appear if the Web user can open the master file—even if the related files are password- or group-protected.

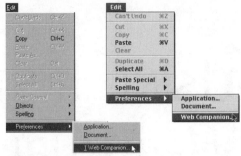

Figure 17.5 Once Web Companion has been enabled, you can quickly reach it via Preferences.

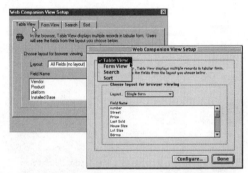

Figure 17.6 Choose one of Instant Web Publishing's four page types using the tabs (top, Windows) or the pop-up menu (bottom, Mac).

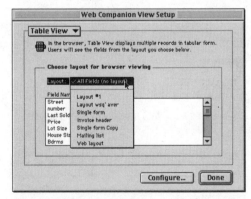

Figure 17.7 Once you've chosen a page type, pick the layout from which it will draw fields.

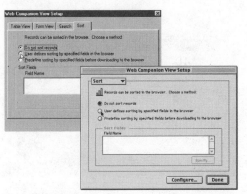

Figure 17.8 and Figure 17.9 Set the Sort view by choosing from one of the three radio buttons: Do not sort records, User defines sorting, or Predefine sorting.

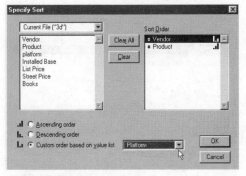

Figure 17.10 The Specify Sort dialog box lets you pick which fields appear for sorting.

To set sort options

1. Choose Preferences from the Edit menu and select Web Companion from the submenu to open the Web Companion View Setup dialog box. When the dialog box appears, choose Sort with the tab (Windows) or pop-up menu (Mac).

2. To set the Web Sort view, click on one of the three radio buttons within the Web Companion View Setup dialog box (**Figure 17.8** and **Figure 17.9**):

   Do not sort records: This option keeps Web users from sorting the file. It also keeps the Sort button from appearing on the Web user's Table View and Form View of the file.

   User defines sorting: This option gives sorting control to the Web user. To pick which fields appear for sorting, click this option and then click Specify to reach the Specify Sort dialog box (**Figure 17.10**). For more information on specifying sorts, see Chapter 5, "Finding and Sorting Records," on page 39.

   Predefine sorting: This option lets you sort the file *before* the Web user sees the file, and the Sort button won't appear in the user's Table or Form views. Set the sort order (ascending, descending, or custom) by clicking Specify to reach the Specify Sort dialog box). For more information on specifying sorts, see Chapter 5, "Finding and Sorting Records," on page 39.

3. When you've finished setting the Sort options, click Done.

SETTING WEB SORT OPTIONS

Browsing Instant pages

Once you've activated Instant Web Publishing, you'll need to tell potential users how to find your Instant home page. (See "Once you're open for business" on page 235 in Chapter 16). The home page will list your various Instant databases with links to each (**Figure 17.11**).

Depending on the view choices you've selected, the databases will be visible to Web users through four standard page views:

Table View: This is the Web Companion's default view (**Figure 17.12**). Exactly what other views Web users can reach will depend on the page types you've selected and the layout fields they are built on. (See "To set view options" on page 238.) Each page's appearance—and whether a user can even see it—also will depend on the access rights you've set for that user. For details on setting access rights, see "Web Security" on page 232 and "Controlling file access" on page 215.

Form View: If the user's Web browser supports Java, the Form View page will look very familiar (**Figure 17.13**). In the upper-left corner, sits the standard flipbook icon for navigating through records one at a time. Instead of menu bar commands, however, the Edit record, New record, Delete record, and Find all commands are triggered by buttons arranged down the page's left margin.

Figure 17.11 Instant Web Publishing presents Web users with a built-in home page featuring links to your Web databases.

Figure 17.12 The fields listed within the Table View will vary depending on the user's access rights.

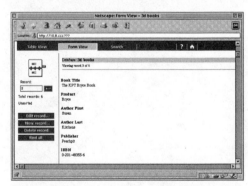

Figure 17.13 For Web browsers that support Java, the Form View sports the familiar record flipbook.

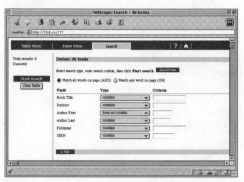

Figure 17.14 Instant Web Publishing's Search page offers a mix of familiar and new elements.

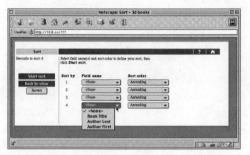

Figure 17.15 The Sort form lets Web users choose the sort type used for each field selected.

Search View: Web users with search privileges will discover that the Search page contains a mix of FileMaker's familiar Find mode and some new elements (**Figure 17.14**). A pair of radio buttons present users with the choice of making AND/OR searches of the listed fields. Users can also choose whether the field should contain or not contain the search criteria. The results are returned in a Table View page.

Sort: Web users with sort privileges will see a Sort button in the left margin of the Table View and Form View pages. Clicking the button presents users with a Sort form in which they can set the sort type for each field sorted (**Figure 17.15**).

Using Custom
Web Publishing

Custom Web Publishing sits at the other end of the spectrum from Instant Web Publishing. While Instant's quick but inflexible, Custom is quite flexible yet takes longer to get the hang of. You'll need to know how to create HTML code or how to use an HTML editing program. You'll also have to understand the gist of FileMaker's own code, Claris Dynamic Markup Language (CDML), which doesn't take long if you're already HTML-savvy.

Here's a quick rundown of the steps involved in using FileMaker's Custom Web Publishing:

- FileMaker and the FileMaker database must be on a machine with a full-time Internet connection. (See Chapter 16's "How it works and what you'll need" on page 226 for details.)

- Make sure the Web Companion plug-in is enabled and configure Web Companion so that it uses the home page you've created. (See "Configuring Web Companion" on page 230.) You'll also want to set your security options and passwords. (See "Web Security" on page 232 in Chapter 16.)

- Use an existing FileMaker database or create a Web-specific version of it.

- Open your Web-bound databases in FileMaker and choose Web Sharing within the File Sharing dialog box for each. (See "To share a file over the Web" on page 229.)

- Create the special format files that Custom Web Publishing requires, along with any HTML pages you'll need. (See "To create format files" on page 250.)

- Move the format files, HTML pages, and any associated image files into FileMaker's Web folder. By the way, it's OK to create subfolders within the Web folder to keep everything organized.

- Let users know the IP address for your database.

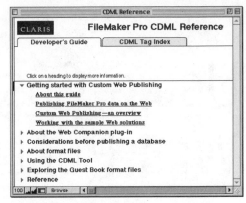

Figure 18.1 The CDML Reference includes a developer's guide to walk you through creating format files and the CDML Tag Index, showing the syntax for every CDML tag.

Figure 18.2 The nine CDML templates found in the Web Tools folder are used to generate format files that control HTML-to-FileMaker interaction.

Figure 18.3 Each CDML template uses HTML coding to present a consistent interface within the user's Web browser.

```
<H2>Sample Delete Record Form</H2>

<P> <!-- Note: Follow the steps below to create an HTML form
that deletes records from a FileMaker Pro database.

<P> <!-- STEP 1. SPECIFY THE FORM ACTION
The form action is already set to "FmPro." When submitting
this form, the Web server is notified to pass this format file to
FileMaker Pro 4.0 for processing. -->
<P> <FORM ACTION="FmPro" METHOD="post">

<P> <!-- STEP 2. SPECIFY THE DATABASE
```

Figure 18.4 Each template's comment tags, which cannot be seen by users, contain step-by-step instructions on how to create a template-based format file.

Understanding CDML

CDML (Claris Dynamic Markup Language) tags and the format files where they reside form the heart of Custom Web Publishing. CDML has about 90 tags, which Web Companion uses to interact with the FileMaker database. Format files are HTML-coded pages that also contain CDML tags. The CDML, in effect, lets Web browsers use HTML Form tags to communicate with FileMaker databases.

Unlike HTML, which can be interpreted by any Web browser program, CDML tags are strictly for Web Companion and FileMaker. If you don't want to learn yet another set of tags, you can use FileMaker's Claris Home Page program (sold separately) to generate your HTML pages. Fortunately, FileMaker comes with four built-in items that make working with CDML fairly painless:

- The CDML Reference, a FileMaker database that can be found in FileMaker's Web Tools folder (**Figure 18.1**). The Reference includes a developer's guide to walk you through creating format files and the CDML Index, which shows examples of and the syntax for every CDML tag.

- A set of nine CDML templates, also found in FileMaker's Web Tools folder (**Figure 18.2**). Each template covers one action, or step, that when used with the CDML Tool lets you control the interaction of the HTML page and FileMaker database. The templates use HTML coding to present a consistent interface to the Web user (**Figure 18.3**) but contain comment tags not seen by the user to guide you in creating them (**Figure 18.4**).

(continued)

■ The CDML Tool, found in FileMaker's Web Tools folder, helps you build format files by acting as a go-between for any open FileMaker database and your HTML editing application (**Figure 18.5**).

■ The Web examples folder, found in FileMaker's Web folder, contains three sample format files—a guest registry, an employee database, and an online shopping cart. Together, they use virtually all of the CDML tags, making them a great way to get a hands-on feel for CDML. To see them in action (**Figure 18.6**), launch your Web browser and navigate within the FileMaker folder to: Web\default.htm. To put them to use, open each of the example databases in FileMaker and then use the CDML Tool to copy their code into an HTML document of your own.

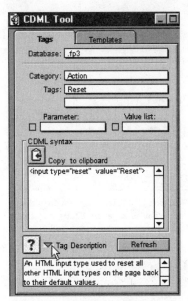

Figure 18.5 The CDML Tool guides you through building format files by using your FileMaker database and the HTML editor of your choice.

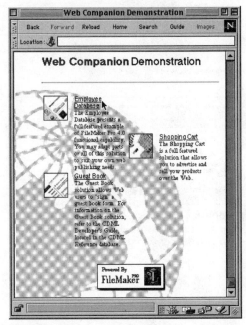

Figure 18.6 The three database examples used in the Web Companion demonstration show virtually every CDML tag in action.

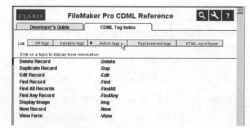

Figure 18.7 The CDML Tag Index lets you view all the tags individually or by type (Variable, Action, and Replacement).

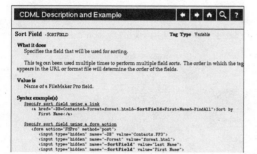

Figure 18.8 Select a CDML tag in the index and you'll see a brief description of what it does, an example of its syntax, and a list of any associated tags required for its use.

Using the CDML Reference

If you want a broad view before diving into the hands-on work of the CDML Tool, start with the CDML Reference, found in FileMaker's Web Tools folder. It contains two items: a Developer's Guide and a CDML Tag Index.

Despite its name, the Developer's Guide isn't just for developers. Instead, it provides a basic orientation to Custom Web Publishing, explaining how it works and how to configure the Web Companion. It also includes solid information on planning a Web site, boosting FileMaker's Web performance, and a brief troubleshooting section.

The CDML Tag Index offers a great way to get an overall sense of CDML. Arranged as a database of all the tags, the index lets you view tags individually or by type (Variable, Action, and Replacement) (**Figure 18.7**). CDML's nine Action tags, as the name suggests, all trigger a FileMaker action, such as deleting, duplicating, or finding a record. Variable tags control options associated with Action tags, such as specifying which database and layout will be acted on. Replacement tags serve as placeholders for data within the FileMaker Web database, such as a field's data, a sort order item, or a value list.

When you select a tag, the index displays a brief description of what the tag does, an example of the tag's syntax, and a list of any associated tags required for its use (**Figure 18.8**). The tag index also includes a section explaining the use and syntax of HTML's eight Input tags, such as check boxes and radio buttons, which are used in tandem with the HTML Form tags that CDML exploits.

Using templates for format files

Format files and CDML templates are really the same things. You create customized format files by copying the templates, which reside in FileMaker's Web Tools folder. While you can just duplicate them and then open them with any HTML editor, it's best to use the CDML Tool (See "To create format files" on page 250).

You'll need to create a separate format file for every interaction you expect between Web users and the particular database you're working with. That's not as daunting as it might sound. There are only nine templates, which mostly pair up in action-reply sets such as Delete and Delete Reply (**Table 18.1**). If you keep the number of layouts you're using for the database under control, the whole process doesn't take that long.

The format files control how Web users interact with your Web database. These files contain HTML and CDML tags. The HTML controls how the pages appear to the Web user. The CDML tags, which are placed inside HTML Form tags, control what the Web server asks for from the FileMaker database stored on it. CDML tags, by the way, can be hidden from the user.

The Form tags in the format files can contain pure HTML or a mix of HTML and CDML. HTML-only forms generate what are called *static* pages, which do not let the Web user interact directly with the FileMaker database. In contrast, forms with HTML and CDML generate dynamic, on-the-fly pages, which reflect the latest updates in the data. Deciding whether to create static or dynamic forms depends on the circumstances: static pages may be less current but serve up fairly quickly, while dynamic pages are up-to-the-minute but take longer to appear in the user's browser as the FileMaker database fetches the required data.

Table 18.1

CDML Templates for Format Files	
THIS TEMPLATE	CREATES A FORMAT FILE THAT
New	Creates new record in FileMaker database
New Reply	Tells Web user that record was created
Edit	Edits records from FileMaker database
Edit Reply	Tells Web user that record was changed
Delete	Deletes record(s) from FileMaker database
Delete Reply	Tells Web user that record was deleted
Search	Searches records in FileMaker database
Results	Shows search info about multiple records
Detail	Shows record information

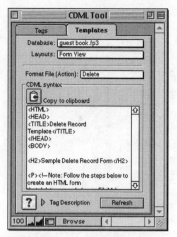

Figure 18.9 The CDML Tool offers two tab-controlled views: one to work with CDML templates, one for CDML tags.

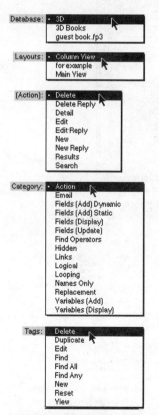

Figure 18.10 A sampling of items controlled by the CDML Tool's drop-down lists. The choices vary depending on what else is selected.

Using the CDML Tool

This is one cool little tool. With a bit of patience you'll find that it guides you right along in the process of using the CDML templates to create custom format files. Tucked into FileMaker's Web Tools folder, the tool offers two tab-controlled views: one to work with CDML templates, one for CDML tags (**Figure 18.9**). Both the Templates and Tags views offer drop-down lists for selecting your database, layout, format file tag category, the fields within your database, parameters, and any value lists you've created for the selected field (**Figure 18.10**). The drop-down choices vary depending on what else is selected.

Every database will need its own set of format files, with the number needed dictated by the types of interactions you want to make available to Web users.

To create format files

1. Open the FileMaker database you want to work on and make sure Web Companion sharing is on for the file. (See Chapter 16's "To share a file over the Web" on page 229.)

2. Open the CDML Tool, which you'll find inside FileMaker's Web Tools folder.

3. When the tool opens, click the Templates tab and use the drop-down list to choose the database you want to work on and a starting-point layout (**Figure 18.11**).

4. Open a new, blank HTML document in the HTML editing application of your choice. Many HTML editors automatically insert start and end Header and Body tags into a new document. In this case, delete them since the template will be adding its own Header and Body tags.

5. Position the HTML document window where you can see it and the CDML Tool window.

6. Back within the CDML Tool, use the "Format File (Action)" pop-up menu to pick one of the nine templates.

7. The code (syntax) for the template will appear in the CDML Tool's main window. Click the "Copy to clipboard" icon just above the window (**Figure 18.12**).

8. Switch over to your HTML editor and paste in the template code (**Figure 18.13**). Look at what's been pasted into the HTML document and you'll find within the HTML comment tags <!- - which look like this - -> containing step-by-step instructions on how to finish coding the format file.

Figure 18.11 To create a format file, click the CDML Tool's Templates tab and use the drop-down list to choose a database to work on and a layout.

Figure 18.12 Once you've used the drop-down lists to pick the right format file, click the "Copy to clipboard" button.

Figure 18.13 Paste the format file into a blank HTML document, then follow the instructions within the HTML comment tags.

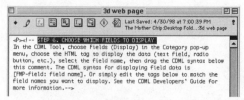

Figure 18.14 Creating CDML tags works just like the template procedure: Follow the comment tags' step-by-step instructions for using the CDML Tool. Use the drop-down lists to specify the database fields, values, and records.

Figure 18.15 Once you've used the drop-down lists to specify a field, value, or record, click the Copy button and paste the coding back into the HTML document.

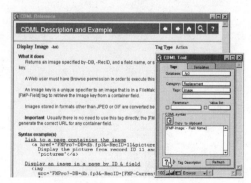

Figure 18.16 Clicking the **?** button within the CDML Tool calls up syntax help from the CDML Reference.

9. Follow the step-by-step comments you've pasted into your HTML document, which from this point on usually require that you switch over to the Tags tab of the CDML Tool. Creating tags with the tool works much like using the templates: following the step-by-step comments (**Figure 18.14**), you use the tool's drop-down lists to specify the database's fields, values, and records. The tool generates the appropriate CDML tags in the syntax window, which you then copy to the clipboard and paste into your HTML document (**Figure 18.15**).

10. Repeat Steps 3-9 until you've created all the format files you need for the open database. Remember to place the format files inside FileMaker's Web folder on the Web server when you're done.

✔ Tips

■ You may need to occasionally click the CDML Tool's lower right Refresh button as you change your selections within the various pop-up menus.

■ If you get stumped while using the CDML Tool, click the **?** button and the CDML Reference will display an explanation (**Figure 18.16**).

PART VI

APPENDICES

APPENDIX A:
INSTALLING FILEMAKER

Unlike most of the book, this appendix has two separate sections for Windows and Macintosh machines.

For installing FileMaker on computers running Windows (3.1, Workgroups 3.11, 95, 98, or NT), turn to page 256.

For installing FileMaker on computers running the Macintosh operating system, turn to page 262.

Installing the Windows versions of FileMaker

FileMaker runs on a variety of Windows operating systems. It will work with Windows 98, Windows 95, Windows NT 3.51 or later, Windows for Workgroups 3.11, and Windows 3.1.

What you'll need before starting:

- A PC with an Intel-compatible chip equivalent to at least the 486/33 with at least 8 MB of RAM (memory).

- A CD-ROM drive for using FileMaker's installation CD.

- A hard drive with at least 20 MB of free space.

- The installation code for FileMaker. Look for the peel-off label on the sleeve containing the FileMaker CD.

✔ Tip

- If you've been using an earlier version of FileMaker, it's easy to import the old files into FileMaker 4. For more information, see Chapter 7, "Converting Files," on page 67.

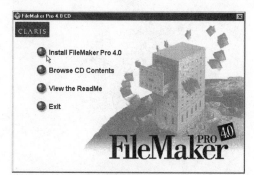

Figure A.1 When the CD's welcome screen appears, click the first install choice to get started.

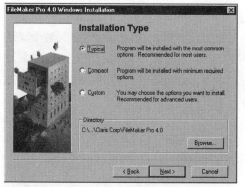

Figure A.2 Unless you're hard pressed for space, click Typical for the full FileMaker installation, and then click Next.

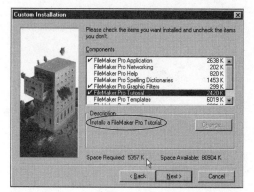

Figure A.3 The Custom installation lets you pick only the files you want. The right column shows each file's size; the lower window displays information on the highlighted file. When you're done, click Next.

To install on a Windows 98, Windows 95 or Windows NT 4.0 computer

1. Exit any other programs you may be running.

2. Put the FileMaker disc into your CD-ROM drive. Once the CD launches, you'll be presented with several choices (**Figure A.1**). Browse the CD contents if you like. The "View the Readme" choice includes information on potential conflicts with other programs. To get started, click "Install FileMaker Pro 4.0." Click Next when the welcome dialog box appears. When the licensing agreement appears, click Accept to move to the next step.

3. The FileMaker Installation dialog box offers three configuration choices: Typical, Compact, and Custom (**Figure A.2**). If the default settings suit your purposes—and in most cases they will—simply click the Next button and skip ahead to step 6. You should choose Typical unless you're short on hard drive space, in which case choose Compact; if you only want to install a few specific files, choose Custom.

   If you want to install FileMaker somewhere other than the drive or folder indicated within the Directory box, follow step 4.

   If you want to change the installation type, skip to step 5.

4. To change where FileMaker will be installed, use the Browse button to select a new destination.

5. To limit the FileMaker installation to the minimum number of files necessary, click Compact (the second choice in Figure A.2). Once you're done, move to step 6.

   To install only certain files, click Custom. When the Custom Installation dialog box

   (continued)

appears (**Figure A.3**), click on the files you need. The size of each file appears to the right of its name. The space required for *all* the files you check appears just above the Back button. The Description area within the dialog box offers information on the purpose of each file you highlight—helping you decide which files to install. Once you're done, move to step 6.

6. Once you select your installation type, FileMaker will ask you what networking protocol you prefer (**Figure A.4**). The default setting is TCP/IP, which will cover most situations, so click Next and move on. For more information on networking, see page 211.

7. Unless you selected too small a hard drive (in which case go back to step 4), the Personalization dialog box should appear (**Figure A.5**). You'll find the 17-digit installation code on the sleeve of your FileMaker CD. Click Next and a dialog box will confirm that you're ready to go.

8. To launch FileMaker, go to your Start menu and navigate to the FileMaker folder and icon (**Figure A.6**).

✔ Tip

■ The Compact and Custom installations require much less space than the Typical installation, but they also restrict what you can do with FileMaker. Consider tidying up your hard drive to make room for the Typical installation.

The Compact installation will leave out the FileMaker tutorial and the Web Companion files. It will also leave out all the dictionary, translator, networking, and example files. Of course, that's not a problem if you just want to set up a PC to read existing FileMaker files and don't need it for importing other databases, designing databases, or publishing files for the Web.

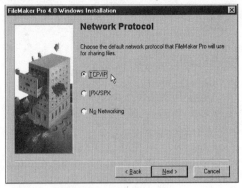

Figure A.4 The TCP/IP default will work for most network installations, so click Next. For more on networking, see page 211.

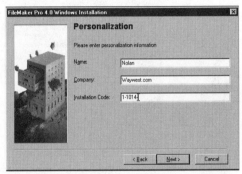

Figure A.5 You'll find the installation code on the sleeve of your FileMaker CD. When you're ready, click Next.

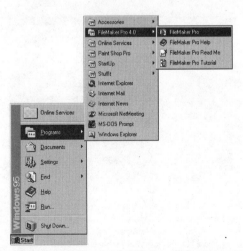

Figure A.6 Navigate via the Windows 95 Start button to launch FileMaker and you're off.

To install on a Windows 3.1, Windows for Workgroups, or Windows NT 3.5.1 computer

1. First make sure you have Win32s 1.30c installed. To check which version you have, go to the File Manager and click on WIN32S16.DLL, which resides in the \Windows\System directory. Now select Properties from the File menu of the File Manager. If your version is older than 1.30c, go on to step 2 to remove it. Otherwise, skip ahead to step 6.

2. To remove an earlier version of Win32s, you'll have to change a line in the Boot section of System.Ini. Change DRIVERS=MMSYSTEM.DLL to DRIVERS=MMSYSTEM.DDL

3. Now remove this line from the 386Enh section of the System.Ini: DEVICE= <WINDOWS>\<SYSTEM>\WIN32S\W32S.386 (Typically this line will read: DEVICE= C:\WINDOWS\SYSTEM\WIN32S\W32S.386).

4. Exit and restart Windows.

5. Now delete these files from the <WINDOWS>\<SYSTEM> subdirectory (or from the SYSTEM directory if you're dealing with a network installation):
   W32.SYS.DLL
   WIN32.S16.DLL
   WIN32S.INI
   WINMM16.DLL

6. Delete all files in the <WINDOWS>\<SYSTEM>\WIN32S subdirectory (or the <SYSTEM>\WIN32S subdirectory for a network installation). Now delete the WIN32S directory itself. You must exit and restart for the changes to take effect.

7. Once you've removed the old files, you're ready to install Win32s 1.30c by going to the Program Manager and clicking the Main group.

(continued)

8. Open the 386 Enhanced control panel (**Figure A.7**) and under New Settings change the Type to Permanent. Under New Size, make sure the file size is at least 20 MB. At the bottom of the control panel, turn on Use 32-Bit Disk Access and Use 32-Bit File Access (if they're available). Now click OK.

9. Restart and insert the FileMaker installation disc into your CD-ROM.

10. Use the File Manager to look within your FileMaker CD for the Win32s directory (**Figure A.8**). Open it, then open the Disk 1 directory. Look for the **Setup.Exe** file and double-click it. Now follow the Win32s instructions.

11. Once you're done with the Win32s installation, the FreeCell Setup dialog box will open. Go ahead and install FreeCell. Now restart and go back to page 259 to begin installing FileMaker.

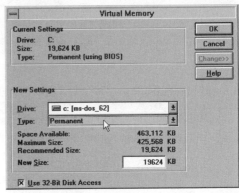

Figure A.7 Within your 386 Enhanced control panel (path: \Program Manager\Main\), set the Type and New Size text boxes as shown, and mark the bottom two check boxes, if they're visible.

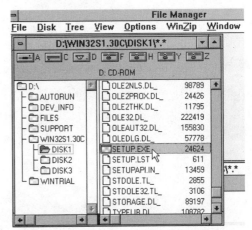

Figure A.8 Use the File Manager to find the Setup.Exe file within Win32s directory on your FileMaker CD. Double-click it and follow the instructions.

Installing the Macintosh version of FileMaker

Unlike so many software programs, the newest version of FileMaker doesn't demand the very latest operating system software to work. It will run just fine with the older System 7.1 as well as the current OS 8.

What you'll need before starting:

- A Macintosh or Mac OS-compatible computer with at least 4 MB of RAM (8 MB if you're using a computer with a Power PC chip or if you intend to use FileMaker's Web Companion, which is the reason for using FileMaker 4).

- A hard drive with at least 20 MB of free space. If you simply can't free up the space for the regular installation, see the Tips on page 263 for help on creating a minimum installation.

- A CD-ROM drive for using the FileMaker installation CD.

- The installation code for FileMaker. Look for the peel-off label on the sleeve containing the FileMaker CD.

INSTALLING MACINTOSH VERSION OF FILEMAKER

To install on a Macintosh

1. Turn off any anti-virus program you may have running in the background. Such programs sometimes cause problems for FileMaker's installer program.

2. If it's running, turn off File Sharing by clicking on the Apple at the upper-left corner of your screen. Hold down the mouse button and navigate to the Control Panels folder. Continue holding the mouse button down until you locate the File Sharing control panel, then release the mouse button. When the File Sharing control panel opens, click the Cancel button, then close the control panel. (Remember to turn File Sharing back on once you're done with the installation.)

3. Put the FileMaker disc into your CD-ROM drive.

4. Once the CD launches, double-click the Start Here icon (**Figure A.9**), which will present the software license agreement. Click Accept to move to the next step.

5. The FileMaker installer dialog box will appear. Easy Install, the default setting, will install all the FileMaker files.

6. Select the hard drive on which you want to install FileMaker. By default, your startup hard drive is chosen. If you wish to install FileMaker on a different drive, select it via the Install Location pull-down menu at the bottom of the window (**Figure A.10**). Note that the approximate disk space needed to install FileMaker appears on the right just above the Quit button.

7. Once you've selected your hard drive, click Install. Fill out the registration dialog box when it appears (**Figure A.11**). You'll find the 17-digit installation code on the sleeve of your FileMaker CD. Click OK and you're ready to go.

Start Here

Figure A.9 Double-click the Start Here icon to begin installation on the Macintosh.

Figure A.10 If you choose Easy Install, be sure to note the default destination drive in the lower left and change it if necessary. The disk space needed appears above the Quit button.

Figure A.11 You'll find the installation code on the sleeve of your FileMaker CD. When you're done, click OK.

Figure A.12 To perform a custom installation of FileMaker, use your cursor to toggle the install button in the upper left of the registration window.

Figure A.13 Within the Custom Install window, click the [I] if you want a description of a file's purpose.

✔ Tips

■ If you do not have enough hard drive space to install all the FileMaker files, click the Easy Install button in the upper left of the installation window and choose Custom Install (**Figure A.12**). You can then select only the files you need. The Approximate disk space needed figure in the lower right will change as you check or uncheck items, helping you decide how many FileMaker items to install.

The Custom installation requires much less space than the Easy Install but also restricts what you can do with FileMaker. Consider tidying up your hard drive to make room for the Easy Install.

The Compact installation will leave out the FileMaker tutorial and Web Companion files. It will also leave out all the dictionary, translator, networking, and example files. Of course, that's not a problem if you just want to set up a Mac to read existing FileMaker files and don't need to import other databases, design databases, or publish to the Web.

■ In making a Custom Install, if you're not sure which items you truly need, click on the [I] to the right of any item for more information on its purpose (**Figure A.13**).

APPENDIX B:
SETTING PREFERENCES

FileMaker gives you control over three kinds of preferences: application, document, and Web. Application-level preferences affect *every* document used by FileMaker. Document-level preferences apply only to the *open* database, which if you like, lets you create a different set of preferences for a particular database. The Web preferences are covered separately in Chapter 16's "Setting up Web Companion" on page 229.

Application preferences

Before you start setting preferences, here's a quick rundown of the application-level choices:

General Preferences: Most items in this dialog box are fairly self explanatory (**Figure B.1**). The status bar option will display an icon at the bottom of your screen showing which of FileMaker's four modes you're in. The Templates option is great if you'll regularly use templates as layout starting points; otherwise it adds an extra step to the file-opening process.

Layout Preferences: Most items in this dialog box are fairly self explanatory (**Figure B.2**). The "Always lock layout tools" option helps keep you from accidentally deselecting a tool, though you can also lock any tool by double-clicking it as you work within in a particular file.

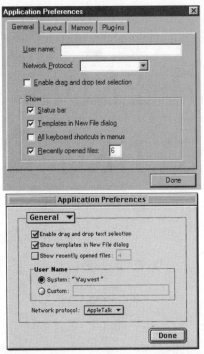

Figure B.1 The application-level General preferences dialog box affects every FileMaker database.

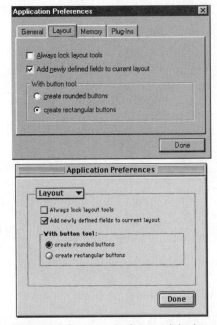

Figure B.2 The Layout preferences dialog box.

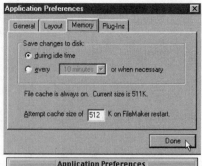

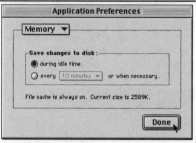

Figure B.3 Use the Memory preferences dialog box to set how often FileMaker automatically saves your database.

Memory Preferences: Unlike many programs, FileMaker has no Save command and instead saves automatically. Here's where you control how often it saves—an interval based on your own comfort zone—and whether it saves only when the computer's idle, which is the default (**Figure B.3**).

Modem Preferences: In Windows 95 and Windows NT, modem settings are controlled with the Modem control panel: Settings\Control Panel\Modems. On the Mac, most of the items in this dialog box are fairly self explanatory (**Figure B.4**). Unless you know your AT modem control commands cold or have specific settings recommended by your modem manufacturer, leave the Modem Commands settings alone. As for the lower panel's Connection settings, check the modem speed—it's easy to forget to bump it up as you upgrade your modems.

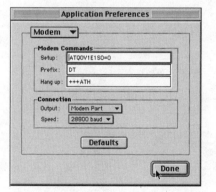

Figure B.4 The Mac's Modem preferences dialog box (Windows' settings are controlled in the Modem control panel).

APPLICATION PREFERENCES

Dialing Preferences: In Windows 95 and Windows NT, dialing settings also are controlled with the Modem control panel: Settings\Control Panel\Modems. On the Mac, FileMaker uses the Dialing settings as part of the Dial Phone script to call numbers in a database. The entry boxes let you account for the varying dialing needs of phone systems in handling outside, long-distance, and local extension calls (**Figure B.5**).

Plug-Ins Preferences: This dialog box is used to enable plug-ins, which in FileMaker's case means Web Companion (**Figure B.6**). For details, see "Setting up Web Companion" on page 229 in Chapter 16.

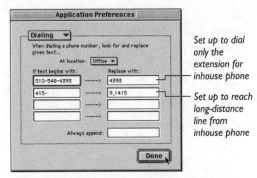

Set up to dial only the extension for inhouse phone

Set up to reach long-distance line from inhouse phone

Figure B.5 The Mac's Dialing preferences dialog box lets you control outside, long-distance, and extension settings. (Windows' settings are controlled in the Modem control panel).

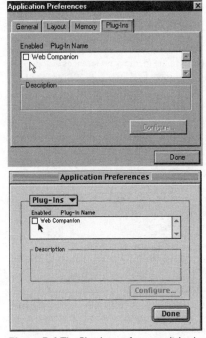

Figure B.6 The Plug-Ins preferences dialog box.

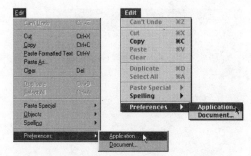

Figure B.7 To reach the application-level preferences, choose Preferences from the Edit menu and choose Application from the submenu.

To set application preferences

1. Open a FileMaker database (Ctrl O in Windows/⌘ O on the Mac), then choose Preferences from the Edit menu and select Application from the submenu (**Figure B.7**).

2. When the Application Preferences dialog box appears, choose a category with the tabs (Windows) or the pop-up menu (Mac).

3. Make your choices based on the information described in the preceding section. Click Done.

APPLICATION PREFERENCES

Document preferences

If a document is shared, only users who know the master password can change its preferences. (For more on passwords, see Chapter 15, "Networking," on page 211.) Before you start setting preferences, here's a quick run-down of the document-level choices:

General Preferences: The options in this dialog box give you a fair amount of control over individual databases (**Figure B.8**).

- Check "Use smart quotes" to automatically substitute the more typographically polished curly quotes for straight quotes.

- Check "Store compatible graphics" to automatically store database objects in cross-platform formats such as JPEG, GIF, or PICT. This will take a little more space on your hard drive but make cross-platform work more consistent.

- Check "Try default password" and type in a password if you want FileMaker to automatically enter that password when you open the database. Obviously, this option only makes sense for password-protected databases.

- Check "Switch to layout" and enter a specific layout name if you want FileMaker to automatically change to that layout whenever this document is open. This can be particularly handy if you're spending multiple sessions designing a complicated database.

- Check either of the two "Perform script" boxes and enter a script's name (one to run upon opening a file, the other upon closing it) if you want a particular set of actions performed at that time. This is very useful if, as host of a database, you regularly work on a database but want guests to see it presorted or set up in a particular view.

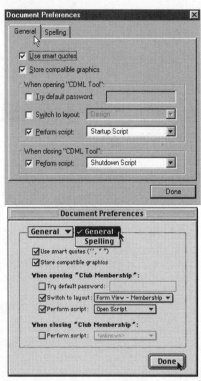

Figure B.8 The document-level General preferences dialog box affects only the currently open database.

DOCUMENT PREFERENCES

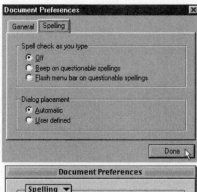

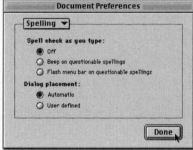

Figure B.9 The Spelling preferences, again, apply only to the currently open database.

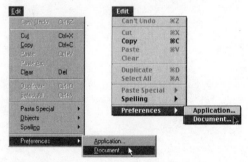

Figure B.10 To reach the document-level preferences, choose Preferences from the Edit menu and choose Document from the submenu.

Spelling Preferences: Most items in this dialog box are fairly self explanatory (**Figure B.9**). Some users love check-as-you-go spelling: others can't stand it. Selecting "User defined" under Dialog placement, lets you move the Spelling dialog box when it appears the first time to a set spot on your screen. Unless you move it again for this database, it will appear in that same spot every time, making it quick to find.

To set document preferences

1. Open a FileMaker database ($\boxed{\text{Ctrl}}\boxed{\text{O}}$ in Windows/$\boxed{\text{⌘}}\boxed{\text{O}}$ on the Mac), then choose Preferences from the Edit menu and select Document from the submenu (**Figure B.10**).

2. When the Document Preferences dialog box appears, choose a category (General or Spelling) with the tabs (Windows) or the pop-up menu (Mac).

3. Make your choices based on the information in the preceding section and click Done.

DOCUMENT PREFERENCES

Appendix C:
Using FileMaker's
Help and Tutorial

FileMaker has perhaps the best built-in Help of any software program. But it can be a bit confusing simply because it offers so many ways to get the same information. FileMaker's Help options include getting contextual answers for items on your screen or getting topical help via a table of contents, an index, or by searching for a specific word or phrase. Knowing which route to go can get complicated, so read on.

In contrast, FileMaker's built-in tutorial is pretty straightforward, so the explanations required for it are blessedly few.

Getting contextual help

If you have a fairly simple question, such as "What's that thingamabob," FileMaker offers a handy—though limited—feature called context-sensitive help. Using it, you can get a quick explanation for any tool, button, or menu bar that appears within your FileMaker screen.

To start/stop contextual help

1. From the Help menu, select FileMaker Help (Windows) or Show Balloons (Mac) (**Figure C.1**).

2. Once you start up FileMaker's contextual help, just move your cursor to any FileMaker item you have a question about.

Win Windows shows a floating question icon (**Figure C.2**), which you can use to click on any tool, button, or menu bar for a quick explanation of its purpose (**Figure C.3**). To get back to FileMaker's main window, close or Exit the FileMaker Pro Help window.

Mac On the Mac, the cursor immediately turns into a cartoon-style speech balloon whenever you drag it across any of FileMaker's program-wide features (**Figure C.4**). However, it will not tell you anything about items confined to an individual FileMaker file. While handy, a little bit of this feature goes a long way as balloons start popping up everywhere, including all your other applications. To turn it off, scoot back up to the Help menu and select Hide Balloons (**Figure C.5**).

Figure C.1 For contextual information, go to FileMaker's Help menu and choose based on your platform: Windows on the left, Mac on the right.

Figure C.2 Within Windows 95, click with the floating question icon ...

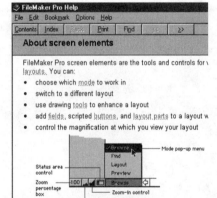

Figure C.3 ... for a quick explanation of any FileMaker tool, button, or menu bar.

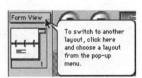

Figure C.4 On the Mac, contextual help comes via a speech balloon dragged over any FileMaker tool, button, or menu bar.

Figure C.5 Go to the Mac's Help menu to turn off the balloons—please.

Figure C.6 For a broad search, choose FileMaker Help Topics from the Help menu.

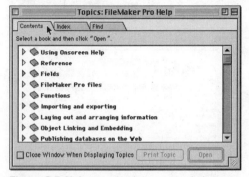

Figure C.7 Click on any book icon to reach the topics within.

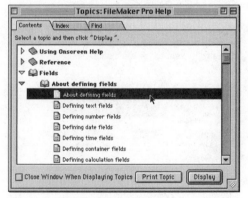

Figure C.8 Double-click the document icon to open the topic you're seeking.

Figure C.9 Once you've read a topic, use the menu buttons to move on.

Getting help by topic

If you're looking to get a big-picture feel for some aspect of FileMaker, searching by topic is your best bet. This approach allows you to cast a broad net, then gradually burrow down to the exact bit of information you need. A word of warning: sometimes FileMaker calls this Help Topics, sometimes it's called Contents, as you'll see in step 2.

To search Help by topic

1. From the Help menu select FileMaker Help Topics (**Figure C.6**).

2. FileMaker's Help will present a three-tab screen with Contents on top (**Figure C.7**). Within the Contents window appears a list of topics, much like a book's table of contents. Each book icon represents a related group of topics. Click on any book icon to reach the topics within. You may need to click down several levels to reach what you're looking for (**Figure C.8**).

3. Once you reach a relevant topic, double-click its icon and a screenful of information will appear (**Figure C.9**). The Help program's menu bar allows you to retrace your route by clicking Go Back. You can return directly to the original top-level table of contents by clicking Contents. Clicking Index takes you, where else, to Help's index, whose use is explained on the next page. Jumping from topics to the index is often handy when you find the topics approach too broad.

   Within the topics screen, you'll notice colored, underlined words. Clicking on any of these keywords reveals their definitions. For more on keywords, see the next page.

Using the Help index

Narrower than Help's Topics but broader than a direct search, the Index works best for that mid-level information hunt.

To use Help's index

1. From the Help menu select FileMaker Help Index (**Figure C.10**).

2. FileMaker's Help will present a three-tab screen with Index on top. As soon as you begin typing a word into the top entry box, FileMaker displays related items in the lower window (**Figure C.11**).

3. Double-click on the entry highlighted in the lower window and you'll be presented with several items containing the word you're seeking. The nice thing about this is it often allows you to spot a relevant, but easily overlooked, index entry. Double-clicking on the item you find most relevant presents the index entry itself (**Figure C.12**).

Within the index screen, you'll notice colored, underlined words. Clicking on any of these keywords reveals their definitions (**Figure C.13**). Click outside the definitions window to close it.

Figure C.10 For a relatively narrow search, choose FileMaker Help Index from the Help menu.

Figure C.11 As you type in the Index's upper window, potential matches appear in the lower window. Double-click any list item to see the details.

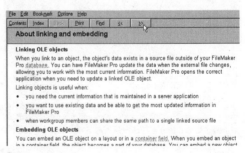

Figure C.12 Once you've read an index entry, use the menu buttons to move on.

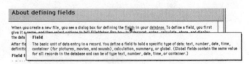

Figure C.13 You can double click on any underlined word within a Help screen to see its definition. Close the definition by clicking off the window.

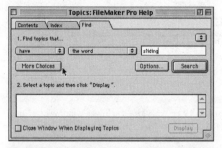

Figure C.14 To use the Find/Search feature, you must first select FileMaker Help's Topics or Index. Either one takes you to the same place.

Figure C.15 Use Find's dialog boxes to refine your search, then click Search.

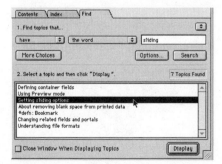

Figure C.16 In Windows, a dialog box appears the first time you use Find. Choose Minimize, then click Next.

Figure C.17 Double-click the topic of your choice to see the full entry.

Directly searching Help

Using Help's direct search feature works best in two almost opposite situations: when you need to find an exact phrase or when you have only the vaguest sense of what you're looking for. The reason is simply because Help's search feature will fetch each and every instance of a word, which allows you to search narrowly and widely.

To use Find to directly search Help

1. Unlike Help's Topics or Index features, the Find/Search feature cannot be reached directly from FileMaker's Help menu. Instead you reach it by selecting FileMaker Help Topics or FileMaker Help Index from the FileMaker Help menu (**Figure C.14**).

2. Once FileMaker's Help presents its three-tab screen, click the Find tab. The Find window then offers a variety of ways to tailor your search (**Figure C.15**). The default is set for finding topics that *have* the *word*, but you can toggle the boxes to find topics that *don't* have the word or have words *starting with* that topic. Clicking the More Choices and Options boxes enable you to further refine your search.

   Win The first time you use Help's Find feature, you'll be presented with the Find Setup Wizard (**Figure C.16**). Choose the default (Minimize) and click Next.

3. Once you've entered the word you're seeking, click Search, then double-click which one of the resulting items you want displayed (**Figure C.17**).

4. Within the find screen—amid all the high-lighted search terms—you'll also notice colored, underlined words. These are key-words and clicking on any of them reveals their definitions. For more, see page 276.

Using Help's bookmarks

True to their name, bookmarks help you quickly relocate a Help topic. They're particularly helpful for that seldom-used but hard-to-remember procedure. You can add or delete them at any time, enabling you to build up a bookmark collection tailored to your needs.

To add or delete a Help bookmark

1. You can only add bookmarks while you're using FileMaker's Help. So first find a Help topic you'll want to save as a bookmark, then choose Bookmark from the FileMaker Help menu. Use your cursor to select Define (Windows) or Set Bookmark (Mac) (**Figure C.18**).

2. A dialog box appears with the name of the Help item. You can accept the default name, which is the same as the actual index entry, or name it something that will jog your memory later (**Figure C.19**). You also can use this same dialog box to delete bookmarks or to change their names.

3. Once you define a bookmark, it's available any time by selecting Help's Bookmark menu. Bookmarking topics of interest as you look them up allows you to build a time-saving collection of your most-used topics (**Figure C.20**).

Figure C.18 Once you've found a Help item you want to mark, go to the Help menu and choose Define (Windows) or Set Bookmark (Mac).

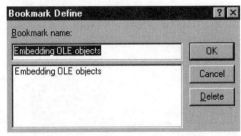

Figure C.19 You may use the lower window's default name or change it. When you're done, click OK.

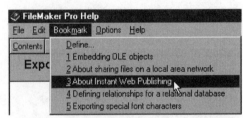

Figure C.20 Avoid repetitive searches by bookmarking your most-used Help topics. The numbers just left of the topics give you keyboard access to each bookmark.

✔ Tip

■ If you repeatedly look up a particular Help topic, you can skip the Bookmark menu by using a keyboard command to instantly reach any bookmark.

Win In Windows, type [Alt] M and the number just left of the bookmark you want (**Figure C.20**).

Mac On the Mac, you can assign a key during the Set Bookmark process or do so later by selecting Edit Bookmarks from the Bookmarks menu. Selecting Edit Bookmarks will open a dialog box where you can assign keys to, or rename, any of your bookmarks.

USING HELP'S BOOKMARKS

Adding notes in Help

People are a bit like computers: You can never have too much memory. Adding electronic notes within FileMaker's Help allows you to reconstruct that earth-shattering insight you had the last time you looked up a knotty topic.

To add notes to Help

1. Just like the Bookmark feature, Help Notes can only be created while you're using FileMaker's Help. So first find a Help topic that needs a note of explanation. Once you've got an item on your screen, you're ready to add a note.

Win Within the FileMaker Help program, use your cursor to select Annotate under the Edit menu (**Figure C.21**). The Annotate window will open (**Figure C.22**), allowing you to type in your note. When you're done, click Save.

If you change your mind in mid entry, just click Cancel. To delete an existing annotation, click on it, then select Delete from within the Annotate window.

Figure C.21 For Windows, add notes by selecting Annotate from Help's Edit menu.

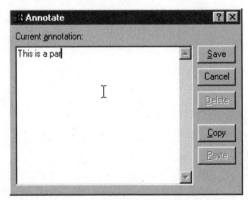

Figure C.22 For Windows, Annotate allows you to save, edit, or delete your note.

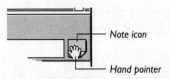

Note icon

Hand pointer

Figure C.23 For the Mac, add notes by grabbing the note icon in the upper right of the FileMaker Help window and dragging it to anywhere inside the topic window.

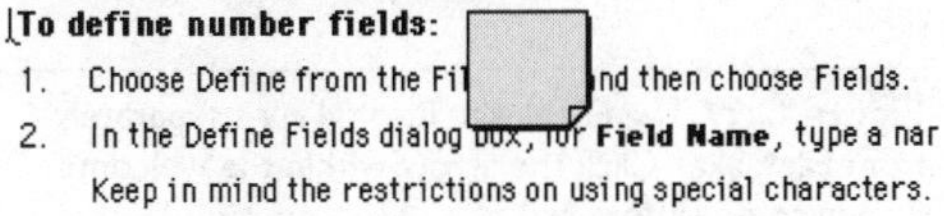

To define number fields:

1. Choose Define from the Fil[   ]nd then choose Fields.

2. In the Define Fields dialog box, for **Field Name**, type a nar Keep in mind the restrictions on using special characters.

Figure C.24 Once the Mac's note icon is in place, enter your text.

Figure C.25 Within Windows, clicking on the paper clip icon opens the note.

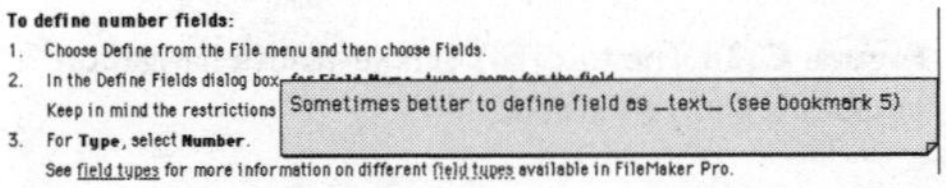

To define number fields:
1. Choose Define from the File menu and then choose Fields.
2. In the Define Fields dialog box, for Field Name, type a name for the field
   Keep in mind the restrictions Sometimes better to define field as ...text... (see bookmark 5)
3. For **Type**, select **Number**.
   See field types for more information on different field types available in FileMaker Pro.

Figure C.26 On the Mac, the full note's visible. If the note blocks your view of the Help topic, just click on the note and drag it.

Mac Whenever the FileMaker Help window is open, you'll notice a yellow note icon on the right side of the menu bar. To make a note, move your cursor over the note icon. The cursor will become a hand (**Figure C.23**). Hold down the cursor and drag a copy of the note icon to anywhere within the Help screen. Once you release the cursor, the note is ready for your entry (**Figure C.24**).

If you change your mind in mid entry, just click anywhere else on the screen and the note will disappear. If you want to delete an existing note, move your cursor over it until it becomes a hand. Now hold the cursor and drag the icon out of the document.

Now whenever you return to this particular Help topic, the note will be there to jog your memory.

✔ Tips

Win If a Help topic contains a note, a paper clip icon appears at the upper left of that topic's text. To see the note, move your cursor over the paper clip and click when the cursor becomes a hand (**Figure C.25**).

Mac If a Help topic contains a note, you'll see a yellow note icon with the full text inside (**Figure C.26**). If a long entry obstructs your view of the topic screen, click your cursor on the note and drag it out of your way. You can also hide or show all your notes by going to the View menu and selecting Show Notes or Hide Notes.

ADDING NOTES IN HELP

Using the FileMaker tutorial

Every copy of FileMaker comes with a tutorial that covers the basic concepts and uses of the program. It's not as detailed as the manual, or this book, but it's great for getting a quick overview or for brushing up on a topic.

To start the FileMaker tutorial

Win If you're using Windows 95, press the Start button, then navigate to: Programs\FileMaker Pro 4.0\FileMaker Pro Tutorial. For all other Windows versions, navigate to: Claris\FileMaker Pro 4.0\Tutorial\ and open Tutorial.

Mac On the Mac, navigate your way to the FileMaker Pro 4.0 Folder\FileMaker Tutorial\ and double-click FileMaker Tutorial.

1. Once the FileMaker Tutorial's welcome screen appears, click the arrow to move on (**Figure C.27**).

2. The tutorial opens with a quick orientation that explains how to get around. It's easy: Click the left-facing arrow to move back, the right-facing arrow to move ahead, and the Main Menu icon to jump to the tutorial's all-important table of contents (**Figure C.28**). Now click the Main Menu icon.

Figure C.27 The FileMaker Tutorial runs separately from FileMaker. Click the arrow within the welcome screen to move forward.

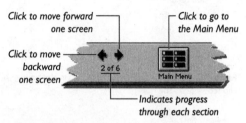

Figure C.28 The tutorial's simple-to-use navigation buttons are always visible.

Figure C.29 Click on any checkbox within the tutorial's table of contents to jump straight to the topic.

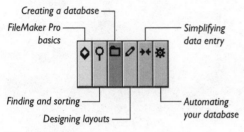

Figure C.30 Clicking on the icons at the top of each tutorial screen allows you to skip to any of six tutorial sections.

3. Up pops the table of contents, which breaks FileMaker into six broad topics (**Figure C.29**). Use your cursor to click on any checkbox to jump straight to that tutorial topic.

4. Once you're done with a tutorial item, you can use the navigation bar's left- and right-facing arrows to move step-by-step through a topic. Or you can skip to another of the six topics by clicking on the icons at the top center of the screen (**Figure C.30**).

5. Within the tutorial's table of contents, red checks mark your progress. To quit the tutorial at any time, go to the File menu and select Exit (Windows) or Quit (Mac).

Appendix D: Online Resources

This list is far from complete. Instead, it highlights major FileMaker areas online where you'll find plenty of ideas, inspiration, and help. Use them—and the other sites linked to them—to discover more about FileMaker as your needs grow.

Official FileMaker Web sites

FileMaker's Home Page Naturally enough, this site's a major source for FileMaker news, tech support, templates, lists of FileMaker-savvy Internet Service Providers, and other helpful items: http://www.filemaker.com

FileMaker's Software Center Quickly find updates, trial software, and pre-built buttons and scripts. A search engine lets you look for items by platform, or general categories, such as business, home, or entertainment: http://www.claris.com/software/software.html

Mailing lists

General FileMaker Dartmouth University hosts a long-standing discussion of all things FileMaker. To subscribe, send an email to: listserv@listserv.dartmouth.edu and include in the body of the message: "subFileMakerPRO-L *yourfirstname yourlastname*"

FileMaker and the Web The FileMaker Web Talk Mailing List, hosted by ISO Productions, focuses on sharing FileMaker databases on the Web. To subscribe, use the list server at: http://www.isoproductions.com/res-fmwebtalk. phtml

FileMaker and the Web This list also focuses on using FileMaker on the Web. It's hosted by Blue World Communications, which makes an advanced Web plug-in called Lasso. FileMaker's own Web Companion is based on technology acquired from Blue World. Subscribe by using the list server Web site at: http://lists.blueworld.com/

Newsgroups

There are two newsgroups where you'll find information on FileMaker.

FileMaker on Windows, go to: news:comp.databases

FileMaker on the Mac, go to: news:comp.sys.mac.databases

Commercial message boards

America Online Use the keyword: CLARIS

CompuServe Use the keywords: GO CLARIS

Third-party Web sites

Database Pros A good site for tips, tricks, and templates: http://www.best.com/~jmo/index.shtml

ClickWorld This site features a nice mix of tips, discussions, templates, and commercial solutions: http://www.clickworld.com/

Shopping Carts on the Web A directory of FileMaker Pro-powered e-commerce sites with real-world tips from each: http://www.blueworld.com/fmpro/carts/ default.html

FMPro.org The site includes tips, templates, and FileMaker-related shareware: http://www.fmpro.org

Database Publishing with FileMaker Pro on the Web Author Maria Langer's companion Web site for her Peachpit book is packed with tips and tricks for using FileMaker on the Web: http://www.gilesrd.com/fmproweb/index.html

APPENDIX E:
FUNCTIONS

Here's an all-in-one-place listing of
FileMaker's various functions, organized by
type. Before digging into these tables, be sure
you understand formulas and how to use
expressions, constants, and operators. If you
don't, these tables won't make much sense. For
more information, see Chapter 9, "Defining
Fields," on page 85. We'll wait here until you
come back.

Text Functions

SYNTAX	DEFINITION
Exact *(original text, comparison text)*	Returns a comparison of *original text* and *comparison text* in two text strings
Exact *(original container, comparison container)*	Returns a comparison of *original container* and *comparison container* in two container fields
Left *(text, number)*	Returns the specified *number* of characters in the supplied *text*, counting from the left
LeftWords *(text, number of words)*	Returns a text result containing the specified *number of words* in the supplied *text*, counting from the left
Length *(text)*	Returns the number or characters of *text*, including all spaces, numbers, and special characters
Lower *(text)*	Converts all letters in the given *text* to lowercase
Middle *(text, start, size)*	Returns characters from the supplied *text*, counting from *start* through number of characters in *size*
MiddleWords *(text, starting word, number of words)*	Returns the middle words from the supplied *text*, from *starting word* through the *number of words*
PatternCount *(text, search string)*	Returns the number of occurrences of the *search string* in *text*
Position *(text, search string, start, occurrence*	Scans the supplied *text* from *start* for the nth *occurrence* of a *search string*
Proper *(text)*	Converts first letter in each word of *text* to uppercase and rest to lowercase
Replace *(text, start, size, replacement text)*	Substitutes a series of characters for others in a string
Right *(text, number)*	Returns the specified *number* of characters in the supplied *text*, counting from the right
RightWords *(text, number of words)*	Returns a text result containing the specified *number of words* in the supplied *text*, counting from the right
Substitute *(text, search string, replace string)*	Substitutes every occurrence of a specified set of characters in a text string with another set of characters you specify, and returns the revised text string
TextToDate *(text)*	Returns the date equivalent of the supplied *text*, for use with formulas involving dates or date-oriented functions
TextToNum *(text)*	Returns the numeric equivalent of the supplied *text*, for use with formulas involving numbers or numeric functions
TextToTime *(text)*	Returns the time equivalent of the supplied *text*, for use with formulas involving time or time-oriented functions
Trim *(text)*	Returns the supplied *text*, stripped of all leading and trailing spaces
Upper *(text)*	Converts all letters in the given *text* to uppercase
WordCount *(text)*	Returns a count of the total number of words in the given *text*

FUNCTIONS

Number Functions

SYNTAX	DEFINITION
Abs *(number)*	The absolute value (a positive value) of the *number* supplied
Exp *(number)*	The value of the constant "e", raised to the power specified by the supplied *number*
Int *(number)*	The integer part of the supplied *number*, dropping any digits to the right of the decimal point
Mod *(number, divisor)*	The remainder after the specified *number* is divided by a *divisor*
NumToText *(number)*	The text equivalent of the specified *number*
Random	A random number between 0 and 1
Round *(number, precision)*	The supplied *number*, rounded off to the number of decimal places supplied in *precision*
Sign *(number)*	One of three possible values, representing whether the supplied *number* is negative, zero, or positive
Sqrt *(number)*	The square root of the supplied *number*
Truncate *(number, precision)*	The supplied *number*, truncated to the specified number of decimal places supplied in *precision*

Date Functions

SYNTAX	DEFINITION
Date *(month, day, year)*	The calendar date
DateToText *(date)*	The text equivalent of the supplied *date*
Day *(date)*	A number representing the day of the month for the given *date*
DayName *(date)*	Text containing the name of the weekday for the given *date*
DayOfWeek *(date)*	A number representing the day of the week for the given *date*
DayOfYear *(date)*	A number representing the number of days since January 1 for the given *date*
Month *(date)*	A number representing the month of the year for the given *date*
MonthName *(date)*	Text containing the name of the month for the given *date*
Today	The current date
WeekOfYear *(date)*	The number of weeks since January 1 for the given *date*
WeekOfYearFiscal *(date, starting day)*	A number between 1 and 53 representing the week containing the given *date*, figured according to the *starting day* used as the first day of the week
Year *(date)*	A number representing the year for the given *date*

Time Functions

SYNTAX	DEFINITION
Hour *(time)*	A number representing the number of hours embedded in a *time* value
Minute *(time)*	A number representing the number of minutes embedded in a *time* value
Seconds *(time)*	A number representing the number of seconds embedded in a *time* value
Time *(hours, minutes, seconds)*	A time result with the given number of *hours*, *minutes*, and *seconds*, counting from zero and adding the supplied duration of time to each unit
TimeToText *(time)*	The text equivalent of the supplied *time*, for use with formulas involving text or text-oriented functions

Aggregate Functions

SYNTAX	DEFINITION
Average (*field*) Average (*relationship::field*)	Returns the average for all non-blank values in a single repeating field (*field*) or (*relationship::field*)
Average (*field1, field2,...*) Average (*relationship::field1, relationship::field2...*)	Returns the average for all non-blank values in each corresponding repetition of one or more repeating fields or non-repeating fields (*field1, field2,...*) or (*relationship::field1, relationship::field2...*)
Count (*field*) Count (*relationship::field*)	Returns the number of valid, non-blank entries in a repeating field (*field*) or (*relationship::field*)
Count (*field1, field2,...*) Count (*relationship::field1, relationship::field2...*)	Returns the number of valid, non-blank values in each corresponding repetition of one or more repeating fields or non-repeating fields (*field1, field2,...*) or (*relationship::field1, relationship::field2...*)
Max (*field*) Max (*relationship::field*)	Returns the highest non-blank value in a repeating field (*field*) or (*relationship::field*)
Max (*field1, field2,...*) Max (*relationship::field1, relationship::field2...*)	Returns the highest non-blank values in each corresponding repetition of one or more repeating fields or non-repeating fields (*field1, field2,...*) or (*relationship::field1, relationship::field2...*)
Min (*field*) Min (*relationship::field*)	Returns the lowest non-blank value in a repeating field (*field*) or (*relationship::field*)
Min (*field1, field2,...*) Min (*relationship::field1, relationship::field2...*)	Returns the lowest non-blank values in each corresponding repetition of one or more repeating fields or non-repeating fields (*field1, field2,...*) or (*relationship::field1, relationship::field2...*)
StDev (*field*) StDev (*relationship::field*)	Returns the standard deviation of the sample represented by a series of non-blank values in a repeating field (*field*) or (*relationship::field*)
StDev (*field1, field2,...*) StDev (*relationship::field1, relationship::field2...*)	Returns the standard deviation of the sample represented by a series of non-blank values in each corresponding repetition of one or more repeating fields or non-repeating fields (*field1, field2,...*) or (*relationship::field1, relationship::field2...*)
StDevP (*field*) StDevP (*relationship::field*)	Returns the standard deviation of a population represented by a series of non-blank values in a repeating field (*field*) or (*relationship::field*)
StDevP (*field1, field2,...*) StDevP (*relationship::field1, relationship::field2...*)	Returns the standard deviation of a population represented by a series of non-blank values in each corresponding repetition of one or more repeating fields or non-repeating fields (*field1, field2,...*) or (*relationship::field1, relationship::field2...*)
Sum (*field*) Sum (*relationship::field*)	Returns the sum of non-blank values in a repeating field (*field*) or (*relationship::field*)
Sum (*field1, field2,...*) Sum (*relationship::field1, relationship::field2...*)	Returns the sum of non-blank values in each corresponding repetition of one or more repeating fields or non-repeating fields (*field1, field2,...*) or (*relationship::field1, relationship::field2...*)

Summary Functions

SYNTAX	DEFINITION
GetSummary (*summary field, break field*)	Returns the value of the specified *summary field* for the current range of records when the database is sorted by *break field*; otherwise returns an empty result. (Equivalent to calculating a sub summary.)
GetSummary (*summary field, summary field*)	Returns the value of the *summary field* for the current found set of records. (Equivalent to calculating a grand summary.)

Repeating Functions

SYNTAX	DEFINITION
Extend *(non-repeating field)*	Allows the value of a *non-repeating field* (a field defined to contain only one value) to be used in calculations involving repeating fields
GetRepetition *(repeating field, repetition number)*	Returns the contents of the *repetition number* specified in a *repeating field*
Last *(repeating field)*	Returns the last valid, non-blank value in a *repeating field*. The Last function can also return the contents of the last related record.

Financial Functions

SYNTAX	DEFINITION
FV *(payment, interest rate, periods)*	The future value of an investment, based on a constant *interest rate* and *payment* amount for the *periods*
NPV *(payment, interest rate)*	The net present value of a series of unequal *payments* made at regular intervals, assuming a fixed *interest rate* per interval
PMT *(principal, interest rate, term)*	The payment required to meet the requirements of the *term, interest rate,* and *principal* supplied
PV *(payment, interest rate, periods)*	The present value of a series of equal *payments* made at regular intervals (*periods*), assuming a fixed *interest rate* per interval

Trigonometric Functions

SYNTAX	DEFINITION
Atan *(number)*	The trigonometric arc tangent (inverse tangent) of the *number* supplied
Cos *(number)*	The cosine of the angle (in radians) of the *number* supplied
Degrees *(number)*	The supplied *number* (in radians) converted to degrees
Ln *(number)*	The base-e (natural) logarithm of the *number* supplied
Log *(number)*	The common logarithm (base 10) of any positive *number*
Pi	The value of the constant *pi* (approximately 3.14159)
Radians *(number)*	The supplied *number* (in degrees) converted to radians
Sin *(number)*	The sine of an angle expressed in *number* of radians
Tan *(number)*	The tangent of an angle in *number* of radians

Logical Functions

SYNTAX	DEFINITION
Case *(test1, result1 [, test2, result2, default result]...)*	Evaluates each in a series of expressions, in order, and when a True expression is found, returns the result supplied for that expression. Returns one of any number of results from a supplied list.
Choose *(expression, result0 [, result1, result2]...)*	Searches a list of arguments and returns a result. Returns one of any number of results from a supplied list. Use Choose to look up one value in a list of possibilities.
If *(test, resultIfTrue, resultIfFalse)*	Tests the number or expression for a True or False condition
IsEmpty *(value)*	Determines whether a *value* is an empty (null) value
IsValid *(field)*	Determines if a given *field* is missing or contains an invalid entry

Status Functions

SYNTAX	DEFINITION
Status (CurrentAppVersion)	The FileMaker Pro version number that is currently in use
Status (CurrentDate)	The current calendar date
Status (CurrentError)	A number representing the current error value
Status (CurrentFieldName)	The name of the field currently containing the insertion point
Status (CurrentFileName)	The name of the file currently in use
Status (CurrentFileSize)	The size (in bytes) of the current file
Status (CurrentFoundCount)	The number of records in the current found set
Status (CurrentGroup)	The group (or groups) that the current user is a member of, based on the current password
Status (CurrentHostName)	The host name FileMaker Pro registers on the network
Status (CurrentLanguage)	The current language set on the current system
Status (CurrentLayoutCount)	The total number of layouts defined in the database file
Status (CurrentLayoutName)	The name of the layout currently displayed in the file
Status (CurrentLayoutNumber)	The number of the current layout in the file
Status (CurrentMessageChoice)	A number indicating user input from an alert message displayed using the Show Message step in a script
Status (CurrentMode)	The FileMaker Pro mode at the time of the calculation
Status (CurrentModifierKeys)	A number representing which keyboard modifier keys (for example, Shift) are being pressed by the user
Status (CurrentMultiUserStatus)	A value representing single user file, multiuser file on the host computer, or multiuser file on a guest computer
Status (CurrentNetworkChoice)	The name of the network protocol that is currently loaded
Status (CurrentPageNumber)	The current page being printed or previewed
Status (CurrentPlatform)	A value representing the current platform (Windows or Mac OS)
Status (CurrentPortalRow)	The number of the current row in a selected portal (when no portal is selected, returns 0)
Status (CurrentPrinterName)	A text string identifying the current printer type
Status (CurrentRecordCount)	A number that represents the total number of records in the current file
Status (CurrentRecordID)	The unique ID of the current record
Status (CurrentRecordNumber)	The number of the current record in the found set
Status (CurrentRepetitionNumber)	A number representing the current (active) iteration of a repeating field
Status (CurrentRequestCount)	The total number of find requests currently defined in the database file
Status (CurrentScreenDepth)	The number of bits needed to represent the color of a pixel on the main screen
Status (CurrentScreenHeight)	The number of pixels displayed vertically on the screen in which the window of the current file is open
Status (CurrentScreenWidth)	The number of pixels displayed horizontally on the screen in which the window of the current file is open
Status (CurrentScriptName)	The name of the script currently running (or paused)
Status (CurrentSortStatus)	A value representing whether the records in the current file are unsorted, sorted, or partially sorted
Status (CurrentSystemVersion)	A text string containing the current system version
Status (CurrentTime)	The current time
Status (CurrentUserCount)	The number of users currently accessing the file
Status (CurrentUserName)	The name of the FileMaker Pro user, as specified in the General area of the Application Preferences dialog box

Design Functions

SYNTAX	DEFINITION
DatabaseNames	The names of the currently opened databases
FieldBounds (*database name, layout name, field name*)	The location and size of a specified field
FieldNames (*database name, [layout name]*)	The names of fields in a specified database file
FieldRepetitions (*database name, layout name, field name*)	The number of repetitions of a specified repeating field
FieldStyle (*database name, layout name, field name*)	How a specified field is formatted on a layout (for example, a radio button), and whether a value list is associated with the field
FieldType (*database name, field name*)	The field definition for a specified field
LayoutNames (*database name*)	The names of layouts in a specified database file
RelationInfo (*database name, relationship name*)	The name of the related file for a specified relationship
RelationNames (*database name*)	The relationships defined in a specified database file
ScriptNames (*database name*)	The scripts defined in a specified database file
ValueListItems (*database name, value list name*)	The values defined for a specified value list
ValueListNames (*database name*)	The value lists defined in a specified database file

FileMaker Pro Web Companion External Functions

SYNTAX	DEFINITION
External ("Web-Version", 0)	The version of FileMaker Pro Web Companion that loads when you open FileMaker Pro
External ("Web-ClientAddress", 0)	The domain name (for example, www.filemaker.com) of a Web user whose HTTP request is being processed by FileMaker Pro Web Companion
External ("Web-ClientIP", 0)	The IP address (for example, 12.34.56.78) of the Web user whose HTTP request is being processed by FileMaker Pro Web Companion
External ("Web-ClientName", 0)	The value that the Web user types for user name in the Web browser password dialog box
External ("Web-ClientType", 0)	The name and version of the Web browser being used by the Web user
External ("Web-ToHTML", field name or text value)	The contents of the specified field or text value encoded in HTML
External ("Web-ToHTTP", field name or text value)	The contents of the specified field or text value encoded in HTTP

APPENDIX F: SCRIPT COMMANDS

Virtually any script step you can think of has been predefined within FileMaker. You build scripts within ScriptMaker's Script Definition dialog box where all the available script steps are listed in the left-hand column (**Figure F.1**). Use this appendix as you work within the dialog box to quickly look up what actions each script step will trigger. The appendix is arranged in the same order and groups as the steps displayed in the left-hand column. For more on using FileMaker's ScriptMaker, see Chapter 12, "Using Templates and Scripts," on page 179.

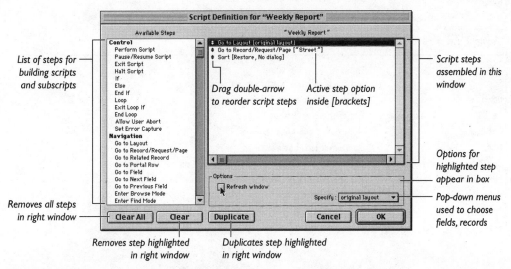

Figure labels:
- List of steps for building scripts and subscripts
- Drag double-arrow to reorder script steps
- Active step option inside [brackets]
- Script steps assembled in this window
- Options for highlighted step appear in box
- Pop-down menus used to choose fields, records
- Removes all steps in right window
- Removes step highlighted in right window
- Duplicates step highlighted in right window

Figure F.1 Use this appendix to help you quickly decipher the Script Definition dialog box's left-hand column, which lists all of FileMaker's available script steps.

Control Script Steps

USE	TO
Perform Script	Run another script, specified by options, within a script
Pause/Resume Script	Pause (or resume) script, based on option chosen
Exit Script	Exit the current script
Halt Script	Stop current script (allowing for user inputs)
If	Perform script if calculation is True
Else	Perform another step if calculation is False
End If	Mark end of script started by If script
Loop	Repeat a set of steps
Exit Loop If	Exit a loop if a calculation is True
End Loop	Mark end of Loop script
Allow User Abort	Let user stop (or not stop) script, based on option chosen
Set Capture Error	Move (or not move) error messages to Status function, based on option chosen

Navigation Script Steps

USE	TO
Go to Layout	Move to layout specified by option
Go to Record, Request, Page	Move to record, request, or page specified by option
Go to Related Record	Move to record in related database specified by option
Go to Portal Row	Move to portal row or field in portal row specified by option
Go to Field	Move to field specified by option
Go to Next Field	Move to next field in current layout
Go to Previous Field	Move to previous field in current layout
Enter Browse Mode	Switch to Browse mode with option to pause

Sort, Find, Print Script Steps

USE	TO
Sort	Sort records in found set based on current sort settings
Unsort	Restore records to unsorted state
Find All	Find all records in database
Find Omitted	Find records not in found set
Omit	Omit current record from found set
Omit Multiple	Omit number of records from found set, starting with current record
Perform Find	Find records matching current find request
Modify Last Find	Change find request
Page Setup/Print Setup	Open Page Setup dialog box (Mac); Open Print Setup dialog box (Windows)
Print	Print current record

Editing Script Steps

USE	TO
Undo	Undo last action
Cut	Delete contents of field specified by option and place in Clipboard
Copy	Copy contents of field specified by option and place in Clipboard
Paste	Paste Clipboard contents into field specified by option
Clear	Delete contents of field specified by option
Select All	Select all items in layout

Field Script Steps

USE	TO
Set Field	Replace contents of field specified by option with results of calculation, also specified by option
Paste Literal	Paste text specified by option into field specified by option
Paste Result	Paste result of calculation specified by option into field specified by option
Paste from Index	Paste contents of field specified by option
Paste from Last Record	Paste contents of field, specified by option, from last active record
Paste Current Date	Paste current system date into field specified by option
Paste Current Time	Paste current system time into field specified by option
Paste Current User Name	Paste current user name into field specified by option
Insert Object	Insert embedded or linked object into container field (Windows only)
Update Link	Update an OLE link in container field (Windows only)

Record Script Steps

USE	TO
New Record/Request	Add a new record or find request
Duplicate Record/Request	Duplicate a record or find request
Delete Record/Request	Delete current record or find request
Delete Portal Row	Delete current portal row
Revert Record/Request	Revert current record or find request to state before most recent action
Exit Record/Request	Leave current record or find request, with no field selected
Copy Record	Copy contents of current record to Clipboard
Copy All Records	Copy contents of records in found set to Clipboard
Delete All Records	Delete all records in found set
Replace	Replace contents of field, specified by options, within current record
Relookup	Update current record from lookup value

Import, Export Script Steps

USE	TO
Import Picture	Import graphic, specified by options, to current container field
Import Movie/Import QuickTime	Import QuickTime movie, specified by options, to current container field (Mac/Windows)
Import Records	Import records, specified by options, to current field
Export Records	Export records, specified by options, to another database format

Window Script Steps

USE	TO
Freeze Window	Hide action from user
Refresh Window	Update screen
Scroll Window	Scroll window to position specified by options
Toggle Window	Toggle window size to choice specified by options
Toggle Status Area	Toggle status area to choice specified by options
Toggle Text Ruler	Show or hide text ruler based on options
Set Zoom Level	Change window's zoom based on options
View As	Show single record or list of records, based on options

File Script Steps

USE	TO
New	Create new database
Open	Open a database specified by options
Close	Close a database specified by options
Change Password	Change existing password
Set Multi-User	Allow or block network access to current file
Set Use System Formats	Use date, time, number formats of current file or use system formats
Save Copy As	Save a database specified by options
Recover	Recover a damaged database specified by options

Spelling Script Steps

USE	TO
Check Selection	Check spelling in field specified by options
Check Record	Check spelling in record specified by options
Check Found Set	Check spelling in all records within found set
Correct Word	Display Spelling dialog box so user can correct misspelled word
Spelling Options	Display Spelling Options dialog box
Set Multi-User	Display Select Dictionaries dialog box
Edit User Dictionary	Display Edit User Dictionary dialog box

Open Menu Item Script Steps

USE	TO
Open Application Preferences	Display Application Preferences dialog box
Open Document Preferences	Display Document Preferences dialog box
Open Define Fields	Display Define Fields dialog box
Open Define Relationships	Display Define Relationships dialog box
Open Define Value Lists	Display Define Value Lists dialog box
Open Help	Display FileMaker's Help contents window
Open ScriptMaker	Display Define Scripts dialog box and halt current script
Open Sharing	Display File Sharing dialog box

Miscellaneous Script Steps

USE	TO
Show Message	Display specified text message for user
Beep	Play system alert sound
Speak	Generate speech from text specified by options (Mac only)
Dial Phone	Dial phone number specified by options
Open URL	Open a Web URL specified by options
Send Mail	Send e-mail with To, Cc, Subject, and Message fields specified by options
Send Apple Event	Start Apple Event specified by options (Mac only)
Perform AppleScript	Run AppleScript specified by options (Mac only)
Send DDE Execute	Send a Dynamic Data Exchange command to application specified by options (Windows only)
Send Message	Start or print using another application specified by options (Windows only)
Comment	Add explanatory note to a script
Flush Cache to Disk	Save FileMaker internal cache to disk
Exit Application	Close all files and exit FileMaker

APPENDIX G: KEYBOARD SHORTCUTS

This appendix aims to help you quickly find the FileMaker keyboard command shortcuts you need. For that reason, they are organized by menu and by function—reflecting the two most common ways people remember commands and do their work.

Shortcuts by menu: Sometimes you really have to dig around in a menu to find all the available commands. The Shortcuts by menu tables list every keyboard shortcut hiding beneath FileMaker's nine menus. Many keyboard shortcuts, however, do not appear under any menu. That's where the Shortcuts by function tables come to the rescue.

Shortcuts by function: FileMaker's menus arrangement sometimes does not really mirror the way you use the program. If you're deep into creating a new layout, for example, it's easier to see all the layout-related functions at a glance rather than listed under a bunch of menus. The same goes for text selection and formatting.

Shortcuts by menu

The File Menu

To	WINDOWS	MACINTOSH	WORKS IN MODE
Create new file	none	none	All
Open file	Ctrl O	⌘ O	All
Close file	Ctrl W	⌘ W	All
Open Define fields dialog box	Ctrl Shift D	Shift ⌘ D	All
Redefine field	Double-click field	Double-click field	Layout
Print	Ctrl P	⌘ P	All
Print without dialog box	Ctrl Alt P	Option ⌘ P	All
Exit/Quit	Alt W	⌘ Q	All

The Edit Menu

To	WINDOWS	MACINTOSH	WORKS IN MODE
Undo an action	Ctrl Z	⌘ Z	All
Cut a selection	Ctrl X	⌘ X	All
Copy a selection	Ctrl C	⌘ C	All
Paste a selection	Ctrl V	⌘ V	All
Delete a selection	Del	Del	All
Duplicate object	Ctrl D	⌘ D	Layout
Select All	Ctrl A	⌘ A	All
Paste Special—From Index	Ctrl I	⌘ I	Browse, Find
Paste Special—From Last Record	Ctrl ' (apostrophe)	⌘ ' (apostrophe)	Browse, Find
Paste Special—Current Date	Ctrl – (hyphen)	⌘ – (hyphen)	Browse, Find
Paste Special—Current Time	Ctrl ;	⌘ ;	Browse, Find
Paste Special—Current User Name	Ctrl Shift N	Shift ⌘ N	Browse, Find
Paste Special—Merge Field	Ctrl M	⌘ M	Layout
Spelling—Correct Word	Ctrl Shift Y	Shift ⌘ Y	Browse, Find, Layout

The Mode Menu

To switch to	Windows	Macintosh	Works in Mode
Browse mode	Ctrl B	⌘ B	All
Find mode	Ctrl F	⌘ F	All
Layout mode	Ctrl L	⌘ L	All
Preview mode	Ctrl U	⌘ U	All
Create new record	Ctrl N	⌘ N	Browse
Duplicate record	Ctrl D	⌘ D	Browse
Delete record	Ctrl E	⌘ E	Browse
Delete record w/o dialog confirmation	Ctrl Shift E	Option ⌘ E	Browse
Sort records	Ctrl S	⌘ S	Browse, Preview
New find request	Ctrl N	⌘ N	Find
Duplicate request	Ctrl D	⌘ D	Find
Delete find request	Ctrl E	⌘ E	Find
Delete find request w/o dialog confirmation	Ctrl Shift E	Option ⌘ E	Find
Create new layout	Ctrl N	⌘ N	Layout
Duplicate layout	none	none	Layout
Delete layout	Ctrl E	⌘ E	Layout

The Select Menu (appears in Browse & Find only)

To	Windows	Macintosh	Works in Mode
Find all records	Ctrl J	⌘ J	Browse, Find
Modify Last Find	Ctrl R	⌘ R	Browse
Perform Find	Enter	Return	Find
Omit record	none	⌘ M	Browse
Omit multiple records	none	Shift ⌘ M	Browse

The Show Menu (appears in Layout only)

To	Windows	Macintosh	Works in Mode
Turn on/off T-squares	Ctrl T	⌘ T	Layout

The Arrange Menu (appears in Layout only)

To	WINDOWS	MACINTOSH	WORKS IN MODE
Group selected objects or fields	Ctrl G	⌘ G	Layout
Ungroup selected object(s) or field(s)	Ctrl Shift G	Shift ⌘ G	Layout
Lock selected object(s) or field(s)	Ctrl H	⌘ H	Layout
Unlock selected object(s) or field(s)	Ctrl Shift H	Shift ⌘ H	Layout
Bring selected object(s) to front	none	Shift Option ⌘ F	Layout
Bring selected object(s) forward	Ctrl Shift F	Shift ⌘ F	Layout
Send selected object(s) to back	none	Shift Option ⌘ J	Layout
Bring selected object(s) backward	Ctrl Shift J	Shift ⌘ J	Layout
Rotate selected object(s) or part(s)	none	Option ⌘ R	Layout
Align selected object(s)	Ctrl K	⌘ K	Layout
Open alignment dialog box	Ctrl Shift K	Shift ⌘ K	Layout
Turn on/off autogrid	Ctrl Y	⌘ Y	Layout

The Format Menu

TO FORMAT	WINDOWS	MACINTOSH	WORKS IN MODE
Selected text via Text Format dialog box	Alt +Double-click	Option +Double-click	Browse, Layout
Size—Increase by one point size	Ctrl Shift >	Shift ⌘ >	Browse, Layout
Size—Decrease by one point size	Ctrl Shift <	Shift ⌘ <	Browse, Layout
Size—Select menu's next larger size	Ctrl .	Shift Option ⌘ >	Browse, Layout
Size—Select menu's next smaller size	Ctrl ,	Shift Option ⌘ <	Browse, Layout
Style—Plain text	Ctrl Shift P	Shift ⌘ P	Browse, Layout
Style—**Bold**	Ctrl Shift B	Shift ⌘ B	Browse, Layout
Style—*Italic*	Ctrl Shift I	Shift ⌘ I	Browse, Layout
Style—Outline	none	Shift ⌘ O	Browse, Layout
Style—Shadow	none	Shift ⌘ S	Browse, Layout
Style—Underline	Ctrl Shift U	Shift ⌘ U	Browse, Layout
Style—Superscript	none	Shift ⌘ +	Browse, Layout
Style—Subscript	none	Shift ⌘ −	Browse, Layout
Align Text—Left	Ctrl [	⌘ [	Browse, Layout
Align Text—Center	Ctrl \	⌘ \	Browse, Layout
Align Text—Right	Ctrl]	⌘]	Browse, Layout
Align Text—Full (Justify)	none	Shift ⌘ \	Browse, Layout
Field Format	none	Option ⌘ F	Browse, Layout
Field Borders	none	Option ⌘ B	Browse, Layout

The Script Menu

(no keyboard shortcuts)

The Window Menu

(no keyboard shortcuts)

The Help Menu

TO	WINDOWS	MACINTOSH	WORKS IN MODE
Launch Help	F1	⌘ ?	All

Shortcuts by function

Navigating

TO MOVE TO	WINDOWS	MACINTOSH	WORKS IN MODE
Beginning of line	Home	⌘ ←	Browse, Find, Layout
End of line	End	⌘ →	Browse, Find, Layout
Previous word	Ctrl ←	Option ←	Browse, Find, Layout
Next word	Ctrl →	Option →	Browse, Find, Layout
Beginning of text	Ctrl Home	⌘ ↑	Browse, Find, Layout
End of text	Ctrl End	⌘ ↓	Browse, Find, Layout
Next character	→	→	Browse, Find, Layout
Previous character	←	←	Browse, Find, Layout
Next line	↓	↓	Browse, Find, Layout
Previous line	↑	↑	Browse, Find, Layout
Next field	Tab	Tab	Browse, Find
Previous field	Shift Tab	Shift Tab	Browse, Find
Next record, layout, request	Ctrl ↓	⌘ Tab	Browse, Find
Previous record, layout, request	Ctrl ↑	Ctrl ↑ or Shift ⌘ Tab	Browse, Find
Flipbook icon if nothing selected	none	Esc	All

Editing

To	Windows	Macintosh	Works in Mode
Select a word	Double-click	Double-click	All
Select a line	Triple-click	Triple-click	All
Select a paragraph	Four clicks	Four clicks	All
Select All	`Ctrl` `A`	`⌘` `A`	All
Select back to beginning of line	`Shift` `Home`	`Option` `⌘` `←`	Browse, Find, Layout
Select back to beginning of previous word	`Shift` `Ctrl` `←`	`Shift` `Option` `←`	Browse, Find, Layout
Select back to beginning of text block	`Ctrl` `Shift` `Home`	`Shift` `Option` `⌘` `↑`	Browse, Find, Layout
Select to end of line	`Shift` `End`	`Shift` `Option` `⌘` `→`	Browse, Find, Layout
Select to end of next word	`Shift` `Ctrl` `→`	`Shift` `Option` `→`	Browse, Find, Layout
Select to end of text block	`Ctrl` `Shift` `End`	`Shift` `Alt` `⌘` `↓`	Browse, Find, Layout
Select next character	`Shift` `→`	`Shift` `→`	Browse, Find, Layout
Select next line	`Ctrl` `Shift` `↓`	`Ctrl` `Shift` `↓`	Browse, Find, Layout
Select previous character	`Shift` `←`	`Shift` `←`	Browse, Find, Layout
Select previous line	`Ctrl` `Shift` `↑`	`Ctrl` `Shift` `↑`	Browse, Find, Layout
Delete a selection	`Del`	`Del`	Browse, Find, Layout
Delete next character	`Del`	`⌦` (below Help key)	Browse, Find, Layout
Delete next word	`Ctrl` `Del`	`Option` `⌦`	Browse, Find, Layout
Delete previous character	`←Backspace`	`Delete`	Browse, Find, Layout
Delete previous word	none	`Option` `Delete`	Browse, Find, Layout
Undo	`Ctrl` `Z`	`⌘` `Z`	Browse, Find, Layout
Copy selection	`Ctrl` `C`	`⌘` `C`	Browse, Find, Layout
Copy all text in record (nothing selected)	`Ctrl` `C`	`⌘` `C`	Browse, Find, Layout
Cut selection	`Ctrl` `X`	`⌘` `X`	Browse, Find, Layout
Paste a selection	`Ctrl` `V`	`⌘` `V`	Browse, Find, Layout
Paste from index	`Ctrl` `I`	`⌘` `I`	Browse, Find
Paste from last record	`Ctrl` `'` (apostrophe)	`⌘` `'` (apostrophe)	Browse, Find
Paste from last record & move to next field	`Ctrl` `Shift` `'`	`Shift` `⌘` `'`	Browse, Find
Paste current date	`Ctrl` `−` (hyphen)	`⌘` `−` (hyphen)	Browse, Find
Paste current time	`Ctrl` `;`	`⌘` `;`	Browse, Find
Paste current user name	`Ctrl` `Shift` `N`	`Shift` `⌘` `N`	Browse, Find
Paste merge field	`Ctrl` `M`	`⌘` `M`	Layout
Paste without styling	`Ctrl` `Shift` `V`	`Option` `⌘` `V`	Browse, Find
Replace current field contents in found set	`Ctrl` `=`	`⌘` `=`	Browse
Spelling—Correct Word	`Ctrl` `Shift` `Y`	`Shift` `⌘` `Y`	Browse, Find, Layout

Formatting

To Format	Windows	Macintosh	Works in Mode
Size—Increase by one point size	Ctrl Shift >	Shift ⌘ >	Browse, Layout
Size—Decrease by one point size	Ctrl Shift <	Shift ⌘ <	Browse, Layout
Size—Select menu's next larger size	Ctrl .	Shift Option ⌘ >	Browse, Layout
Size—Select menu's next smaller size	Ctrl ,	Shift Option ⌘ <	Browse, Layout
Style—Plain text	Ctrl Shift P	Shift ⌘ P	Browse, Layout
Style—**Bold**	Ctrl Shift B	Shift ⌘ B	Browse, Layout
Style—*Italic*	Ctrl Shift I	Shift ⌘ I	Browse, Layout
Style—Outline	none	Shift ⌘ O	Browse, Layout
Style—Shadow	none	Shift ⌘ S	Browse, Layout
Style—Underline	Ctrl Shift U	Shift ⌘ U	Browse, Layout
Style—Superscript	none	Shift ⌘ +	Browse, Layout
Style—Subscript	none	Shift ⌘ -	Browse, Layout
Align Text—Left	Ctrl [	⌘ [	Browse, Layout
Align Text—Center	Ctrl \	⌘ \	Browse, Layout
Align Text—Right	Ctrl]	⌘]	Browse, Layout
Align Text—Full (Justify)	none	Shift ⌘ \	Browse, Layout
Insert tab into text	Ctrl Tab	Option Tab	Browse, Layout
Insert nonbreaking space	Ctrl Spacebar	Option Spacebar	Browse, Layout

Switching modes

To switch to	Windows	Macintosh	Works in Mode
Browse mode	Ctrl B	⌘ B	All
Find mode	Ctrl F	⌘ F	All
Layout mode	Ctrl L	⌘ L	All
Preview mode	Ctrl U	⌘ U	All

Working with records

Creating, duplicating records

To	WINDOWS	MACINTOSH	WORKS IN MODE
Switch to Browse mode	Ctrl B	⌘ B	All
Create new record	Ctrl N	⌘ N	Browse
Duplicate record	Ctrl D	⌘ D	Browse
Copy the found set (no fields selected)	Ctrl Shift C	Option ⌘ C	Browse

Finding records

To	WINDOWS	MACINTOSH	WORKS IN MODE
Switch to Find mode	Ctrl F	⌘ F	All
Find all records	Ctrl J	⌘ J	Browse, Find
Modify Last Find	Ctrl R	⌘ R	Browse
New find request	Ctrl N	⌘ N	Find
Duplicate request	Ctrl D	⌘ D	Find
Delete find request	Ctrl E	⌘ E	Find
Delete find request w/o dialog confirmation	Ctrl Shift E	Option ⌘ E	Find
Perform Find	Enter	Return	Find

Omitting records

To	WINDOWS	MACINTOSH	WORKS IN MODE
Omit record	none	⌘ M	Browse
Omit multiple records	none	Shift ⌘ M	Browse

Deleting records

To	WINDOWS	MACINTOSH	WORKS IN MODE
Delete record	Ctrl E	⌘ E	Browse
Delete record w/o dialog confirmation	Ctrl Shift E	Option ⌘ E	Browse

Sorting records

To	WINDOWS	MACINTOSH	WORKS IN MODE
Sort records	Ctrl S	⌘ S	Browse, Preview

Working with layouts

Layout tools, formats

To	WINDOWS	MACINTOSH	WORKS IN MODE
Switch current tool to pointer tool (and back)	`Enter`	`Return`	Layout
Constrain line tool to 45 degree increments	`Ctrl` +drag	`Option` +drag	Layout
Constrain movement horizontally/vertically	`Shift` +drag	`Shift` +drag	Layout
Constrain oval tool to a circle	`Ctrl` +drag	`Option` +drag	Layout
Constrain rectangle tool to a square	`Ctrl` +drag	`Option` +drag	Layout
Constrain resize to horizontal/vertical	`Shift` +drag handle	`Shift` +drag handle	Layout
Square object being resized	`Ctrl` +resize	`Option` +resize	Layout
Turn on/off T-squares	`Ctrl` `T`	`⌘` `T`	Layout
Turn on/off autogrid	`Ctrl` `Y`	`⌘` `Y`	Layout
Open alignment dialog box	`Ctrl` `Shift` `K`	`Shift` `⌘` `K`	Layout
Display selected object's format	`Alt` Double-click	`Option` Double-click	Layout
Reset default field format	`Ctrl` Click field	`⌘` Click field	Layout
Open define fields dialog box	`Ctrl` `Shift` `D`	`Shift` `⌘` `D`	All
Redefine a field	Double-click field	Double-click field	Layout
Field Format	none	`Option` `⌘` `F`	Browse, Layout
Field Borders	none	`Option` `⌘` `B`	Browse, Layout

Moving, selecting layout objects

To	WINDOWS	MACINTOSH	WORKS IN MODE
Move object	Click+drag	Click+drag	Layout
Move selected object pixel by pixel	Arrow keys	Arrow keys	Layout
Drag layout *part* past object	`Alt` +drag part	`Option` +drag part	Layout
Duplicate *object* by dragging	`Ctrl` +drag part	`Option` +drag part	Layout
Turn off autogrid while dragging	`Alt` +drag	`⌘` +drag	Layout
Resize object	Drag handle	Drag handle	Layout
Turn off autogrid while resizing	`Alt` +drag handle	`⌘` +drag handle	Layout
Bring selected object(s) to front	none	`Shift` `Option` `⌘` `F`	Layout
Bring selected object(s) forward	`Ctrl` `Shift` `F`	`Shift` `⌘` `F`	Layout
Send selected object(s) to back	none	`Shift` `Option` `⌘` `J`	Layout
Bring selected object(s) backward	`Ctrl` `Shift` `J`	`Shift` `⌘` `J`	Layout
Rotate selected object(s) or part(s)	none	`Option` `⌘` `R`	Layout
Reorder selected part	`Shift` +drag part	`Shift` +drag part	Layout
Reorient part labels (horizontal/vertical)	`Ctrl` Click	`⌘` Click	Layout
Align selected object(s)	`Ctrl` `K`	`⌘` `K`	Layout
Select objects by type	`Ctrl` `Shift` `A`	`Option` `⌘` `A`	Layout
Select objects via marquee	`Ctrl` +drag	`⌘` +drag	Layout
Group selected objects or fields	`Ctrl` `G`	`⌘` `G`	Layout
Ungroup selected object(s) or field(s)	`Ctrl` `Shift` `G`	`Shift` `⌘` `G`	Layout
Lock selected object(s) or field(s)	`Ctrl` `H`	`⌘` `H`	Layout
Unlock selected object(s) or field(s)	`Ctrl` `Shift` `H`	`Shift` `⌘` `H`	Layout

SHORTCUTS BY FUNCTION

Working with windows

To	Windows	Macintosh	Works in Mode
Scroll document window down	Page Down	Page Down	All
Scroll document window up	Page Up	Page Up	All
Scroll left in document window	Ctrl Page Up	none	All
Scroll right in document window	Ctrl Page Down	none	All
Show/Hide mode status area	Ctrl Shift S	Option ⌘ S	All
Maximize/Restore (Toggle full size/previous)	Ctrl Shift Z	Shift ⌘ Z	All
Cascade windows	Shift F5	none	All
Tile windows	Shift F4	none	All
Zoom in	F3	none	All
Zoom out	Shift F3	none	All

Working with files, dialog boxes

To	Windows	Macintosh	Works in Mode
Quit FileMaker	Ctrl Q , Alt F4	⌘ Q	All
Close database	Ctrl W , Ctrl F4	⌘ W	All
Save	Automatic	Automatic	All
Print	Ctrl P	⌘ P	All
Print without dialog box	Ctrl Shift T	Option ⌘ P	All
Open a dialog box	Ctrl O	⌘ O	All
Cancel a dialog box	Esc	Esc	All
Open Hosts/Network dialog box	Ctrl Shift O	Option ⌘ O	All
Cancel an operation	none	⌘ . (period)	All
Cancel a paused script	Alt N	none	All
Move object up in dialog box list	Ctrl ↑	⌘ ↑	All
Move object down in dialog box list	Ctrl ↓	⌘ ↓	All
Select layout in Layout pop-up menu	F2 ↑ or ↓ Enter	none	Layout
Select symbol in Symbols pop-up menu	Alt B ↑ or ↓	none	Find
Check/Uncheck Omit box in status area	Alt O	⌘ M	Find

INDEX

INDEX

INDEX

Listing 1: **Search.htm page**—Here's an example of the HTML code needed to generate this page.

```
<HTML>
  <HEAD><TITLE>Search</TITLE></HEAD>
  <BODY BGCOLOR=#FFFFFF>
    <FORM ACTION="FMPro" METHOD="POST">

      <INPUT TYPE="hidden" NAME="-db" VALUE="cars.fp3">
      <INPUT TYPE="hidden" NAME="-lay" VALUE="web">
      <INPUT TYPE="hidden" NAME="-format" VALUE="list.h
      <INPUT TYPE="hidden" NAME="-error" VALUE="errors.
      <TABLE>
        <TR>
          <TD ALIGN=CENTER COLSPAN=2>
            <FONT SIZE=5>Search For A Car/Van/Sport Utilit
          </TD>
        </TR>
        <TR>
          <TD ALIGN=RIGHT
            <B>Make:</B>
          </TD>
          <TD>
            <SELECT NAME="make">
              <OPTION VALUE="" SELECTED>- Sele
              <OPTION>Chevrolet
              <OPTION>GMC
              <OPTION>Nissan
              <OPTION>Toyota
            </SELECT>
          </TD>
        </TR>
        <TR>
          <TD ALIGN=RIGHT>
            <B>Type:</B>
          </TD>
          <TD>
            <SELECT NAME="Type">
              <OPTION VALUE="" SELECTED>- Sel
              <OPTION>Car
              <OPTION>Van
              <OPTION>Sport Utility
            </SELECT>
          </TD>
        </TR>
        <TR>
          <TD ALIGN=RIGHT>
```

by, and all **<OPTION>** tags specify values wi
you know to exist in your database.

Use the pop-up menu to search the make
and type (i.e., car, van, and sport utility). T
menus listed are cool! They let you specify
to sort the search results by. For you
the **<OPTION VALUE="" SELECTED>- f**
beginning of each pop-up menu will be er
VALUE="") if you don't select anythii
menu. So, if you click the Search butte
anything to search by, then you'll
the database.

These sort pop-up menus diff
simple way: Rather than '
NAME="-sortfield" and '
the field names that you
of these **"-sortfield"** c
than one, the results wi
field" tags are placed i
the first sortfield to l
field to be **"Model"**
"Make" field then

We interrupt this book

to announce that database development with FileMaker® Pro just got even easier...